Lithic Technology

World Anthropology

General Editor

SOL TAX

Patrons

CLAUDE LÉVI-STRAUSS
MARGARET MEAD
LAILA SHUKRY EL HAMAMSY
M. N. SRINIVAS

MOUTON PUBLISHERS · THE HAGUE · PARIS
DISTRIBUTED IN THE USA AND CANADA BY ALDINE, CHICAGO

Lithic Technology

Making and Using Stone Tools

Editor

EARL SWANSON †

MOUTON PUBLISHERS · THE HAGUE · PARIS
DISTRIBUTED IN THE USA AND CANADA BY ALDINE, CHICAGO

General Editor's Preface

What must be among the oldest of human interests — the chipping of stone to be used as tools — has waited long to become the subject of a book. Anthropological interest in stone-age tools dates from at least 1865, when Lord Avebury first published the terms Paleolithic and Neolithic. By then Europeans had long lost the art of chipping and flaking flint; and it was necessary for archeologists to reconstruct the technique in order to understand and in turn to reconstruct human prehistory. The present book, providing the results of two decades of new research and experimentation in flintknapping, well exemplifies the updating functions of an international Congress.

Like most contemporary sciences, anthropology is a product of the European tradition. Some argue that it is a product of colonialism, with one small and self-interested part of the species dominating the study of the whole. If we are to understand the species, our science needs substantial input from scholars who represent a variety of the world's cultures. It was a deliberate purpose of the IXth International Congress of Anthropological and Ethnological Sciences to provide impetus in this direction. The *World Anthropology* volumes, therefore, offer a first glimpse of a human science in which members from all societies have played an active role. Each of the books is designed to be self-contained; each is an attempt to update its particular sector of scientific knowledge and is written by specialists from all parts of the world. Each volume should be read and reviewed individually as a separate volume on its own given subject. The set as a whole will indicate what changes are in store for anthropology as scholars from the developing countries join in studying the species of which we are all a part.

The IXth Congress was planned from the beginning not only to include as many of the scholars from every part of the world as possible, but also with a view toward the eventual publication of the papers in high quality volumes. At previous Congresses scholars were invited to bring papers which were then read out loud. They were necessarily limited in length; many were only summarized; there was little time for discussion; and the sparse discussion could only be in one language. The IXth Congress was an experiment aimed at changing this. Papers were written with the intention of exchanging them before the Congress, particularly in extensive pre-Congress sessions; they were not intended to be read aloud at the Congress, that time being devoted to discussions — discussions which were simultaneously and professionally translated into five languages. The method for eliciting the papers was structured to make as representative a sample as was allowable when scholarly creativity — hence self-selection — was critically important. Scholars were asked both to propose papers of their own and to suggest topics for sessions of the Congress which they might edit into volumes. All were then informed of the suggestions and encouraged to re-think their own papers and the topics. The process, therefore, was a continuous one of feedback and exchange and it has continued to be so even after the Congress. The some two thousand papers comprising *World Anthropology* certainly then offer a substantial sample of world anthropology. It has been said that anthropology is at a turning point; if this is so, these volumes will be the historical direction-makers.

As might have been foreseen in the first post-colonial generation, the large majority of the Congress papers (82 percent) are the work of scholars identified with the industrialized world which fathered our traditional discipline and the institution of the Congress itself: Eastern Europe (15 percent); Western Europe (16 percent); North America (47 percent); Japan, South Africa, Australia, and New Zealand (4 percent). Only 18 percent of the papers are from developing areas: Africa (4 percent); Asia-Oceania (9 percent); Latin American (5 percent). Aside from the substantial representation from the U.S.S.R. and the nations of Eastern Europe, a significant difference between this corpus of written material and that of other Congresses is the addition of the large proportion of contributions from Africa, Asia, and Latin America. "Only 18 percent" is two to four times as great a proportion as that of other Congresses; moreover, 18 percent of 2,000 papers is 360 papers, 10 times the number of "Third World" papers at previous Congresses. In fact, these 360 papers are more than the total of ALL papers after the last International Congress of Anthropological and Ethnological Sciences which was held in the United States (Philadelphia, 1956). Even in the beautifully organized Tokyo Congress in 1968 less than a third as many members from developing nations, including those of Asia, participated. The significance of the increase is not simply quantitative. The input of scholars from areas which have until recently been no more than subject matter for anthropology represents both feedback and also long-awaited theoretical contributions from the perspectives of very different cultural, social, and historical traditions. Many who attended the IXth Congress were convinced that anthroplogy would not be the same in the future. The fact that the next Congress (India, 1978) will be our first in the "Third World" may be symbolic of the change. Meanwhile, sober consideration of the present set of books will show how much, and just where and how, our discipline is being revolutionized.

Fifty years ago, books on primitive techniques — pottery, basketry, metallurgy, etc. — received major attention from anthropologists and ethnologists. However, at this Congress there were only three sessions (aside from the one on lithic technology) which dealt directly with such techniques: one major session on the Ethnographic Atlas of agricultural implements and two on the origins of agriculture. The present book, however, is also closely related to the wealth of material on archeology and prehistory that occupied the Congress, and which now enrich this series of books on world anthropology.

Chicago, Illinois   SOL TAX
March 17, 1975

Table of Contents

General Editor's Preface   v

Introduction   1
   by *Earl H. Swanson*

PART ONE: LITHIC TECHNOLOGY AND TAXONOMY

Lithic Reduction Sequences: A Glossary and Discussion   5
   by *Bruce A. Bradley*
Lithic Technology as a Means of Processual Inference   15
   by *Michael B. Collins*
Idiosyncratic Behavior in Chipping Style: Some Hypotheses and
   Preliminary Analysis   35
   by *Joel Gunn*
Graph Theoretic Analysis of Lithic Tools from Northern Chile   63
   by *L. Lewis Johnson*
"Punch Technique" and Upper Palaeolithic Blades   97
   by *M. H. Newcomer*

PART TWO: EXPERIMENTAL ANALYSIS OF TOOLMAKING

Comments on Lithic Technology and Experimental Archaeology   105
   by *Don E. Crabtree*
The Experimental Study of Bipolar Flakes   115
   by *Hiroaki Kobayashi*

Remarks on Fragments with *Languette* Fractures 129
by *M. Lenoir*
Fractures for the Archaeologist 133
by *Barbara A. Purdy*

PART THREE: APPLICATION OF ANALYSIS TO ARCHAEOLOGY

The Trimmed-Core Tradition in Asiatic-American Contacts 145
by *Don W. Dragoo*
McKean and Little Lake Technology: A Problem in Projectile Point
Typology in the Great Basin of North America 159
by *James P. Green*
Toolmaking and Tool Use Among the Preceramic Peoples of
Panama 173
by *Anthony J. Ranere*
A Study of Cuts, Grooves, and Other Marks on Recent and Fossil
Bone: II Weathering Cracks, Fractures, Splinters, and Other
Similar Natural Phenomena 211
by *George J. Miller*

PART FOUR: DISCUSSION

Comments
by *Joffre Coe and Jeremiah Epstein* 229
Replies
by *James P. Green, Joel Gunn, L. Lewis Johnson. Hiroaki Kobayashi,
M. H. Newcomer, Barbara A. Purdy* 236

Biographical Notes 241

Index of Names 245

Index of Subjects 249

Plates, i–xl between 102–103

Introduction

EARL H. SWANSON

This volume is one of the flowers of research in lithic technology in the past twenty years. For most of that time the research and teaching have been the work of two men: François Bordes and Don Crabtree. Each has been at work independently for many years, each writing about his experiments, and each instructing apprentices in the craft and perhaps the art of flintworking. Both men span the vast reach of time and mind from the modern industrial universe to the world of primitive man. If their reach of mind has sometimes exceeded their brilliant grasp of a hammerstone, it is this gap which has excited the imagination of students who are represented in this volume and others yet to come.

The foundation of modern lithic technology rests on fine experimental work. It is the acute observation of archaeological phenomena and the deductions made therefrom which led to the discovery of heat treatment of raw materials and of the probable manufacturing sequences used to manufacture many prehistoric stone tools. These flintworkers have replicated the debris as well as the finished products of prehistoric tool makers exposing the possible processes by which distinctive cultural features were established in man's remote past. It has never been enough merely to produce copies of attractive archaeological specimens and the work of Don Crabtree has been focused especially on the replication of flakes and other by-products in the prehistoric manufacturing process. It is in the nature of the method that proof for a single prehistoric technique will never be obtained. But the likelihood of a limited number of manufacturing techniques used to make any given tool type can be increased. For this reason there is a continuing need for experimental work and for teaching new students how to use known flaking techniques.

Descriptive papers have been and will continue to be published, but the making of flaked stone tools can only be learned by doing and can be learned best by apprenticeship under a master. Fortunately, the students of Bordes at Bordeaux and of the Idaho State University Museum flint-working school under Don Crabtree have taken up such teaching at several institutions in Europe and America.

One of the benefits of modern lithic technology has been the realization that the same tool type has been made by different techniques in different geographic areas as in the case of the Clovis point in North America. Another has been the discovery that artifacts identified as knives or bifacial scrapers are sometimes blanks and preforms which bear witness to unfinished steps in the prehistoric manufacturing process. We have come to recognize that some tools classified by supposed function may be the by-products of tool making and be part of the tool making kit. Perhaps the best example is the arrowshaft smoother which may have served no arrows at all but was, in fact, the whetstone on which a tool maker kept his fabricator pointed. These are small straws in the wind of archaeological change but they indicate the diversity which has only begun to be examined in the analysis of archaeological remains of flaked stone tools. Whether the expanding possibilities will require more quantitative analyses or whether experimental results will eliminate some of the numerical possibilities will probably never be decided by any procedure except the decision of the individual investigator.

Lithic analysis should make it possible to discriminate between some artifact populations which are now thought to be essentially the same, yet permit the synthesis of some populations identified on stylistic grounds alone. Clearly, we have now the possibility of identifying the products of the individual flintworker. These possibilities illustrate the enormous impact of Don Crabtree and François Bordes on a generation of archaeologists. Their impact reaches in another direction as well because classification has already started in an effort to synthesize the results of experimental analysis. The taxonomic efforts illustrate rather nicely the induction of different generalizations from similar data. New classifications are bound to occur as the expansion of information continues apace. They are even more likely to occur as a result of the application of experimental analyses to archaeological site and area reports. If the results of analysis and classification sometimes seem to be confusing it should be remembered that flowering of lithic technology has yet to occur. When all or almost all archaeologists are capable of such analysis or make use of such specialists in their own work, we will have arrived not at the flowering of lithic technology but at its Indian summer.

PART ONE

Lithic Technology and Taxonomy

Lithic Reduction Sequences: A Glossary and Discussion

BRUCE A. BRADLEY

One of the fundamental problems of dealing with a lithic reduction sequence is dividing it into specific stages. Once this is done the interpretive potentials are greatly increased. A necessary prerequisite is a standardized terminology. The glossary that follows aims to deal with terms that may be used in the discussion of lithic reduction sequences.

GLOSSARY

ASSEMBLAGE: all artifacts (including debitage etc.) found in a given layer at a site (Bordes 1972: 185).

BLANK: any piece of lithic material that has been modified to an intended stage of a lithic reduction sequence in a specified assemblage. It must be demonstrable that it is not a finished implement and that it is intended for further modification. Furthermore it must have the morphological potential to be modified into more than one implement type within the assemblage. The method of its manufacture is not important in its initial identification.

IMPLEMENT: any piece of lithic material that has been modified to an intended stage of a lithic reduction sequence in a specified assemblage. It must be demonstrable that it is the final intended stage and is not intended for further modification (other than by use). The method of its manufacture is not important to its initial identification.

MODIFICATION: the act of morphological alteration of a unit of lithic material by a human agent. A core is a modified piece of stone, whereas a flake struck from the core is a distinct unmodified lithic unit until it is subsequently altered by human activity.

MORPHOLOGY: the three dimensional form (size, shape and volume) of any object.

PREFORM: any piece of lithic material that has been modified to an intended stage of a lithic reduction sequence in a specified assemblage. It must be demonstrable that it is not a finished implement and that it is intended for further modification. Furthermore, it must have the morphological potential of being modified into only one implement type within the assemblage. The method of its manufacture is not important to its initial identification.

PRELIMINARY MODIFICATION: the first step or steps that modify a piece of raw material into any other stage.

PRIMARY CORE: any piece of raw material that has had flakes struck from it, the desired product being the flakes. A handaxe made directly from a piece of raw material is not a primary core if it can be demonstrated that it was the handaxe, not the flakes, that was the intended product.

PRIMARY FLAKE-BLANK: any flake removed from a primary core for the purpose of further modification.

RAW MATERIAL: any unmodified piece of lithic material that is structurally and morphologically suitable for modification into implements.

SECONDARY CORE: any primary flake-blank that has had flakes struck from it, the desired product being the flakes.

SECONDARY FLAKE-BLANK: any flake removed from a secondary core for the purpose of further modification.

STAGE: a knapper's intended previsualized goal in a lithic reduction sequence.

STEP: a change in a knapper's process orientation which may or may not involve a change of technique. When a knapper is striking flakes from a core, he has a flake production orientation; however, when he begins to modify one of these flakes, his process orientation changes. Each of these changes constitutes a step.

ASSUMPTIONS, EVIDENCE, AND PROCEDURE

When using these terms a certain amount of information must already be available. It should be demonstrable that a valid sample of a specific assemblage is being studied. This assemblage should have an identifiable implement typology and lithic reduction sequences. Deriving this information is not always easy and in some cases virtually impossible. Identification of the implements can be approached functionally, typologically, and ethnologically. Once the implements have been identified, it is possible to deal with the implement and nonimplement evidence separately. Next, the lithic reduction sequences for each implement type should be reconstructed. This may be approached in various ways. Carefully controlled experimental analogy is probably the most useful. This involves careful examination and quantification of the nonimplement material. Quantifications of the experimental material can then be used for comparison. This allows conclusions about techniques, methods, and sequences of reduction to be made. Once the lithic reduction sequences have been reconstructed, they may be divided into stages and steps of manufacture.

The stages I suggest are preliminary modification, blank, preform, and implement. The preliminary modification stage may be subdivided into four steps: primary core, primary flake-blank, secondary core, and secondary flake -blank. This does not include all possible steps. There may be several in each of the other stages; however, the scope of this paper will be limited to those defined in the glossary.

The next, and probably most difficult, task is to demonstrate intent. When dealing with steps of reduction, this is less difficult if it is assumed that "...flintknapping was not a haphazard art but, rather, a carefully planned process of making stone tools..." (Crabtree 1972:2). It is reasonable to conclude that a change in techniques and process orientation is a step intended by the flintknapper. The demonstration of intended stages must be approached differently. Specific kinds of evidence may be used. If the nonimplement materials are carefully examined it may be possible to divide them into modified and unmodified categories. The modified material may then be divided into core and noncore categories. It is the modified, nonimplement, noncore category that may be used to determine intended stages. Within this category there may be typological groups identifiable by clustering of morphological and technological attributes. Once these groups are defined, the nonmaterial evidence (recovery associations) may be examined to determine whether or not there is a high correlation between the two. In an archaeological context this is most likely to be encountered in the form of caches or closely associated (spatially) groupings. If there is a statistically valid correlation, it may be inferred that these groups represent intended stages. These stages may then be classified as preliminary modification, blank, or preform.

APPLICATION

Two hypothetical assemblages have been constructed as a means of clarifying the way in which these terms can be applied. Below is a description

of each, including a statement of context, a comprehensive lithic reduction
sequence for each implement type, and a statement of the evidence upon
which assumptions are based.

GUMU-SANA ASSEMBLAGE

Context and Evidence

I propose that the Gumu-sana assemblage (see Figure 1) comes from one
geological layer of a dry cave site in North Africa. The layer is dated at
around 1400 B.C. From the nonlithic evidence it has been concluded that
the site represents a continuous year round occupation of about 150 years.
The lithic evidence has been divided into implement and nonimplement
categories. The implements were identified by functional analysis (wear
patterns) and by observation of hafted specimens. It has thus been established that five implement types are present: knives, spear points, arrow
points, scrapers, and drills. The nonimplement material includes a complete range of flakes and debitage and has been sorted and identified, by
experimental analogy, as units of lithic reduction sequences of each implement type. Several caches of modified nonimplement, noncore objects
were also recovered.

Reconstructed Lithic Reduction Sequences

KNIFE: A primary core was produced from a flint nodule by the removal
of a series of primary flakes with a large hammerstone, using direct percussion with thigh support. One of the primary flakes was then bifacially
modified to an oval shape with a small hammerstone, using direct percussion with freehand support. This object was bifacially modified to a leaf
shape with a bone billet, using direct percussion with thigh support. This
was finally modified to a leaf shape with a horn, using diagonal parallel
pressure flaking with hand support.

SPEAR POINT: A primary core, primary flake-blank, and oval shaped object were produced with the same techniques used for the knife. It was
then bifacially modified to a subtriangular shape with a bone billet, using
direct percussion with thigh support. This was finally bifacially modified
to a stemmed subtriangular shape with a horn, using collateral pressure
flaking with grooved block support.

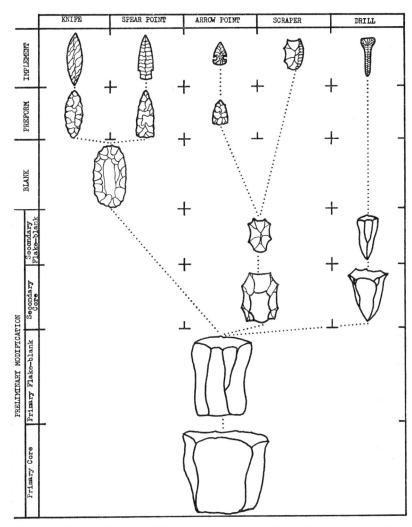

Figure 1.   Stages and steps of lithic reduction sequences in the Gumu-sana assemblage

ARROW POINT: A primary core and primary flake-blank were produced as above. A primary flake-blank was bifacially modified to a "disc" with a small hammerstone, using direct percussion with freehand support. A large flake was struck from the "disc" (secondary core) with a medium hammerstone, using direct percussion with freehand support. This secondary flake-blank was bifacially modified to a subtriangular shape with a bone billet, using direct percussion with freehand support. This object was bifacially modified to a side-notched subtriangular shape with a horn, using nonpatterned pressure flaking with hand support.

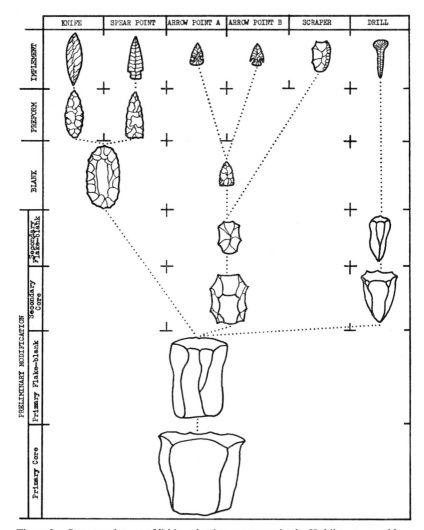

Figure 2.   Stages and steps of lithic reduction sequences in the Kukiksaut assemblage

SCRAPER: A primary core, primary flake-blank, secondary core, and secondary flake-blank were produced with the same techniques used for the arrow point. The secondary flake-blank was unifacially modified along one margin with a bone billet, using direct percussion with freehand support.

DRILL: A primary core and primary flake-blank were produced with the same techniques used for the knife. A primary flake-blank was unifacially modified, producing a series of secondary flake-blanks, with a bone punch, using indirect percussion with foot support. A secondary flake-blank was unifacially modified to a "T" shape, using serial pressure flaking with hand support.

KUKIKSAUT ASSEMBLAGE

Context and Evidence

I propose that the Kukiksaut assemblage (see Figure 2) comes from one geological layer of a dry rock shelter site in eastern Alaska. Various independent methods of dating the deposit agree with ethnological information, which places the occupation of the site at about A. D. 1550. Faunal evidence suggests that the site was only seasonally occupied. the lithic evidence has been divided into implement and nonimplement categories. The implements were identified by functional analysis (wear patterns), observation of hafted specimens, and ethnological information. It has been established that six implement types are present; knives, spear points, hunting arrow points (Type A), fishing arrow points (Type B), scrapers, and drills. The nonimplement material includes a complete range of flakes and debitage and has been sorted and identified, by experimental analogy, as units of lithic reduction sequences of each implement type. Several closely associated groupings of modified nonimplement, noncore objects were also recovered.

Reconstructed Lithic Reduction Sequences

All of the implements were produced with the same techniques as their corresponding types in the Gumu-sana assemblage. Arrow point type A and B were produced with the same techniques.

DISCUSSION

From the evidence described above, it is now possible to determine stages for each reduction sequence. In the Gumu-sana assemblage there are groups of modified nonimplement, noncore objects. These can be divided technologically and morphologically (typologically) into four distinct categories. Examination of the archaeological evidence demonstrates that these four categories have a high correlation with the groups recovered in caches. First there is a group of bifacially modified oval direct percussion with freehand support, with a small hammerstone. Within the assemblage there are two implement types that can be made by further modification of these objects; the knife and the spear point. By definition, these objects must be assumed to be blanks. Another group of objects can be identified as the above defined blank that was bifacially modified to a leaf shape by a bone billet, using direct percussion with thigh support. These have the morphological potential of modification to only one implement type, that is, the knife. By definition, they must be assumed to be preforms. This same procedure makes it possible to identify a preform for the spear point and a preform for the arrow point.

In the Kukiksaut assemblage, using the same procedure, it is possible to identify a blank for the knife and spear point, a preform for the knife, a preform for the spear point, and a blank for the arrow points (types A and B).

It will now be noted that there is a group of objects in both assemblages that share the same characteristics, yet are identified as different stages. The arrow point preform in the Gumu-sana assemblage is an arrow point blank in the Kukiksaut. This clearly demonstrates that the identification of stages must rely upon their context. This conclusion raises an important point. If the identification of stages is to be of any value in the interpretation of cultural phenomena, they cannot be defined by typological characteristics alone. Therefore to define a preform as "... an unfinished, unused form of the proposed artifact... with deep bulbar scars... irregular edges and no means of hafting... generally made by direct percussion" (Crabtree 1972:85) is of little interpretive value. Indeed an object of this description may be a preform in one assemblage and a blank in another! As an example, if a cache of modified nonimplement, noncore objects is recovered without any cultural context, it is not possible to say whether the cache is of blanks or preforms. It is possible however to make a statement that within the context of the Gumu-sana assemblage it is a cache of arrow point preforms.

CONCLUSION

Before lithic studies can be of interpretive value of prehistoric culture it is necessary to construct a standardized vocabulary and a standardized analytical approach. It is essential to know the interpretive potentials of lithic assemblages before deciding what questions can and cannot be answered.

I propose that it is possible to identify stages of lithic reduction sequences. This, however, can be accomplished only after conclusions about context, technology, and implement typology have been derived. It is my contention that the major interpretive value of identification of stages is to make possible positive statements about specific intention within the framework of specified assemblages.

REFERENCES

BORDES, F.
1972　*A tale of two caves.* New York: Harper and Row.
CRABTREE, DON E.
1972　"An introduction to flintworking," in *Occasional Papers of the Idaho State University Museum* 28, part two. Edited by Earl H. Swanson, Jr. and B. Robert Butler. Pocatello, Idaho.

Lithic Technology as a Means of Processual Inference

MICHAEL B. COLLINS

Because they survive where less durable items do not, and also because among stone age peoples they constitute an integral part of the adaptive mechanism, chipped stone tools are one of the most important classes of evidence by which we may view the record of human evolution. Although the student of the first 99 percent of the hominid record must deal almost entirely with bones, teeth, artifacts of stone and bone, and sometimes charcoal, he must not lose sight of the fact that the RELATIVE IMPORTANCE of such nonperishable objects to perishable ones, such as wooden tools, is usually unknown. He must then devote the bulk of his analytical efforts toward what is a crucial but perhaps relatively meager item of culture. It is imperative, therefore, that his analytical procedures be capable of extracting the maximum possible understanding of human behavior from the limited data. Although this situation is widely recognized, archaeologists have not developed a comprehensive framework suited to the integration of technological and typological analytical procedures, the explication of specific lithic technologies, and the examination of the adaptive role of lithic technology in the broader cultural context.

As a first step toward achieving such a framework, the following model of chipped stone tool manufacture is suggested. Virtually all chipped stone artifacts in any assemblage can be identified according to the activity set which produced them; in this way, all of the activities represented in the assemblage can be inferred. The inference in each case is by analogy with experimentally determined correlates between behavior and artifact attributes. These inferences are strongest in the case of artifact "populations" where consistent patterns are observable (inferences based upon single specimens are not reliable). The various activities inferred for a particular assemblage are then organized according to their proper place in the model to produce a description of the sequence of manufacturing activities represented in that assemblage. This description forms the basis for interpreting the adaptive role of the lithic technology within the culture or cultures whose remains are under examination. For example, in a complex village it might be observed that all residences reduplicated the entire manufacturing process, and therefore, that specialization was not practiced in the production of stone tools. Or through time, changes in patterns of exploiting material sources may reflect responses to changes in the physical environment. Some assemblages may include evidence of activities which are dependent upon earlier manufacturing steps that are not evidenced. The interpretive framework below allows identification of these missing activities and leads to the inference that they must have been accomplished outside of the area sampled by the assemblage at hand.

THE MODEL

The manufacture of chipped stone tools is a reductive technology dependent upon that property of conchoidal fracture which characterizes many microcrystalline and cryptocrystalline masses. The technology is bounded by rather stringent limitations imposed by the behavior of the conchoidal fracture, the nature of occurrence of rocks and minerals possessing chippable properties, and the capacities of primitive cultures for exerting and controlling forces (Berry and Mason 1959: 255; Goodman 1944; Speth 1972). Within these bounds, which to a certain extent can be described empirically, there are certain basic and unavoidable reductive steps involved in producing useful objects. Stone must be acquired and reduced until the desired form is achieved; generally, the more complex the form, the greater the amount of reduction that is required.

Although the process is linear, it is convenient to divide it into a series of steps. These steps are not sharply delimited one from another, but they are sufficiently distinct in terms of their procedures and output to merit separation. The output from each manufacturing step, here designated as "product groups," contains a number of individual specimens sharing certain qualities different from those of the output from other steps AND WHICH DETERMINE THE SUBSEQUENT UTILITY OF THE OUTPUT IN THE MANUFACTURING PROCESS. In this model, five steps account for the manufacturing and rejuvenating activities involved in producing even the most complex chipped stone objects. Certain less complex items can be produced by omitting the optional trimming steps, and, of course, rejuvenation is an optional step. The linear relationship of the steps in the model is determined by the fact that all but the initial step are dependent upon the output qualities of the prior steps as preconditions for their initiation. Except in very rare cases, none of the basic steps can be omitted nor can their order be changed. Each of the steps, however, whether basic or optional, may be achieved by a variety of specific techniques, and certain other manipulations of part of any product group — such as heat treating or storage — may intervene between any two steps.

Any particular culture may be expected to manufacture its chipped stone objects using only a very limited set of the possible combinations of techniques and options. In other words, any EMIC (specific) lithic technology is structured in response to the needs of the culture as well as to the choice, skill, and knowledge on the part of the artisans combined with such factors as the kind, quantity, and quality of raw material. There is the potential operation of a "feedback" relationship between steps in the manufacturing process as changes in output requirements in one step may necessitate changes in earlier steps. The basic structure of the model presented below derives from the experimentally determined physical properties of chippable stone and the linear feedback relationships among the reductive steps. The articulation of the model with other aspects of culture, society, and the physical environment, as well as possible techniques by which manufacturing steps may be accomplished, is derived from ethnographic and experimental data.

The generalized — or ETIC — model is composed of the five steps: ACQUISITION OF RAW MATERIAL, CORE PREPARATION AND INITIAL REDUCTION, optional PRIMARY TRIMMING, optional SECONDARY TRIMMING AND SHAPING, and optional MAINTENANCE/MODIFICATION. The linear relationship among these steps is illustrated in Figure 1. Each of these steps is composed of one or more activity sets and each activity set results in a product group of chipped stone artifacts. An activity set may include one or more specific activities and each product group (except the first) consists of two kinds of materials — waste by-products and objects destined for further reduction or for use. The specific activities which were employed in any given activity set impute certain discernible attributes in the product group. If isolated, product groups can be described in terms of their technological attributes and inferences can be drawn concerning the specific activities by which the particular manufacturing step was accomplished. The waste, or debitage, is particularly amenable to this technological analysis. Those objects in any product group which seem to be destined for use rather than for discard or further reduction are

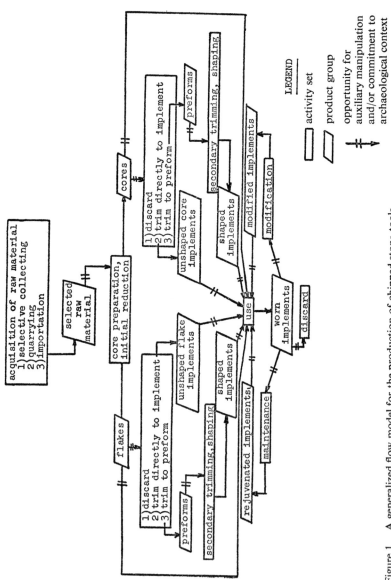

Figure 1.   A generalized flow model for the production of chipped stone tools

properly treated typologically (in the usual sense of categorizing for descriptive purpose the finished objects in any assemblage). Except in unusual circumstances, debitage remains at the locus of manufacture and finished objects are subject to relocation with use. In evaluating the spatial relationships between manufacturing activities, the debitage is, therefore, the more reliable source of data

Acquisition of Raw Material

Raw material is a very broad category and refers to stones or minerals that are chippable. These include rocks, minerals, natural glasses, crystalline aggregates, and, rarely, large crystals which exhibit a conchoidal fracture pattern. Such materials may occur in sedimentary, intrusive igneous, extrusive igneous, metamorphic, or secondary geologic hosts and are widely available on the Earth's surface. In some places, primitive man was able to select among a variety of available materials, but in others he was limited to scarce or inferior resources. There is ample evidence that desirable materials were often transported long distances (Griffin, Gordus, and Wright 1969; Hole, Flannery, and Neely 1969). The activity set, acquisition, supplies the artisan with suitable pieces of chippable stone selected from available resources. The most common means of acquiring raw material are collecting, quarrying, and some form of importation.

Where chippable stones occur on the surface in portable pieces, selective collecting is the only necessary acquisition activity. Such occurrences include stream gravels, terrace gravels, glacial drifts, beaches, colluvial deposits, and pieces dropped by erosion of a softer matrix. These kinds of exposures are subject to the effects of seasonal or long-term environmental changes such as vegetation cover, snowfall, burial or dislocation by wind or water, and similar processes. It should be noted that in addition to these and other naturally occurring sources of material, any but the earliest inhabitants of a particular region may pick over the stone waste or abandoned implements left by earlier inhabitants as a source of raw materials.

It is frequently the case that desirable raw material must be extracted from its geologic host by quarrying. Usually the material is exposed at the surface — in insufficient quantity or inferior quality — with indications that more or better material could be had by working into the deposits. There exists a continuum from the very simple extraction of materials from unconsolidated deposits (Holmes 1890) through the dislodging or breaking away of exposed nodules or other masses from solid deposits (Ronen and Davis 1970) to actual mining (Clark and Piggott 1933).

If raw material desired for chipping is not locally available, some form of importation may be employed. It is sometimes rather simple to demonstrate that importation has occurred. For example, in the Llano Estacado in western Texas and eastern New Mexico (United States), virtually all of the cherts, all of the obsidian, and most other chipped stones found in prehistoric sites had to have been imported as there are no local sources of these materials (Collins 1971:92). Furthermore, it is often possible not only to demonstrate that a given material is not locally obtainable, and therefore imported, but also confidently to identify its point of origin (e.g. Cann and Renfrew 1964). However, after it has been demonstrated that a material was imported, it is quite a different matter to determine the mechanism by which it was imported. As Wilmsen (1970:66) points out, social exchange, trade, direct acquisition expeditions, and other activities with indistinct archaeological indications are undoubtedly involved.

Material acquisition, in summary, may be accomplished in a variety of ways. It provides the artisans with materials needed or desired for the production of chipped stone objects through either direct or indirect articulation with the physical environment. The cultural system cannot exceed the limitations imposed by that articulation. The kinds of raw material, their mode of occurrence, and the means of their acquisition determine the qualities to be found in the resulting product group. In processual inferences, the basic information about the acquisition activities include the following: kind or kinds of raw material, acquisition techniques, selective criteria, and any particulars which apply to the cultural system under observation.

Once material has been acquired, and prior to the next step of initial reduction, it is possible that various auxiliary manipulations may be required. One may begin reduction immediately at the locus of acquisition or he may transport the materials to another locality. It is possible for materials in an unreduced state to be stored, traded, exchanged socially, or altered by heating or submersing in water. In general, evidence for auxiliary manipulation — if any — will be in the form of patterned attributes or distributions among specimens of this product group (product GROUP I).

Core Preparation and Initial Reduction

The principal features of the product group resulting from the acquisition activities and any intervening auxiliary manipulations are size, quality, shape of pieces and nature of surfaces, abundance, and condition. How the artisan prepares the materials and begins reduction depends largely upon these features, but is dictated as well by his objectives. In this activity set, he must transform the raw material into a form suited either for use as tools or for further reduction. Three basic options present themselves: he may concentrate on shaping the parent piece (core) and discard all detached pieces (flakes); he may optimize the detachment of suitable flakes or blades and discard the exhausted core; or he may compromise and retain both the core and a portion of the detached pieces. At this step in manufacture, the frequently applied distinction between core tools and flake tools is useful if further reduction is absent or very limited. In technologies where items in this product group undergo considerable additional reduction so as to obscure the attributes acquired at this step, the distinction loses its usefulness to typology.

In simpler technologies, core preparation need involve nothing more than selecting the most expedient place to begin. With more sophisticated objectives, the core must be prepared with careful attention to the form of the core face, core platform, and the angle between these surfaces (examples include blade cores, Lavallois cores, and discoidal cores). The cores and flakes — including nondescript debris — resulting from these activities is designated as product GROUP II. Also included are "rejects" (items which were abandoned because of flaws in the material or failures in manufacture).

Optional Primary Trimming

Either the cores or flakes resulting from the above activity may be trimmed prior to use or further reduction. Other auxiliary activities may have intervened, and the activities of this set are dependent upon the qualities of the incoming materials as well as upon the desired output characteristics. Shaping is the principal objective of this activity set. Simple retouched implements receive their final shaping here and are ready for use, whereas more complex implements will receive secondary shaping in the next step before they are functional.

Three aspects of shaping must be considered. The first of these is outline, usually modified by retouching the edges of the core or flakes along all or part of their periphery on one or both faces. The second aspect is section — longitudinal, transverse, or both. Flaking across one or both faces is the usual procedure in modifying any section. Finally, the edge is shaped — beveled, aligned in a single straight plane, curved, or otherwise formed in the desired shape. In the case of implements which receive their final shaping in this step, all of these aspects of shape are attained in a single operation. Those destined for further reduction are termed "preforms" and usually receive only their sectional shape and approximate outline at this time. The rejects, debitage, preforms, or finished implements produced by these activities comprise product GROUP III.

Optional Secondary Trimming and Shaping

The preforms among the above product group constitute the input into this activity set. Preforms are generally bifacially flaked and exhibit the general outline and sections of the ultimate finished product. This step is predominantly the bifacial edge trimming process which refines a preform into a specific form of bifacial implement. Common variations of this trimming include notching, serrating, denticulating, beveling, or straightening edges. The products of this activity set are usually among the most variable in any assemblage and their forms probably include the greatest amount of "stylistic" expression among chipped stone tools. It is with these items that typological analyses have the greatest promise for delimiting time/space patterns of distribution. Debitage, rejects, and finished objects make up the output, or product GROUP IV.

Use

Strictly speaking, use of chipped stone implements is not a part of the reductive technology, but it is included in the model as an activity set which produces a product group (GROUP V) of worn and/or damaged objects. These may be taken out of active participation in the cultural system or they may be recycled. Many objects seem to become part of the archaeological record at this step by simple loss or discard at or near the place of habitation or use. If it is not possible to identify the means whereby objects are removed from active service, those objects are assigned to the product group resulting from use. If, on the other hand, specialized techniques for taking items out of service are indicated, another designation may be desirable. In this case, the activity set would be specialized disposal, and would result in its own product group (GROUP VII). Examples include objects intentionally buried with the dead, purposefully destroyed (as in potlatching), or disposed of in trash pits.

Optional Maintenance and Modification

After chipped stone objects have been subjected to use, they may become broken, worn, or slightly damaged. If they are not discarded or recycled directly into another task — a worn cutting edge, for example, may serve as a scraping edge — these used items may be further reduced in the optional chipping step of maintenance or modification. Maintenance, or rejuvenation, is simply restoration of the originally desired attributes, such as sharpness of edge. Modification, on the other hand, transforms a worn or broken implement from one form to another. The modified implement may be another form of the same general category, as from end- to side-scraper, or a completely different kind of tool (e.g. small bifaces broken transversely are easily modified into burins by striking the surface of the transverse fracture plane). This activity produces an output, product GROUP VI, composed of distinctive debitage, such as scraper renewal flakes (Jelinek 1966; Shafer 1970) and of implements with evidence that their working surfaces or edges have been either maintained or modified.

Experimental manufacture of stone tools and examination of the attributes imparted to the discarded waste and rejects as well as to the end products provide the basis for inferring manufacturing steps and techniques from archaeological evidence. The investigator should avail himself of all sources of information including the chipped stone artifacts, the fabricators, and setting of the assemblage he wishes to describe. There should be correspondence between various lines of evidence and consistency among the patterns observed in each. For example, in a well-preserved assemblage where bifacial implements were thinned with some sort of soft billet, characteristic "billet" flakes and possibly preserved antler or wooden billets should be expected.

LITHIC TECHNOLOGY, THE PHYSICAL ENVIRONMENT, AND THE CULTURAL SYSTEM

It is now appropriate to examine briefly the way in which the above activities articulate with the remainder of the larger system of which they are a part. The lithic technological system may be viewed as a throughput system in which raw material is extracted from the physical environment (see Spier 1970; Schiffer 1972).

The physical environment is neither static nor uniform, and the technological system reflects its articulation with this dynamic entity in the form of the materials it processes, the fabricators with which it accomplishes the processing, the techniques of acquisition it employs, the kind of reduction that it uses, and in other details.

The knapper is an enculturated member of a group. His learning experience begins early in life and continues, perhaps intensively, over some years. As a participant in a culture largely dependent upon its lithic technology he will have the opportunity — or the necessity — to develop considerable skill. His skill may center around relatively few techniques and a very limited array of raw materials. The present-day experimental knapper, with access to knowledge about a wide array of techniques and materials, may develop a much greater repertory of skills and be able to shape a variety of kinds of stone. But it is unlikely that he will ever develop an acquaintance with specific materials as intimate as that achieved by a knapper who spends his entire life with a specific resource base. An important area of inquiry in need of enlightened students is the nature of this fundamental learning process: From whom does the knapper learn his skill? Is the less skillful able to exchange goods or services for chipped stone tools? Is there need to master certain realms of the supernatural in order to become a successful knapper? Does one alter his social status by his mastery of all or part of the technology?

Inter-group, or political, boundaries may affect the lithic technological system and impart discernible patterning to the archaeological record. In fact, the lithic technological system may be influenced by virtually every aspect of life among stone age peoples. If it is possible to identify properly the source of these influences with their consequences in the material remains, lithic technological data can be used in the interpretation of a variety of aspects of culture.

Processual inference — that is, interpreting the form of a culture's activities and discovering the reasons for that form — rests, in the case of chipped stone tool production, upon interpretation of objects recovered from archaeological context. Basically, this context is part of the physical environment, but it has significance only in a broader interpretive setting (such as dating, validity of associations, etc.). The various chipping activity sets discussed above result in the production of materials, some of which become a part of the physical environment (archaeological context) without further participation in the cultural system and others of which may remain in the cultural system for further reduction or for utilization. Schiffer (1972) has discussed this relationship between archaeological context and the cultural system in general and very useful terms. Schematized in Figure 2 are the relationships between the various chipped stone products, the activities which produced them, and their

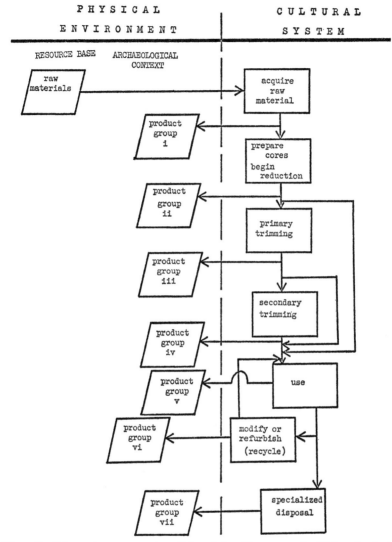

Figure 2.   Schematic representation of the relationships among the lithic technological system, the various product groups, and the physical environment

archaeological context. This may be considered a specific example of the general perspective outlined by Schiffer.

APPLICATION OF THE MODEL

Presented above is a model of lithic technology which purports to account for each manufacturing step in any and all specific, or emic, technologies. Limitations of space precluded any but the briefest mention of the various steps in the model; these same limitations now constrain our discussion of the application of the model. To date, three archaeological assemblages have been analyzed using the model as a framework, and the results have been very satisfactory. As examples of the application of the model, some of the results of two of these can now be briefly summarized.

Arenosa Shelter

This site is beneath a shallow overhanging limestone ledge along the right bank of the Pecos River, near its mouth, in western Texas. Stratified deposits, attaining a total thickness of just over fourteen meters, contained cultural materials representing approximately 8,000 years of occupation, beginning near the end of the Pleistocene (Dibble 1967). The cultural configuration is referred to as "Archaic," or "Desert Culture," and represents a mesolithic subsistence based upon intensive plant food collecting, supplemented by small game hunting, fishing, and shell fishing. There were twenty-five sterile and twenty-four cultural strata defined in the excavations at Arenosa Shelter. Among the latter, the following are discussed: (1) stratum 5, dated to about A.D. 1, in the upper levels of the deposit; (2) combined strata 11–18, dated to about 500 B.C., near the middle of the deposit; and (3) combined strata 23–23d, dated to about 2100 B.C., in the lower deposits.

Stratum 5 yielded 2 unmodified river cobbles of chert, which would appear to be chippable raw material assignable to product GROUP I; these indicate the exploitation of river gravels for chert cobbles. This inference is corroborated by examination of cortex remnants on other artifacts where about 95 percent of the identifiable pieces are river cobble cherts and 5 percent include all other kinds of material and sources (e.g. upland chert nodules, river cobbles of metamorphic rock, etc.). Collecting of river cobble cherts, then, is inferred to be the major acquisition activity.

Products assignable to GROUP II of stratum 5 include an estimated 3,803 flakes, 49 chert cobble cores, 4 cores of other kinds of material, and 7 miscellaneous chunks of broken chert. (Several items produced in the step of initial reduction were utilized, and are discussed below as part of product GROUP V.) A predominant number of flakes and cores in this group exhibit the attributes of direct hard hammer percussion. The cores are not uniform and seem to indicate no reductive procedure other than the expedient removal of flakes.

Also present in stratum 5 were approximately 1,560 flakes and 121 rejected bifaces and biface fragments whose stage of refinement conforms to product GROUP III expectations — that is, resulting from the primary trimming activity. A number of implements produced by primary trimming are assumed to have been used and are described below as part of GROUP V. Most primary trimming seems to have been accomplished by hard hammer percussion and by pressure flaking.

In stratum 5, GROUP IV, are included the waste product of secondary trimming. These include about 448 flakes and 22 rejected bifaces and biface fragments. Even though the objects in this group include a few examples of apparent soft hammer percussion, pressure flaking and direct hard hammer percussion continue to predominate as the trimming techniques.

The products of use (GROUP V) are numerous in stratum 5 and consist of the output of initial core reduction (9 utilized flakes and 14 core-choppers), of primary trimming (1 denticulated flake, 1 burin on a flake, 1 unifacial graver, and 55 unifaces), and of secondary trimming (2 ovate bifaces, 63 projectile points, and 2 bifacial drills). Typologically, these materials can be assigned to a number of descriptive categories, including 5 projectile point types (see Dibble 1967). Twenty of the unifaces exhibit a high sheen, or use polish, not unlike sickle sheen. This is thought to result from collecting or processing such desert plants as *Agave*, whose leaves were evidently eaten in large quantities.

No specialized disposal activities are indicated for lithic materials in stratum 5.

Recycled objects from stratum 5 (GROUP VI) include 13 resharpened unifaces (partial removal of use polish), 1 scraper renewal flake, and a snapped biface modified into a burin. Resharpening of unifaces, therefore, seems to have been an important activity.

The collections from strata 11 through 18 included no examples of unmodified GROUP I raw materials; however, collecting activities are inferred to have been similar to those evidenced in stratum 5. About 82 percent of the observable cortex remnants are of river cobble cherts, and about 18 percent are equally divided among different materials (igneous and metamorphic cobbles) and non-cobble cherts. Collecting is the only acquisition activity for which there is evidence.

The GROUP II waste products in strata 11–18 include about 2,152 flakes, 23 cores of cobble chert, and 5 other cores. Implements produced by initial reduction are described with the GROUP V materials. Direct hard hammer percussion seems to have been the technique used in initial core reduction.

The strata 11–18 waste products of primary trimming (GROUP III) include 2,328 flakes and 244 rejected or fragmentary bifaces. Implements supposedly finished with this step are included in GROUP V as it is assumed that most were used. This product group is composed almost entirely of objects reduced by direct soft hammer percussion. Some form of billet (antler or wood?) was evidently employed in most primary thinning activities.

Materials discarded during secondary trimming in strata 11–18 (GROUP IV) include about 2,260 flakes and 67 bifaces and bifacial fragments. Virtually all of these exhibit the attributes of soft hammer direct percussion. One of the biface fragments appears to have been heat treated after primary trimming. Evidently, as trimming was resumed after heating, the piece broke and was discarded.

The various implements of strata 11–18 which seem to represent the discards after use (GROUP V) include the output from initial reduction (1 utilized flake and 5 core-choppers), from primary trimming (3 handaxe-like bifaces, 3 gravers, a burin on a flake, and 23 unifaces), and from secondary trimming (25 thin bifaces, 28 projectile points, and 5 drills). Typologically these may be grouped into several categories, including 5 projectile point types, all but one of which are distinct from those of stratum 5. As a group, the thinned bifaces from this time period are thinner and more regular than those produced during the time of stratum 5. Several of the bifaces in this assemblage exhibit a polish like that found on unifaces in stratum 5. This may be evidence that similar tasks were being accomplished using different kinds of tools.

There is limited evidence from strata 11–18 that worn or broken objects were refurbished on occasion. These constitute GROUP VI and include 3 bifaces exhibiting use polish which has been partially removed by resharpening, 2 scraper renewal flakes, and 1 secondary burin spall with evidence of wear on the earlier burin surface.

Nothing indicating specialized disposal activities was found in strata 11–18.

Even though no GROUP I artifacts were recovered from strata 23–23d, acquisition is inferred from other evidence to have involved mostly selective collecting of chert cobbles from stream gravels. In addition there evidently was limited collecting of cherts from upland exposures as well. Very few chipped pieces of materials other than chert were recovered.

The GROUP II materials from this lower group of strata include about 730 flakes, 12 cobble cores of chert, 2 cores of upland chert, and 1 miscellaneous chunk of chert. Direct percussion using a hard percussor appears to have been the major technique employed in initial reduction.

The products of primary trimming (GROUP III) are numerous and include about 2,000 flakes and 176 rejected bifaces and biface fragments. Here, as in strata 11–18, soft hammer percussion appears to have been the predominant technique.

Secondary trimming is evidenced in strata 23–23d to have involved mostly soft hammer thinning of preforms. A specialized "twist" or alternate bevel was imparted to many bifaces at this stage of manufacture. GROUP IV artifacts include about 1,650 flakes and 50 rejects and broken bifaces (one of which had evidently been heat treated after primary trimming).

The finished implements thought to have been used (GROUP V) were manufactured by initial reduction (4 core-choppers and 3 utilized flakes), primary trimming (3 gravers, 1 burin on a flake, and 16 unifaces), and secondary trimming (26 ovate bifaces, some of which are beveled, 1 drill, and 80 projectile points, of which 12 are beveled). The bifaces in this group are less evenly thinned than those of strata 11–18. Typologically, this assemblage is distinct. Only one type of projectile point (8 specimens) resembles forms found in the deposits discussed above; the remaining 72 specimens are subdivided into 7 descriptive categories.

Evidence for the refurbishing of worn objects from strata 23–23d is 2 resharpened unifaces, a scraper renewal flake, and a secondary burin spall.

These materials indicate no specialized disposal procedure.

In general, the technology of these three time periods reflects a relatively uniform pattern of reliance upon stream cherts as the major source of raw material. During the time represented by strata 11–18, however, this practice was augmented by greater exploitation of other forms of chert. Strata 11–18 are very thin deposits alternating between sterile silts and cultural debris. The interpretation seems warranted that these represent brief occupations interrupted by frequent flooding of the nearby Pecos River. Perhaps silting and flooding of the valley floor necessitated greater use of upland chert sources.

In the two earlier periods under examination (represented by strata 11–18 and strata 23–23d), soft hammer thinning of bifaces was a conspicuous manufacturing technique. Its refinement seems greater in the period represented by strata 11–18, but in both periods it produced the majority of the chipped stone artifacts. In contrast, during the period represented by stratum 5, bifaces were thinned rather ineffectively by hard hammer percussion and pressure flaking (edges are less even, sections are thicker and less regular, and outlines are less symmetrical than in the other two periods).

Implements during the period of stratum 5 were produced by initial reduction and primary trimming (95 specimens) more often than by secondary trimming (68 specimens). In strata 11–18, 38 specimens were produced by initial reduction and primary trimming whereas many more (61) were produced by secondary trimming. In strata 23–23d, the ratio is 33 implements produced by primary trimming and initial reduction to 107 produced by secondary trimming.

In the case of the use polish exhibited by bifaces in strata 11–18 and by unifaces in stratum 5, it appears that similar tasks were being performed by implements produced in quite different ways. Among stone tools from strata 23–23d, there is no use polish. It is not certain whether this reflects different activities or accomplishment of similar tasks with different kinds of implements.

Laugerie Haute Ouest

The stratified deposits beneath and in front of a large overhanging lime-stone ledge on the right bank of the Vezere River some two kilometers above Les Eyzies, Dordogne, France, constitute the important Upper Paleolithic site of Laugerie Haute. Excavations by Smith and Bordes in the western part of the shelter in 1959 produced a very well documented sequence of sixteen Solutrean levels (Smith 1966a). A brief description of the technological data from two of these, levels 12c and 10, is presented here. Level 12c is considered by Smith to be Lower Solutrean, and level 10 is Middle Solutrean, datable to about 20,000 and 19,000 years ago, respectively (Smith 1966a, 1966b).

In level 12c, no unmodified GROUP I pieces of raw material were re-covered. Examination of cortical remnants on cores and flakes, however, does indicate that collection of nodules and cobbles of local chert was the major acquisition activity.

Discarded GROUP II products include an estimated 2,000 flakes and 10 globular and irregular cores. These form the basis for the inference that irregular to well-rounded nodules and cobbles of chert were reduced by simply removing a sequence of flakes in a fashion governed more by expedience than by adherence to any particular core form. The flakes include a variety of cortical and heavy angular forms. Direct percussion with a hard percussor is indicated as the usual activity although the blades in the collection (see below) may have been produced by indirect percussion at least part of the time.

In GROUP III discards from level 12c are found an estimated 2,400 flakes whose patterns of size, platform preparation, and shape suggest that they were produced in the primary trimming of implements by the application of pressure and direct, hard hammer percussion. In the absence of wear pattern data on these implements, it is assumed that ALL were used, and, therefore, are described below as part of product GROUP V.

There are no artifacts from level 12c which indicate the practice of secondary trimming (i.e. no GROUP IV materials were found).

The products of use, GROUP V, are numerous in level 12c and include an estimated 700 untrimmed blades suitable for use. These were produced by the initial reduction of blade cores. Also present are various trimmed flakes and blades produced by primary trimming. Typologically these are end scrapers (72), perforators (2), burins (28), truncated blades (5), unifacial points (19), and various retouched blades (16) and flakes (88). Technologically, these remains indicate that almost all Lower Solutrean implements were produced by primary trimming of flakes and blades or initial reduction of blade cores.

Level 12c produced only two items assignable to GROUP VI. These are unifacial points which appear to have been resharpened. No debitage was clearly assignable to this product group.

There was no evidence for specialized disposal in the Solutrean of Laugerie Haute Ouest.

The materials from level 10 at Laugerie Haute Ouest indicate a more complex technology than that inferred for level 12c. No artifacts representing GROUP I products were recovered from level 10. However, as in level 12c, the collecting activities, inferred from other evidence, were virtually the same as before, with the very uncommon addition of the importation of jaspers and other exotic materials. The mechanisms whereby these few exotic items were imported is unknown.

Level 10 GROUP II consists of 2 prismatic, 1 pyramidal, 1 discoidal, and about 30 irregular cores as well as an estimated 1,770 flakes. Direct hard hammer percussion, with the occasional addition of indirect percussion, seems to have been the major technique of initial core reduction.

The debitage assigned to GROUP III, level 10, includes waste flakes estimated to number about 1,000 and a total of 25 rejected biface preforms (23 made from cores, 2 from large flakes). Implements produced by initial trimming are described below as part of product GROUP V. Although some of the materials in this group show evidence of hard hammer percussion, by far the larger number indicate that primary thinning was accomplished by some sort of soft hammer percussion.

The most abundant material from level 10 is the debitage assigned to product GROUP IV. This includes an estimated 5,860 flakes of bifacial retouch as well as 33 bifaces broken during the secondary trimming step.

Soft hammer percussion and pressure are the flaking techniques indicated by these remains.

GROUP V specimens from level 10 include approximately 920 blades produced by initial core reduction, 40 broken bifaces, and a variety of implements produced by the primary trimming of flakes and blades. Typologically, these items are laurel leaf bifaces (40), end scrapers (61), perforators (17), burins (13), unifacial points (10), and various retouched flakes and blades (240).

Worn and modified items from level 10 (GROUP VI) number only 3. These are a snapped unifacial point modified into a burin, a biface re-shaped into a perforator, and a fragment of a biface modified into a dihedral burin.

None of the materials from level 10 seems to have been disposed of in any specialized manner.

In summary, there are two contrasts in the lithic technology between these two Solutrean levels. One noticeable though minor difference is the addition of a few imported raw materials during the Middle Solutrean. The other is the practice of secondary thinning of bifaces during the Middle Solutrean. As can be seen by comparing the numbers of imple-ments in GROUP V of each of these levels, the numerical consequences of this practice are not too great (40 bifaces to 351 simple retouched tools in the Middle Solutrean, and no bifaces to 230 simple retouched tools in the Lower Solutrean). However, the contrast in debitage is striking. There is no evidence for secondary trimming among the 4,400 flakes and 10 cores of level 12c, whereas in level 10, 58 rejected bifaces and 5,860 of the 8,630 flakes represent secondary trimming byproducts. This reflects the fact that bifacial thinning produces a great number of flakes for each implement (cf. Newcomer 1971). This relationship must be kept in mind to avoid attributing too great a significance to the abundant debitage of bifacial retouch as Smith (1966a:147–148, and Figure 32) did when he referred to this assemblage as representing a virtual manufacturing center for bifaces.

CONCLUSIONS

These few and brief examples, it is hoped, will suffice to demonstrate the utility of a general framework by which to view lithic technology. By properly identifying chipped stone artifacts with the activities which produced them and by knowing the place of those activities relative to other activities in the technology, a major component of the adaptive configuration of stone age culture can be described. From this description, the investigator may proceed on firmer ground to draw typological comparisons with other assemblages or to examine the mechanisms by which any particular culture operated. All too often these tasks have been performed using descriptions which confused technological and typological variables or which failed to provide reliable means of inferring activities from artifact assemblages.

It should be emphasized that the strongest inferences come from assemblages in good context where various lines of evidence may be checked for agreement. Also, there is need for a great deal more experimental production of stone tools to isolate more fully the correlations between specific flaking activities and the attributes which they impart to various artifacts.

REFERENCES

BERRY, L. G., B. MASON
  1959   *Mineralogy: concepts, descriptions, determinations.* San Francisco: W. H. Freeman.
CANN, J. R., C. RENFREW
  1964   The characterization of obsidian and its application to the Mediterranean region. *Proceedings of the Prehistoric Society for 1964* 30: 111–33.
CLARK, G., S. PIGGOTT
  1933   The age of the British flint mines. *Antiquity* 7:166–183.
COLLINS, M. B.
  1971   A review of Llano Estacado archaeology and ethnohistory. *Plains Anthropologist* 16:85–104.
DIBBLE, D. S.
  1967   *Excavations at Arenosa Shelter,* 1965–66. Austin: Texas Archeological Salvage Project.
GOODMAN, M. E.
  1944   The physical properties of stone tool materials. *American Antiquity* 9:415–33.
GRIFFIN, J. B., A. A. GORDUS, G. A. WRIGHT
  1969   Identification of the sources of Hopewellian obsidian in the Middle West. *American Antiquity* 34:1–14.
HOLE, F., K. V. FLANNERY, J. A. NEELY
  1969   *Prehistory and human ecology of the Deh Luran Plain: an early village sequence from Khuzistan, Iran.* Memoirs of the Museum of Anthropology, University of Michigan, 1.
HOLMES, W. H.
  1890   A quarry workshop of the flaked-stone implement makers in the District of Columbia. *American Anthropologist* 3:1–26.

JELINEK, A. J.
  1966   Some distinctive flakes and flake tools from the Llano Estacado. *Papers of the Michigan Academy of Science, Arts, and Letters* 51: 399–405.

NEWCOMER, M. H.
  1971   Some quantitative experiments in handaxe manufacture. *World Archaeology* 3:85–194.

RONEN, A., M. DAVIS
  1970   Un atelier de taille Néolithique au Mt. Carmel – Le Point 355Z. *L'Anthropologie* 74:161–194.

SCHIFFER, M.
  1972   Archaeological context and systemic context. *American Antiquity* 37:156–165.

SHAFER, H. J.
  1970   Notes on uniface retouch technology. *American Antiquity* 35:480–87.

SMITH, P. E.
  1966a   *Le Solutréen en France.* Bordeaux: Delmas.
  1966b   The Solutrean culture. *Scientific American* 211:86–94.

SPETH, J. D.
  1972   Mechanical basis of percussion flaking. *American Antiquity* 37:34–60.

SPIER, R. F. G.
  1970   *From the hand of man.* Boston: Houghton Mifflin.

WILMSEN, E. N.
  1970   Lithic analysis and cultural inference: a paleo-Indian case. *Anthropological Papers of the University of Arizona* 16.

Idiosyncratic Behavior in Chipping Style: Some Hypotheses and Preliminary Analysis

JOEL GUNN

The search for patterned behavior in production of lithic artifacts has largely centered at the cultural level. Projectile point forms, such as Clovis, have served as chronological markers and indicators of social distribution. Recent emphasis on processual archaeology (Binford 1962) suggests to me a need for higher resolution techniques of lithic analysis. L. Binford and S. Binford (1966), for instance, have been criticized for using a typological classification of artifacts in an essentially functional problem.

This paper suggests that problems of social and economic organization and function might be more reliably approached through the identification of artifacts at the level of the individual or, perhaps, of his immediate band society. By tracing the activities of individuals and bands it would be possible to establish the lifeways of prehistoric peoples. J. Adovasio (n.d.), for instance, has been able to detect individual styles in Great Basin prehistoric basket makers.

I wish to extend my appreciation to Don Crabtree, Dr. Earl Swanson, and Guy Muto for advice and encouragement at critical periods during the development of this research. Also, the use of laboratory materials and specimens at Idaho State University, Pocatello, was very helpful. Dr. John Davis of the Kansas Geological Survey supplied the laser diffraction equipment and presided over the beginnings of the analyses. The four knappers, besides myself, who generously contributed time and suggestions to the project were Don Crabtree, Gene Titmus, Guy Muto, and Peter Bleed. All of the personnel of the 1972 Idaho State University Flintknapping School made suggestions. Computer work and writing of the paper was done under the auspices of the Divostin Project, Dr. Alan McPherron. Director, University of Pittsburgh. The manuscript was edited by Maragaret McPherron. Beth Prinz and Dr. Alan McPherron read it and made helpful suggestions.

STONE TOOL PRODUCTION MODEL

Certainly there are cultural elements that contribute to the formation of an artifact. Each artifact, however, also contains characteristics that are a product of the skills, preferences, and ingenuity of the individual who makes it. In the following model, which is intended to be the conceptual framework that guides the study, elements of individual behavior are in-

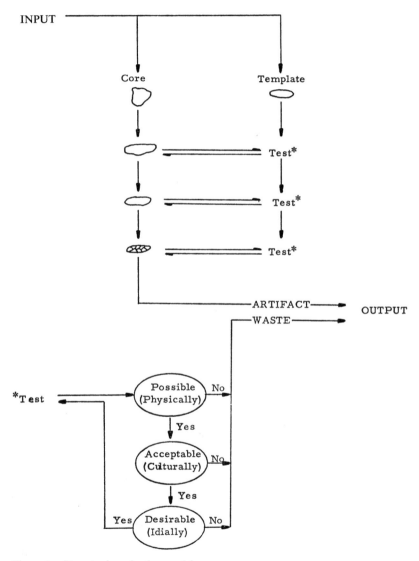

Figure 1.   Stone tool production model

corporated. In the model, Figure 1, the knapper is treated as a production facility that has the ability to manipulate materials and to conduct quality control tests on the results of those manipulations. An artifact is manufactured in a sequence of stages (Muto 1971a, 1971b). At each stage tests are conducted to determine if it will be possible to meet the specifications of a template. For instance, if the core is too small, completion of the artifact is out of the question. The piece is discarded.

Next, is the artifact within acceptable cultural limits? Third, does the tool meet the personal preferences (referred to hereafter as "idial[1] style") of the knapper? One knapper may prefer a slightly more refined scar pattern or a slightly thicker cross section than another. Also involved is the skill of the knapper in executing a more refined design.

Discussion of the testing of this model is not possible here. Its major elements have been a part of the archaeological literature for some time (see for instance, Rouse 1939, on templates). For purposes of this study the model will be assumed to be testable in principle (Hempel 1966: 30–32). It will be assumed that the model has been tested allowing the study to progress to the problems presented in the following pages. This is done with the understanding that if the model proves untenable, adjustments will have to be made in the theory and methodology.

SOME POSSIBLE USES FOR IDIAL STYLE

If prehistoric stone knappers could be detected by idial styles, then habits, social groupings, kinship systems, and ecological practices could be detected by the analysis of lithic assemblages. Three possible examples are:
1.   Suppose that a site were excavated and each piece carefully provenienced. A functional analysis of the stone tools indicates that there was an area of the site for butchering, an area for processing hides, and an area for the manufacture of hunting implements. An analysis of idial style indicates that one person made the tools for hunting and butchering. A second person made the tools for processing hides. These results would strongly suggest specialization by stone knappers.
2.   An analysis similar to the one conducted by J. Deetz (1967: 112–113) on pottery styles might reveal kinship patterns.
3.   If the products of one stone knapper were found at a number of sites over a wide area, but chipping waste was only found at one site, this would suggest that the knapper was making implements for trade. On the other

[1]   Greek idio-, from *idios*. 'One's own, personal, separate, distinct,' as in idiosyncrasy, idiotype. (*Webster's Unabridged Dictionary*) [Second edition], 1237).

hand, if there were chipping waste and implements of a single knapper at several sites, and these sites encompassed more than one ecological zone, it would indicate that the sites were part of one person's (group's) seasonal round.

Based on such findings the lifeways of prehistoric peoples could be determined.

SOME SOURCES OF VARIATION AT THE IDIAL LEVEL

The first step in this study of idial styles was to identify possible sources of variation between stone knappers. Don Crabtree has devoted a great deal of time to the study of stone knapping through replication of implements found in archaeological contexts. I asked his opinions on the subject, once by letter (his reply, January 2, 1972), and once in a personal interview (June 16, 1972). The following catalogue is a compilation of the insights gained on those two occasions. Quotes are taken from the letter.

1.   Platform preparation. Some knappers do not prepare the platforms, while others do, by chipping and grinding. "The detached flakes are often more diagnostic than the finished product since the platform preparation and other diagnostic criteria are removed with the flakes."

2.   Flake scar orientation. The flake scar orientation may vary from knapper to knapper. However, "the early stages of flake removal are often of a random nature in both size and character for they only represent the worker's intent to reduce the magnitude of the piece to workable size."

3.   Bulb of percussion. "The positive and negative bulbar area" may vary in "definition and depth" from worker to worker.

4.   Undulations. The undulations vary in size according to how much force is used and the technique (soft hammer, punch) used to make the removal.

5.   Termination. Some workers can make blades that end in a fine termination each time. Others will tend to take off part of the end of the core. Bifacial thinning flakes may terminate short of the center, continue beyond the center, or, in some cases, hinge slightly in the center, greatly thinning the cross section.

6.   Accuracy. Inaccurate blows will result in crushed edges and hinge fractures on the surface.

7.   Striking angle. The angle at which the blow is struck produces differences in platforms and bulbs.

8.   Thickness of the removal. Some will make thick blades and flakes, others thinner ones.

BIFACE POPULATION

To test the feasibility of identifying stone knappers by scar orientations (see number 2, above), thirty bifaces were collected. Twenty-five were produced by individuals who were modern stone knappers. Each person was asked to make five bifaces according to an established procedure. Five more bifaces were analyzed from the Simon Site Cache in Idaho.

The bifaces were made according to the following procedure:

1. Material—Obsidian, Glass Buttes, Oregon.
2. Chipping implement — soft, sandstone hammerstone (Knapper 3 resorted to a billet occasionally).
3. Product — semioval biface. The first biface (Figure 2) made by the first knapper was used as the template. All succeeding bifaces were supposed to emulate it. The semioval shape, with one end expanded, was chosen to insure a common orientation criterion for the pieces.
4. Extent of chipping — overall thinning flake scars.
5. Flaking technique — percussion.

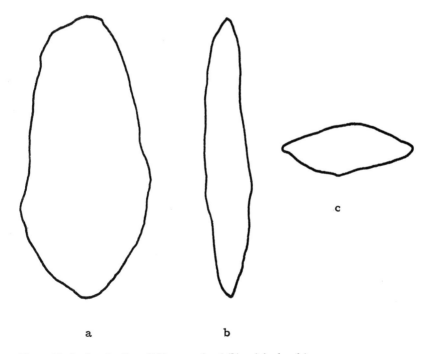

a   b   c

Figure 2(a, b, c).   Outline of biface number 1 ($^3/_5$ original scale)
a.   Plane view
b.   Side view
c.   Cross section

6.   Size — to approximate biface number 1.
7.   Shape — to approximate biface number 1.
8.   The chipping position and techniques of the knapper were photographed when possible.

A series was usually made over a period of two to three days. The latter
specimens in a series were made much more quickly than were earlier ones.
The work was done at the 1972 session of the Idaho State University
Flintworking School.

Both faces of each biface were analyzed, yielding sixty scar patterns. The
following table (see Table 1) gives information on the ordering of the population, the experience of the knappers, whether or not the group was
made as a series, and the handedness of the knappers.

Table 1.   Population information

Knapper	Pattern Numbers	Experience rating	Made as a series for this experiment	Handedness
1	1–10*	3	Yes	Right
2	11–20	1	Yes	Right
3	21–30	4	Yes	Left
4	31–40	5	No	Right
5	41–50	2	Yes	Right
6	51–60	6	No	?

* Biface pattern six had to be dropped because of a faulty negative at a critical
moment

The experience rating is only approximate (1=least experienced, 6=most
experienced). No doubt, any two adjacent positions could be interchanged.
The five bifaces from the Simon Site Cache were selected for closeness
to biface 1. The scar patterns were copied from casts that are in the Idaho
State University Museum (numbers 5541, 5584, 5540, 5463, 5610). References on the site and cache are Butler (1963) and Muto (1971b). Don
Crabtree regards the Simons knapper as very skilled on the basis of his
experience in replicating the Simons bifaces (personal communication).

LASER DIFFRACTION SPECTRA

Once the bifaces were collected, the problem was to convert the scar patterns into numerically analyzable data. The following procedure was used
to obtain measurements of scar orientations.

First, the scar patterns were traced. A sheet of lightweight paper was taped over a scar pattern and rubbed with the flat end of a black crayon. This gave a fairly clear, but more importantly, a very accurate representation of the scar patterns.

Second, with the artifact still in hand, tracing paper was placed over the crayon pattern. A pencil tracing of the scar pattern was then made, checking with the artifact at each line for accuracy. When the scar pattern was satisfactorily transferred to paper, another sheet of tracing paper was placed over the pencil drawing and an inked image made.

Third, the scar pattern inkings were photographed on 35 millimeter Kodak High Contrast Copy Film. The negatives were overdeveloped to get as high a contrast as possible. The time over the recommended developing time was one minute.

Fourth, the negatives were placed in a laser diffraction apparatus. The orientation of scars could then be measured by machinery associated with the laser. Briefly, laser diffraction transforms the scar pattern into a target shaped pattern, or spectrum, like the one shown in Figure 3a. The apparatus used for this experiment does not produce a photograph, so the illustration is material from an earlier pilot study. The outline, Figure 3a, is of the face of a neolithic microblade core. The outline was photographed and the laser diffraction spectrum, the starlike pattern, generated.

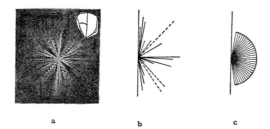

a.   b.   c.

Figure 3 (a, b, c). Making and measuring a laser diffraction spectrum
a. scar outline and spectrum
b. half a spectrum
c. light sensitive surface with 32 segments

Longer rays in the spectrum indicate that more lines in the scar pattern are oriented in that direction. Shorter rays indicate fewer scars similarly oriented.

The process is not unduly complicated (Preston, Green, and Davis 1970: 23). A laser beam is directed through a set of lenses and the negative. Only the lines of the scar pattern let light through the negative. At a distance beyond the negative, the focal point, the spectrum is formed. Either a camera or a light sensitive surface may be located at the focal point to measure its proportions. The spectrum is an optical Fourier transform of the scar pattern.

The apparatus used in this experiment had a light sensitive surface at the focal point. This light sensitive surface measured the concentrations of scar pattern orientations.[2] Because the spectrum is symmetrical, only half of it needs to be measured, as in Figure 3b. The light sensitive surface Figure 3c, is divided into thirty-two wedges of 5 degrees each. Each wedge measures the intensity of the spectrum showing on it, and thus, the relative number of lines in the scar pattern oriented in that direction. These measurements were recorded and used as an indication of scar orientation.

After the data were collected, they were key punched and processed as indicated in the next sections.

The terminology used to refer to the various measurements on the spectrum are as follows (Figure 4c). If a biface is held with the long axis pointing up and down, those scars sloping up to the left will be called "left-oriented" or sloping scars (Figure 4a). If the scar slopes up to the right (Figure 4b), the term "right-oriented" applies. Note that the slope is the same whichever end of the biface is pointed up.

Figure 4c illustrates the part of the 160-degree arc that each of the thirty-two wedges of arc segments measures, and the terms applied to portions of that arc. The six subareas, or subarcs, were defined more or less arbitrarily with some consideration for the modes in the distribution graph in Figure 7. For example, arc segments 1–6, which measure scars sloping very slightly up to the left, are called "left horizontal," etc., around the spectrum until measurements 27–32 are "right horizontal."

The ten degrees, which do not measure light, at the extreme end of the arc are blank because room was needed in the mechanism for electrical leads. If I were to use this apparatus again, I would rotate the negative 90 degrees so the long axis of the biface is horizontal in its holder. This would result in a loss of data in the vertical rather than horizontal elements of the spectrum. Twenty degrees of horizontal data were lost using the approach adopted in this experiment. I think the horizontal elements may have been very important. Results of the experiment might have been better had they been accounted for.

[2] The apparatus used was made available by Dr. John Davis, Chief, Geologic Research Section, Kansas Geological Survey, and of the Center for Research, University of Kansas, Lawrence.

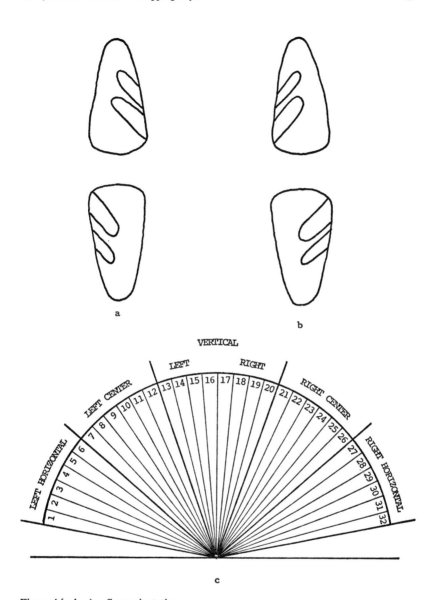

Figure 4 (a, b, c).   Scar orientation
a.   left oriented scars
b.   right oriented scars
c.   terminology for the 32 ace segments

GENERAL DATA DESCRIPTION

The following discussion of the data (see Figures 5 and 6) presents the general form of the data from the laser diffraction analysis and points out some preliminary differences between knappers.

A three decimal number was read from the laser diffraction spectrum for each wedge (5 degrees of arc). Thirty-two readings were taken from each scar pattern. To determine the distribution and dispersion of readings for each scar pattern, a mean, standard deviation and coefficient of variation (S∸X), was calculated. The highest mean was 0.194 (scar pattern 23). The lowest mean was .081 (scar pattern 54). A high mean indi-

Overall distribution of Scar Pattern Means

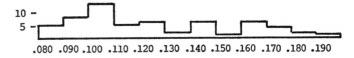

Knapper Means

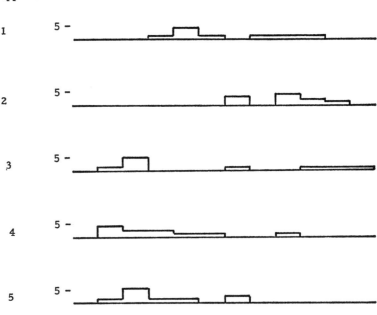

Figure 5.   Distributions of scar pattern means

cates that the photo negative was letting more light through in general, or that there were some very high readings which raised the mean. The coefficient of variation [c.v.], which tells how much dispersion there is from the mean corrected for the size of the numbers, indicates that both kinds of relationships occurred. A high mean and high c.v. would suggest the latter case, i.e. some very high and some very low numbers. Or, in other words, the knapper had a distinct tendency to orient scars in one or a few directions. Scar pattern 23 has the highest mean and c.v.; inspection of the piece confirms the unidirectional orientation of scars. A low c.v. indicates that there is no particular orientation to the scars.

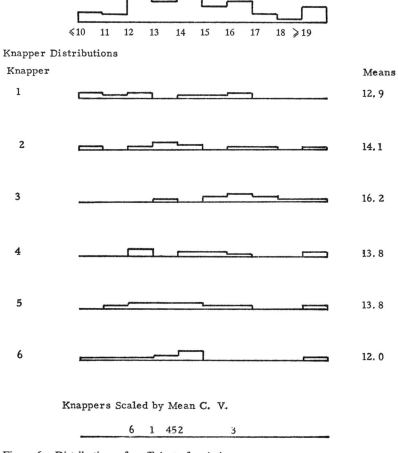

Figure 6. Distributions of coefficient of variation

Table 2. Correlation matrix

CORRELATIONS

	1	2	3	4	5	6	7	8	9	10	11	12	13	14	15	16	17	18	19	20
1 1LH	1.000																			
2 2LH	0.788	1.000																		
3 3LH	0.627	0.717	1.000																	
4 4LH	0.630	0.607	0.780	1.000																
5 5LH	0.331	0.399	0.460	0.735	1.000															
6 6LH	0.324	0.325	0.343	0.610	0.792	1.000														
7 7LC	0.212	0.266	0.337	0.524	0.708	0.824	1.000													
8 8LC	0.027	0.094	0.074	0.201	0.366	0.517	0.600	1.000												
9 9LC	0.001	0.007	0.079	0.178	0.356	0.362	0.611	0.713	1.000											
10 10LC	-0.076	-0.116	-0.011	0.070	0.290	0.179	0.491	0.435	0.773	1.000										
11 11LC	-0.100	-0.084	-0.216	-0.212	-0.118	-0.059	-0.116	0.390	0.257	0.240	1.000									
12 12LC	-0.387	-0.367	-0.195	-0.216	-0.134	-0.174	0.028	0.240	0.450	0.482	0.396	1.000								
13 13LV	-0.313	-0.121	-0.234	-0.350	-0.351	-0.181	-0.256	0.258	0.090	-0.065	0.591	0.416	1.000							
14 14LV	-0.275	-0.064	-0.082	-0.101	-0.140	0.018	-0.006	0.098	0.103	0.001	0.279	0.400	0.687	1.000						
15 15LV	-0.359	-0.116	-0.165	-0.245	-0.140	0.020	-0.022	0.190	0.099	0.054	0.288	0.143	0.502	0.675	1.000					
16 16 V	-0.252	-0.201	-0.323	-0.287	-0.149	-0.080	-0.167	0.161	0.054	0.130	0.459	0.119	0.417	0.502	0.305	1.000				
17 17RV	-0.164	-0.033	-0.195	-0.219	-0.230	-0.173	-0.190	-0.161	-0.135	-0.054	0.058	0.025	0.220	0.417	0.241	0.596	1.000			
18 18RV	-0.201	-0.148	0.019	-0.055	-0.108	-0.136	-0.004	-0.185	-0.140	-0.014	-0.219	-0.020	-0.273	-0.068	-0.095	0.425	0.540	1.000		
19 19RV	-0.341	-0.342	-0.089	-0.093	-0.021	-0.126	-0.181	-0.080	-0.170	-0.068	0.069	0.103	-0.334	-0.059	-0.154	-0.212	0.094	0.463	1.000	
20 20RC	-0.291	-0.324	-0.173	-0.182	-0.073	-0.181	-0.080	-0.184	-0.317	-0.212	-0.455	-0.122	-0.296	-0.201	-0.202	-0.344	-0.163	0.353	0.680	1.000
21 ?1?C	-0.250	-0.187	-0.276	-0.401	-0.233	0.149	0.121	-0.138	-0.168	-0.135	-0.186	-0.001	-0.191	-0.280	-0.227	-0.219	-0.321	0.100	0.357	0.594

24 24RC −0.156 −0.329 −0.099 −0.134 −0.057 −0.095 −0.083 −0.273 −0.024 −0.192 −0.167 −0.114 −0.000 −0.121 0.281
25 25RC −0.164 −0.300 −0.200 −0.254 −0.189 −0.320 −0.338 −0.566 −0.129 −0.289 −0.209 0.012 0.112 0.133 0.336
26 26RL −0.231 −0.215 −0.294 −0.394 −0.373 −0.485 −0.449 −0.424 −0.333 −0.249 −0.234 −0.072 0.042 0.067 0.015 0.215
27 27RL −0.176 −0.203 −0.243 −0.320 −0.472 −0.573 −0.517 −0.605 −0.435 −0.256 −0.146 −0.182 −0.140 −0.145 −0.067 0.088
28 28RL −0.160 −0.227 −0.249 −0.360 −0.515 −0.605 −0.570 −0.523 −0.427 −0.310 −0.278 −0.116 −0.216 −0.322 −0.354 −0.218 −0.127 0.095 0.172 0.140
29 29RL −0.018 −0.156 −0.144 −0.182 −0.274 −0.433 −0.448 −0.587 −0.353 −0.236 −0.345 −0.168 −0.101 −0.012 0.065 0.084
30 30RL 0.043 −0.014 −0.117 −0.176 −0.269 −0.376 −0.377 −0.461 −0.382 −0.316 −0.290 −0.255 −0.328 −0.217 −0.101 −0.045 0.052
31 31RL 0.220 0.074 −0.045 −0.028 −0.184 −0.306 −0.250 −0.441 −0.298 −0.245 −0.352 −0.396 −0.455 −0.473 −0.469 −0.236 −0.035 0.003 0.058
32 32RL 0.290 0.112 0.024 0.026 −0.176 −0.137 −0.222 −0.272 −0.329 −0.370 −0.254 −0.244 −0.423 −0.507 −0.467 −0.405 −0.221 −0.007 −0.134 −0.026

CORRELATIONS

	21	22	23	24	25	26	27	28	29	30	31	32
21 21RC	1.000											
22 22RC	0.422	1.000										
23 23RC	0.241	−0.177	1.000									
24 24RC	0.249	−0.125	0.521	1.000								
25 25RC	0.325	−0.096	0.461	0.450	1.000							
26 26RL	0.289	0.251	0.066	0.145	0.668	0.000						
27 27RL	0.206	−0.140	0.253	0.121	0.506	0.535	1.000					
28 28RL	0.183	0.001	0.023	−0.058	0.231	0.503	0.597	1.000				
29 29RL	0.126	−0.276	0.110	0.054	0.251	0.127	0.532	0.607	01.000			
30 30RL	0.056	−0.124	−0.066	−0.140	0.040	0.153	0.457	0.731	0.738	1.000		
31 31RL	0.053	−0.224	−0.034	−0.050	0.066	0.151	0.396	0.616	0.679	0.853	1.000	
32 32RL	0.006	−0.002	−0.018	−0.083	0.091	0.197	0.304	0.503	0.278	0.540	0.649	1.000

Table 3.   Eigenvalues, cumulative percentage of variance, and unit length eigenvectors. Laser diffraction data on biface scar patterns

	1	2	3	4	5	6	7	8	9	10
Eigenvalues	7.776	5.565	3.568	2.271	2.157	1.962	1.392	1.165	0.972	0.763
Cumulative %	0.243	0.417	0.528	0.599	0.667	0.728	0.772	0.808	0.838	0.862
Unit Length Eigenvectors										
1 1LH	-0.07	-0.31	0.20	-0.06	0.09	0.11	-0.07	0.01	-0.16	-0.08
2 2LH	-0.12	-0.26	0.24	-0.18	0.08	0.06	-0.00	0.21	0.10	-0.19
3 3LH	-0.11	-0.29	0.05	-0.18	0.02	0.13	0.13	0.27	0.04	-0.26
4 4LH	-0.16	-0.32	0.02	-0.11	-0.02	0.09	0.08	0.05	0.05	-0.07
5 5LH	-0.20	-0.25	-0.12	0.00	0.01	0.01	-0.06	-0.23	0.08	-0.09
6 6LH	-0.24	-0.20	-0.09	-0.01	0.12	-0.08	-0.00	-0.31	0.07	0.18
7 7LC	-0.24	-0.18	-0.18	0.10	-0.05	-0.13	-0.06	-0.16	0.20	0.13
8 8LC	-0.27	0.02	-0.05	0.24	0.10	-0.21	-0.04	0.09	-0.01	0.06
9 9LC	-0.24	-0.00	-0.10	0.33	-0.20	-0.03	-0.17	0.09	0.12	0.01
10 10LC	-0.17	0.03	-0.17	0.29	-0.31	0.06	-0.26	0.07	0.01	-0.13
11 11LC	-0.15	0.21	0.16	0.19	0.08	0.04	-0.03	0.22	-0.40	-0.03
12 12LC	-0.10	0.02	-0.13	0.24	-0.26	0.21	0.17	0.29	0.03	-0.03
13 13LV	-0.11	0.30	0.19	0.03	0.11	0.06	0.20	0.16	0.16	0.21
14 14LV	-0.15	0.22	0.09	-0.15	-0.11	0.10	0.44	-0.05	0.28	0.13
15 15LV	-0.15	0.25	0.10	-0.20	-0.03	-0.02	0.12	-0.31	0.13	-0.08
16 16 V	-0.11	0.26	0.13	-0.14	-0.02	0.01	-0.28	-0.26	-0.21	-0.28
17 17RV	-0.03	0.17	0.07	-0.44	-0.22	-0.02	-0.30	-0.02	-0.11	0.13
18 18RV	0.06	0.01	-0.21	-0.35	-0.24	-0.26	-0.11	0.32	-0.12	0.16
19 19RV	0.08	0.01	-0.35	-0.17	-0.22	-0.27	0.15	0.16	-0.02	-0.10
20 20RC	0.15	-0.01	-0.35	-0.11	-0.22	-0.22	0.22	0.01	0.06	-0.12
21 21RC	0.15	0.07	-0.28	0.16	0.12	-0.20	0.08	-0.06	-0.00	-0.19
22 22RC	0.01	0.17	0.05	0.05	0.25	-0.27	-0.03	0.12	-0.06	-0.19
23 23RC	0.11	-0.09	-0.23	0.00	0.51	0.38	0.22	0.07	-0.23	0.05
24 24RC	0.09	-0.00	-0.27	0.01	0.14	0.34	-0.01	-0.17	-0.35	0.27
25 25RC	0.21	0.01	-0.20	-0.07	0.10	0.31	-0.28	-0.05	0.20	0.03
26 26RL	0.22	0.08	-0.03	-0.01	0.09	0.08	-0.41	0.15	0.41	-0.06
27 27RL	0.26	0.03	0.08	0.11	0.17	0.25	0.01	0.00	0.32	-0.06
27 28RL	0.29	0.00	0.12	0.11	-0.05	-0.13	-0.01	0.13	0.09	-0.07
29 29RL	0.24	-0.07	0.11	0.09	0.14	0.02	0.09	-0.23	-0.18	-0.30
30 30RL	0.24	-0.10	0.22	0.15	-0.26	-0.17	0.14	-0.19	0.00	-0.06
31 31RL	0.23	-0.18	0.18	0.16	-0.17	-0.16	0.04	-0.07	-0.09	0.12
32 32PT	0.18	0.17	0.20	0.08	0.08	-0.17	-0.08	0.09	-0.02	0.56

If the average of a knapper's c.v.'s can be taken as an index of his tendency to orient scars in one or a few directions, the knappers studied can be scaled (from high to low) as 3, 2, 4, 5, 1, 6. Interestingly enough, the prehistoric knapper ranks lowest on this scale. With the exception of knapper 3, there seems to be a negative correlation between consistently oriented scars and length of experience.

With regard to experimental control, there is a tendency for the mean to drop as each knapper proceeds through the series. If the experiment were to be repeated, each knapper probably ought to be asked to make two or three trial bifaces before making the collected specimens. I am not sure of all the elements of the scar patterns that the means measures. At least partly it has to do with how well "warmed up" the knapper is.

To find important orientations, a listing of the data was made (Table 4). The data were standardized by rows (the mean for each scar pattern set to zero and measurements converted to units of standard deviation). Pluses were printed where measurements were greater than .5 standard deviations above the mean. Readily apparent is the fact that the most consistent orientations were vertical. High vertical scores mostly represent the ends of scars on the median ridge, and trimming flakes on the ends of the bifaces.

Right-oriented scars are a consistent feature. A histogram of the scores greater than the mean, Figure 7, indicates right high scores group into modes. The left, however, is different. There are no modes, but only erratic highs. The intergroup inconsistency of the left sloping scars will be valuable in distinguishing the tendencies of the various knappers.

TREATING THE DATA AS A POPULATION

Probably the most common situation to be dealt with in the analysis of idiosyncratic behavior in chipping styles will be a population of artifacts collected from a site, or series of sites, with no particular indication as to the maker. In these cases the population will be treated as a unit to be partitioned into subsets, with the assumption that each subset represents a knapper. Appropriate models for this operation are global clustering techniques, such as components-factor analysis and hierarchical clustering.

The diffraction data were standardized by rows (scar patterns). A principal components program (Wahlstedt and Davis 1968) extracted eight components with eigenvalues greater than 1.0. The eight components accounted for 81 percent of the variance. As was mentioned earlier, the

Table 4. Data matrix (+ = .5 standard deviation above the mean)

		Left Horizontal Scores > 0.50						Left Center						Left	
Knapper		1	2	3	4	5	6	7	8	9	10	11	12	13	14
1	1			+									+		
	2			+				+	+	+	+		+		
	3														
	4			+				+	+	+	+		+		
	5														
	6														
	7	+		+	+			+		+	+				
	8							+							
	9														
	10														
2	11												+	+	+
	12	+		+	+										
	13														+
	14	+	+	+	+	+	+	+		+					+
	15														+
	16														
	17	+			+			+	+	+			+		+
	18							+			+		+		+
	19							+			+				
	20									+	+				
3	21														
	22														
	23														
	24														
	25							+							
	26														
	27							+							
	28														
	29														+
	30														+
4	31	+													
	32	+	+	+											
	33														
	34	+			+		+	+							+
	35														
	36						+								
	37			+	+										
	38	+		+	+	+		+							
	39										+				+
	40														
5	41														
	42												+		
	43					+		+							
	44							+		+	+		+		
	45							+							
	46														
	47				+	+									
	48							+							
	49						+	+							
	50					+	+	+			+				
6	51														
	52					+									
	53														
	54														
	55														
	56							+							
	57												+		
	58	+													
	59					+	+	+					+		+
	60	+		+	+	+									

	Vertical			Right		Right Center						Right Horizontal					
5	16	17	18	19	20	21	22	23	24	25	26	27	28	29	30	31	32
	+		+	+				+	+								
	+	+	+										+	+	+	+	+
−	+	+	+					+	+								
	+	+	+					+	+	+						+	
−	+	+	+													+	
−	+	+	+	+				+	+	+						+	+
	+	+												+	+	+	
−	+	+						+	+					+	+	+	
−	+	+			+			+	+	+	+	+		+		+	+
	+							+	+							+	+
−	+	+														+	
	+																
−	+	+	+	+				+					+	+	+	+	+
−	+																+
−	+											+					
−	+	+										+			+	+	+
	+	+						+	+	+				+		+	
−	+	+	+	+									+	+	+	+	+
	+											+	+	+	+	+	+
−	+	+															
	+		+			+			+	+	+	+	+	+	+	+	+
−	+	+	+						+					+		+	
−	+	+	+					+	+					+			
−	+	+	+														
	+	+	+	+													
−	+	+	+	+				+	+								
−	+	+	+														
	+	+	+						+	+						+	+
															+	+	+
	+	+	+	+	+											+	
	+	+	+													+	
	+		+					+	+	+				+	+	+	
	+	+	+						+	+					+	+	+
	+															+	
	+	+	+		+			+	+	+		+	+	+	+	+	+
	+	+															
	+	+	+	+	+			+	+			+		+			
			+	+	+												+
	+	+	+	+		+		+	+			+		+	+	+	
	+		+	+				+	+					+	+	+	+
	+		+	+										+	+	+	+
	+	+	+	+	+			+	+					+	+	+	+
			+	+		+		+	+	+				+			
	+		+	+				+	+	+							
	+			+	+	+		+	+			+		+	+	+	
	+	+	+	+				+	+	+						+	
	+	+	+					+	+	+				+	+	+	+
	+	+	+					+	+	+				+	+	+	+
	+	+	+	+				+	+	+				+	+	+	+
	+		+			+		+	+	+				+		+	+
	+							+	+					+	+	+	
	+								+					+	+	+	+
	+					+		+	+	+		+		+	+	+	+

Tabel 5.

1.731
1.639
1.540
1.454
1.362
1.270
1.178
1.085
0.993
0.901
0.809
0.717
0.625
0.532
0.440
0.348
0.256
0.164
0.071
-0.021
-0.113
-0.205
-0.297
-0.390
-0.482
-0.574
-0.666
-0.758
-0.850
-0.943
-0.035

+32 +14 +12 +47 +37 +38 +60 +58 +34 +36 +55. +54 +40 +16 +17 +64. +35 +48 +59 +22 +19 +9 +10 +31 +24 +6 .25 +26 *+27 +33 +5 +21 +18 +13 +30 +29. +3 +28 +4 *+23 +41 +15

+11

+8

+20

+39   +44

+2

+53

+51

+57

+7 +56   +42 +52

+43 +45

+49

2.8544   2.1908   1.5273   0.8637   0.2001   −0.4634   −1.1270   −7.1905   −2.4541   −3.1176   −3.7812

−1.127
−1.219
−1.311
−1.404
−1.496
−1.588
−1.680
−1.772
−1.865
−1.957
−2.049
−2.141
−2.233
−2.326
−2.418
−2.510
−2.602
−2.694
−2.780
−2.879
−2.971
−3.063
−3.155
−3.247
−3.340
−3.432
−3.524
−3.616
−3.708

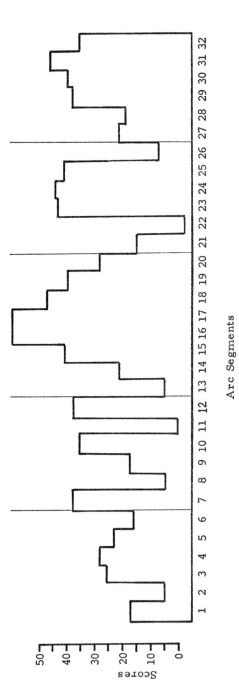

Figure 7.   Distribution of scores greater than the variable means

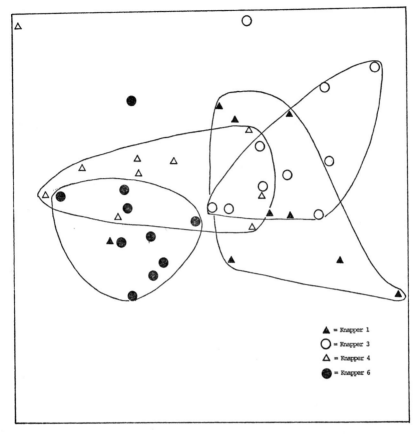

Figure 8.

components accounting for variables on the left side of the laser spectra could be expected to discriminate among the knappers best because of the erratic behavior of that segment of the spectrum. These variables were strongly associated with Component II. As was expected, it separated the knappers best. A search through plots of component scores indicated that Component III was second in discriminatory powers. The others have little discriminatory power. Table 5 is a plot of component scores for II plotted against III. The four most experienced knappers are fairly well divided into two groups of two knappers (Figure 8): knappers 6 and 4 are together on the left, and knappers 1 and 3 appear on the right. There is some overlap of knapper 4 into the other group (three pieces).

The inexperience of knappers 2 and 5 can be seen (Figure 9). Their scar patterns are spread over the entire area on the plot. Even so, the two inexperienced knappers seem to have distinctive enough styles; one appears

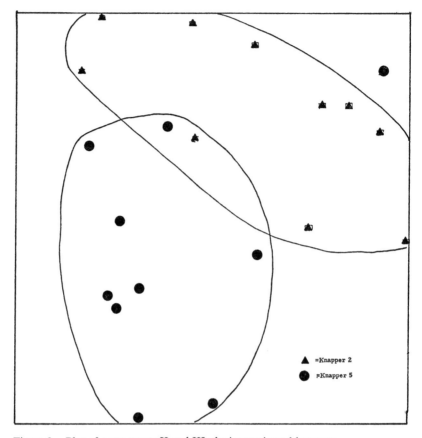

Figure 9.   Plot of components II and III, the inexperienced knappers

at the top of the plot and the other toward the bottom with little overlap in distributions.

(The controlled nature of the diffraction data makes them a very interesting tool for comparison of factoring methods. I tried unrotated principal components, varimax and oblimim rotation (BMDX72). Of course, the factor matrix is more esthetic when rotated. When plotting the component or factor scores, however, unrotated principal components, which are characterized by high correlation with the original data, usually produce the most desirable results in terms of separation of knappers. This has proven to be the case on five sets of lithic data with which I have had experience. There are, of course, still numerous factor analytic techniques with which I have no experience.)

If this particular sample were drawn from a site, it would be hard to separate the population into knappers by principal components. The fact

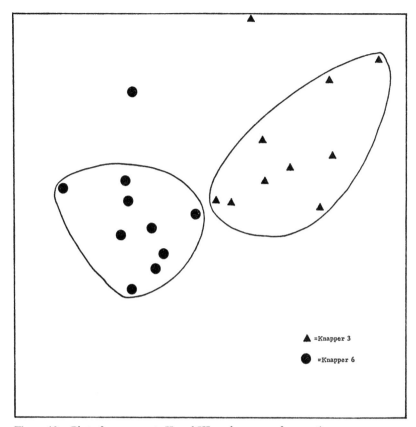

Figure 10.   Plot of components II and III, a clear case of separation

that some knappers can be separated from others, however (e.g. knappers 3 and 6, Figure 10), suggests potential utility for the methodology. The addition of further information on bifaces, such as contextual data and other measurements, would probably separate artifacts into groups attributable to knappers.

As Don Crabtree points out, this may be a particularly difficult sample to deal with:

Our replicas are usually patterned after a particular aboriginal artifact, while prehistoric man made a specific artifact over a long period of time with little or no deviation. Since the purpose of the Bordes and Crabtree experiments have been to replicate a variety of techniques, I think we perhaps would show more variation due to constantly attempting to replicate various tool types of diverse industries (personal communication Jan. 2, 1972).

In support of Crabtree's judgment, I would say that the Simon knapper produced by far the tightest cluster of artifacts of the six knappers used in the experiment. Such tight clustering would additionally contribute to identification of knappers from an archaeological context.

TREATING THE SCAR PATTERNS AS INDIVIDUALS

Cluster analysis techniques give a much higher resolution analysis of a population than do factor analysis techniques. This characteristic was found by Rohlf to make cluster analysis more useful in classification of animals at the specific level, while factor analysis is more satisfactory at higher levels of taxonomy (Rohlf 1968).

A hierarchical clustering program (Veldman 1967) was run on the scar patterns to see how the groups interdigitated at a low level of abstraction. Error showed a marked increase when the program attempted to reduce the number of groups from five to four. Five groups were therefore selected as the most appropriate number of groups. Table 6 shows groups displayed against knappers. The results are essentially the same as the components analysis. Knappers 1 and 3 are largely together, as are knappers 4 and 6.

Table 6.   Knappers classified into groups by hierarchical clustering

		Knappers					
		1	2	3	4	5	6
	1	[3]	[3]	1	1	1	0
	2	[5]	1	[7]	[3]	1	1
Groups	3	1	[3]	2	0	1	0
	4	1	1	0	[6]	[7]	[8]
	5	0	2	0	0	0	0

TREATING THE POPULATION IN GROUPS

The principal components and hierarchical clustering models are convenient because no assumptions have to be made about groups before the analysis is performed. Suppose, however, that two caches of bifaces were known from an area in which several sites had been excavated. An analysis of variance of the two caches leads to the belief that the two caches were made by different people. By use of a discriminant function program it would be possible to: (1) determine a set of functions which would maximally separate the two groups or caches of tools into discrete numerical

Figure 11. Plot of first of two canonical variables (numbers = knappers)

clusters, and (2) classify all of the bifaces excavated from the sites with one of the caches, thus identifying it with the maker of that cache. Only the first step is described here.

To demonstrate this procedure, a discriminant function was performed on the data (BMDO 7M). Based on the results of the discriminant function the program was able to classify all but one of the fifty-nine scar patterns with its maker. Scar pattern 30 was classified as being made by knapper 1 mistakenly. Needless to say, this ability to classify scar patterns with knappers is quite impressive. Figure 11 is a plot of the first two canonical variables from an analysis performed on the diffraction data transformed by the discriminant functions. The plot is equivalent to the plot of component scores (Figures 9–10). The effects of the discriminant function can be seen in the clear separation between knappers 6, 5, 4, and 2. Knappers 1 and 3 are together in the plot. The plot, however, represents only the first two dimensions (71 percent of the dispersion). Knappers 1 and 3 would be separated by the other two significant canonical variables not shown.

CONCLUSIONS

This paper has presented a model for stone tool production which incorporates the concept of idial, or individual, styles. It has further suggested that detection of idial styles would aid in the delineation of the economic and social processes of past societies. Possible sources of variation between stone knappers have been catalogued. One of these sources of variation, scar pattern orientation, was tested using a controlled population of bifaces made by modern stone knappers. Methodology for collecting data on scar patterns and for analyzing those data were outlined and tested. The tests indicate the following results:
1.   There is enough variability in scar pattern orientation to separate some stone knappers.
2.   Separation may not be possible in all cases due to overlap, if the criteria of a more powerful mode of analysis cannot be met (e.g. discriminant function).
3.   The degree of skill, practice, and experience of a knapper will influence the "tightness" of his cluster of scar patterns.
4.   Prehistoric knappers may have tighter clusters than modern knappers, due to long experience at making the same artifacts. Tighter clustering would aid idial classification.

The analyses suggest, further, that scar patterns, possibly in conjunction with other data, make it possible to discriminate among knappers.

REFERENCES

ADOVASIO, J.
   n.d.   *Prehistoric basketry of Western North America.* Smithsonian Institution Contributions to Anthropology. (In preparation.)
BINFORD, L.
   1962   Archeology as anthropology, *American Antiquity* 28:217–225.

BINFORD, L., S. BINFORD
 1966 "A functional analysis of functional variability in the Mousterian of Lavallois Facies," in *Recent Studies in Paleoanthropology*. Edited by J. Desmond Clark and F. Howell. American Anthropologist Special Publication 68 (2).

BUTLER, B. ROBERT
 1963 An early man site at Big Camas Prairie, South Central Idaho. *Tebiwa* 6 (1):22–33.

DEETZ, J.
 1967 *Invitation to Archaeology*. Natural History Press.

DIXON, J. *editor*
 1968 *BMD Manual*. Berkeley: University of California Press.

HEMPEL, C.
 1966 *Philosophy of natural science*. Englewood Cliffs, New Jersey: Prentice-Hall.

MUTO, G.
 1971a "A stage analysis of the manufacture of stone tools," in *Great Basin Anthropological Conference 1970: Selected papers*. University of Oregon Anthropological Papers 1:109–117.
 1971b "A technological analysis of the early stages in the manufacture of lithic artifacts." Unpublished master's thesis, Idaho State University.

PRESTON, F., D. GREEN, J. DAVIS
 1970 *Numerical characterization of reservoir rock pore structure*. Final Report to the American Petroleum Institute Research Project 103. Lawrence, Kansas: University of Kansas, Committee of Research.

ROHLF, F.
 1968 Stereograms in numerical taxonomy. *Systematic Zoology* 17(3):246–255.

ROUSE, I.
 1939 *Prehistory in Haiti, a study in method*. Yale University Publications in Anthropology 21.

VELDMAN, D.
 1967 *Fortran programming for the behavioral sciences*. New York: Holt, Rinehart and Winston.

WAHLSTEDT, W., J. DAVIS
 1968 *Fortran IV program for computation and display of principal components*. Computer Contribution 21. Lawrence, Kansas: State Geological Survey.

Graph Theoretic Analysis of Lithic Tools from Northern Chile

L. LEWIS JOHNSON

One of the aims of archaeological studies is to understand the past cultures of man, and one of the paths we have pursued, particularly in early man research, has been the study of lithic technologies. Classically, this work has included typological and functional studies. Now, however, we are beginning to develop a repertory of new techniques for studying and interpreting tool manufacture – a style of investigation which is coming to be called technological analysis. Among these techniques, two are particularly important: experimental flint knapping and multivariate analysis using computers. Briefly, flint knappers are looking for a general understanding of the physical properties of rock from the point of view of the stone toolmaker. As knappers have mastered more and more of the subtleties of stone working, they have become aware of the many complex factors affecting the shaping of a tool (Crabtree 1969:2). This has led to more detailed studies of lithic waste from sites. The possession of large amounts of carefully described material has led, in turn, to an increasing interest in the possibilities of computer analysis.

Man has often been defined as the toolmaker (e.g. Oakley 1949), patterned toolmaking being the earliest recognizable feature which separates man from the rest of nature, but there has been little interest among archaeologists in technology *per se*. Most preceramic archaeological studies have concentrated on creating seriations, in discovering changes in the form of artifacts through time which can be used as temporal indices. Once these sequences are set up they are used in comparative analyses, to trace changing historical relationships from area to area. Now archaeologists are trying to determine why trajectories parallel each other or diverge from one another.

Another line of archaeological inquiry concerns the uses of stone tools. Traditional archaeological terminology reflects this interest in tool function – such terms as scraper, knife, spokeshave have always been used in archaeological analysis. However, only recently have practical studies been attempted. Information for such studies has come from a number of sources. These include detailed analysis of the association of tools with each other and with other remains in archaeological sites which has provided limits for possible used (Leroi-Gourhan and Brezillon 1966; de Lumley 1969) and microscopic analysis which has allowed the identification of traces of use which can be interpreted in the light of associative possibilities (Semenov 1964). Experimentation with duplicates of archaeological implements and ethnographic analogy with the few people in the world still making and using stone tools have aided the interpretation based on association and microscopic analysis (Gould, et al. 1971). The results emerging from these researches are increasing our understanding of the varied functions of lithic tools in prehistoric life.

Now, in addition to all that the previous work has accomplished, technological analysis is opening doors to aspects of ancient society never before approached. Interest in these aspects is due, primarily, to the flint-knapping of Crabtree, Bordes, and their apprentices. Unlike many people who try to duplicate paleolithic implements, both Crabtree and Bordes are interested in the relationships between their output and ancient stone tools (Crabtree 1969: 5). Many knappers are interested only in the apparent replication of stone tools – in making a Folsom point that looks like one rather than in making one in the way it was actually made by the Folsom hunters (Neill 1952; Mewhinney 1957).

Both Bordes and Crabtree, on the other hand, want not only to replicate the product, but also the process (Crabtree 1966; Bordes and Crabtree 1969). They use the same tools as the prehistoric knappers and compare both the finished tool AND the debitage to archaeological examples. In addition, both Bordes and Crabtree, who use knapping as a scientific aid, enjoy sharing their findings and skill with others – Crabtree has devoted the last few summers to training students in flint-knapping techniques. Knapping ability is very important for a lithic analyst, for, as Leonardo da Vinci wrote, "all sciences are vain and full of errors that are not born of experience, ... that do not at their origin, middle or end pass through any of the five senses (da Vinci 1939: I, 33)."

For example, how many archaeologists who are not knappers know that flakes frequently come off cores with "use wear" already present on their edges? An archaeologist who is a flint knapper may be over-cautious in his analysis, but he is not likely to make completely implausible or impossible interpretations of his data. Many illustrations of knapping show angles of impact which any knapper knows to be impossible (e.g. Bordaz 1970: Figures 4 and 8; Semenov 1964: Figure 4, Number 2; Figure 5, Number 2; Figure 15, Number 4) or interpretations of the formation of use wear on an edge in ways that contradict all of the physical laws of the fracture of lithic materials.

I don't know how many knappers share with me the experience of having done an analysis of a lithic collection before learning to knap and then looking back at it after having become a proficient knapper – it is a sobering experience. For example, retouch on the dorsal surface of the striking platform, which I interpreted as functional retouch (Lewis 1966), I now recognize as core preparation, important for the understanding of manufacture but meaningless in a study of tool function.

Knapping is especially important for someone studying a site in which lithic debris predominates. As Crabtree (1969: 4) has said, waste flakes sometimes furnish more diagnostic traits than the completed artifact. In addition, in many situations, the artifact is gone and all that remains to be studied is the debitage.

In trying to refine the understanding gained through flint knapping and in applying it to the study of archaeological industries, the ideal test case or laboratory would be a quarry containing only one uniform material, which was used by only one group of people for only a short period of time.

Because of vast differences in physical properties from one knappable rock to another, it is difficult to compare two industries, or two tools, made on two different rock types. Thus, there are things that are easy to do when chipping obsidian but are difficult to do when chipping flint. Glassy obsidian pressure-flakes much more easily than flint does. It is even harder to chip stones such as slate or petrified wood which have a definite planer fabric that deflects blows and causes step fractures not intended by the workmen. However, people who use these materials have an easier time than those using stones with irregular fracture strains in them, because they can learn the fracture properties and conform their knapping to them. With heterogeneous materials, the knapper can only hope that he will be able to produce a functional tool. Once studies of lithic technology have advanced it should be possible to sort humanly caused variation from geological variation even in the most difficult cases. However, at present it is easier to hold one variable constant, in this case the structural, while studying variation in the other.

If a test case were available, there would still be the problem of analyzing the vast quantity of evidence. A knapper knows that in order to replicate a single flake, many diverse conditions must be considered, such as the basic nature of the raw material, the shape of the outer surface of the core, the strength of the striking platform and the angle and force of his blow. He also knows that many of these conditions will affect the appearance of the flake produced. In some cases the relation between action and result is clear to knappers – for example, other parameters being constant, changing the angle of percussion will change the shape of the resultant flake. For other flake features the relationship between action and result is not yet understood – among the latter are eraillure flakes and the determinants of their form and size. In lithic analysis, all types of variation that the archaeologist as knapper thinks are important must be considered.

A great many attributes show variation, even when one considers only flake waste. Obviously, all variation cannot be taken into account, nor is all variation pertinent (Clarke 1968: 15). The archaeologist-knapper must select from the total variation those humanly imposed and geological attributes which he knows or suspects to be pertinent to producing the desired tool shape. There is always the possibility that the archaeologist will leave out an important attribute and thus reduce the usefulness of his analysis. Thus, attributes must be consciously and carefully chosen.

The aim of a technological analysis is to discover the humanly deter-mined design which the knappers imposed on their material. Because analysis is a tool to clarify relations between artifacts which are not immediately obvious, although they exist, the attributes chosen for artifact analysis are critical to the results of the analysis. Thus one must be careful not to chose arbitrarily attributes which will impose the analyst's own pattern and thereby obscure the original people's. Although the significance of the analytical results may not be immediately clear, if the attributes are reasonable it should be obvious once the results are studied.

In practice, the archaeologist interested in technological analysis finds himself with many stones which are described by many multistate attributes. In order to continue his analysis he needs to summarize his data so that he can see the patterns present in it. This is where the com-puter becomes a virtual necessity: it would be possible to perform a multivariate analysis on a large collection without using a computer, but it would take years. Even with a large computer this type of analysis is difficult and time-consuming because it is not the class of problem which computers are designed to solve and therefore they are inefficient, in computer terms, when trying to do so.

Once this data manipulation is completed and the computer has shown which attributes are or are not associated, the archaeologist-knapper comes back into the picture. He must analyze and interpret the computer output to discover what its lithic technological meaning is. All the computer does is to find the order present in the data as it has been presented by the archaeologist. It is the job of the archaeologist to find out the causes and significance of the order.

DATA

The lithic material I studied comes from two quarries in northern Chile located on a ridge overlooking the Loa River between the town of Calama and the village of Chiu Chiu. In this area there are many outcrops of silicified tuff, a soft stone, which, however, is eminently chippable. It also has a uniform lithology which means that structural heterogeneity is minimized. The other relevant feature of these outcrops, and of the quarries which are present on most of them, is that the material seems to have been used during only a short time in the prehistoric period. Residents in the later preceramic and ceramic periods preferred to use cherts and basalts, which are available, although rarer, in the region. These latter stones are harder than the tuff and therefore take a better edge that lasts longer.

In the sites of these later people we found VERY LITTLE tuff, certainly not enough to account for the lithic debris found in the quarries. In addition, even in the earlier periods the quarries seem to have been used for a limited time. Thus, our studies of the collections from the sites in different subregions indicate that each region is distinct from the others. This is unlikely to be due to contemporaneous cultural variation, because, even with greater moisture in the area during the late Pleistocene-early post-Pleistocene period, the vegetation would not have increased to the point that more than one group of hunter-gatherers could be sustained by the region at the same time.

The collections analyzed in this report come from two sites belonging to the Aguas Verdes complex. This complex is believed to date to the early post-Pleistocene period, but its absolute dates are not yet known, nor are they essential to the present study. The inhabitants seem to have been generalized hunters and gatherers living off the riverine resources. The Atacama desert, in which these sites are located, is extremely dry and the only vegetation in the area is clustered along the river. However, when there is the least bit of rain, plants do spring up on the desert pavement, so that, if at the time of occupation it was only slightly wetter than it is today, the desert might have been a little more hospitable.

As indicated above, the sites are on the desert pavement on top of their own raw material sources and are, therefore, quarry sites. However, they both are on the crest of a ridge and overlook vegetated areas called *vegas*. In the region of these sites, the major *vegas* are located along the Río Loa, and the two overlook the Salar Brinkerhoff, one of the largest river *vegas*. The significance of this positioning for hunter-gatherers is in being able to spot animals on the move from far away. There is also the possibility of being able to work on manufacturing and mending tools while waiting for the probably scarce fauna to appear. These sites may also have been camps, but there is at present insufficient evidence to identify them definitely as such.

Due to their position on the open pampa, the sites have been stripped by the wind of all material except the lithic implements. The wind has also succeeded in weathering the implements to the point that, on most, any use marks which were once present have been erased.

The first site of interest, RAnL 199B, extends sixty meters along the crest of the hill and twenty meters across it. It is basically a continuous workshop. The second site, RAnL 200B, begins 528 meters to the southwest of RAnL 199 along the same ridge. It is a group of four small workshops strung out along the ridge for a distance of eighty-eight meters. Each workshop is approximately four meters in diameter. The sampling procedure used on these sites was to set up two-by-two-meter squares on the richest sections of the site and to collect all of the material within these squares. This was a method designed to gather a large amount of significant information from the center of workshop areas while limiting the number of squares collected. The largest number of artifacts collected from one square, comprising flakes, blades, cores and tools, was 1,126 and the smallest was 175 artifacts.

The four analyzed collections from RAnL-199B include the surface collections from three two-by-two-meter squares, RAnL 199B-1, RAnL 199B-3, RAnL 199B-7 and the collection from a one-by-one-meter test square excavated under RAnL 199B-1 which is numbered RAnL 199B-12. In this test pit there was no evidence of stratigraphy, and bedrock was encountered at an approximate depth of fifty centimeters. Two collections were analyzed from site RAnL 200B, 200B-1, and 200B-3. These were obtained from the most easterly and most westerly of the workshops.

In the rest of this paper, I will discuss the preliminary analysis of one-half of the cores from the recorded samples from RAnL 199B and 200B. I decided to begin with this small sample in order to test the various methods being used for their success in producing archaeologically meaningful results. I will start with an outline of the system used to record the cores and with the results of a preliminary analysis designed to give a basic count of the representation of the attribute states. This preliminary analysis was performed on the total sample of 345 cores from the six recorded site sections. The half-sample used in the subsequent analytic steps consists of every other core recorded.

CORE RECORDING SYSTEM

In the recording system for the artifacts, an attempt was made to isolate the culturally and technically significant attributes and to set them up quantitatively. These aims were only partially met, but each revision of the system will bring it closer to the final goal of replicability. Only when replication is possible will one researcher really be able to use another's results.

Some of the attributes which were isolated should be universal to lithic implements, others are particular to these collections. The major member of the latter group is the material used for the tools. This attribute needs few states for this collection because only one material was used during this time period in northern Chile. In general, the wide variety of materials from which stone tools can and have been made suggests that this attribute should be left open, to be filled in and described for each collection.

The problems which came up during the recording of the cores and the changes in the system which are already seen to be necessary will be covered below in the discussion of the individual attributes used. A problem which plagues anyone trying to originate and work with a recording system is that, after a certain number of tools have been recorded, it is difficult to continue to modify the system because of the impossibility of re-recording the bulk of the material. Therefore, every system actually used on collections is unsatisfactory by the end of the research because the final revisions have not been entered. However, they can be entered for the next analysis, continuing the improvement of the system.

When I set up the attribute states I was trying to account for all possible variations in the attributes which I thought MIGHT prove important. Some of the attributes were necessary for my information but not for an analysis of the technology of the Aguas Verdes quarries. An example of these is core attribute 17, Weathering. The degree of weathering gives me some idea of the variation in conditions which the site sections have faced since deposition and could indicate why some other attribute had states underrepresented at a particular section. Because the sections occur on various slopes of the hill, they differ in their relationship to the wind. Some of the characteristics of manufacture, particularly fine retouch, can be obscured by wind blasting, particularly on rock as soft as this silicified tuff. However, the weathering in itself can give me no information about the peoples' technology.

Some of the differences between the sites or sections were obvious by inspection and were so strong that including them in the final analysis would overly bias it toward difference. For example, almost all of the artifacts from RAnL 199B were made on tan tuff whereas almost all of those from RAnL 200B were made on light green tuff. Therefore, to include the attribute Material in an analysis aimed, in part, at discovering differences in technology between 199B and 200B would be self-defeating. However, once clusters have been formed, not using this attribute, it is interesting to check them for the odd colors to see if these have clustered. If so, it could be due to the artificers treating them differently or to the rock reacting differently to identical treatment. Finally, in the particular sites with which I was working, many of the states I set up were not important and therefore had to be eliminated before proceeding with the analysis. Occasionally, some straight elimination was possible where no artifact at all possessed a particular state. In this case the state is simply eliminated from consideration and there is no further problem.

A more difficult problem arises when many artifacts possess some of the states and very few possess others. Attributes with state representations which are very off-balanced can bias the results of a cluster analysis by having more influence in the ultimate formation of the clusters than they should. Sometimes, when the states are all very different, the only thing that can be done about this problem is to be aware of it in evaluating the final results of the analysis. At other times it is possible to group similar states into a single larger state which then can be used in the clustering process.

In presenting the recording system for cores, I will discuss it primarily as it finally emerged after the original counts but before the clustering step. Where the preliminary analysis produced clear differences between sites or sections which had not been suspected these will be indicated.

The terminology used in the system owes a great deal to White's description of core analysis (1963). The attributes are numbered according to the computer card column in which they are to be found (Table 1). Attributes 1–6 identify the core according to its provenience (A 1–2), its nature (A 3) and its individual number (A 4–6). Attribute 7, Core Preparation, refers to the shaping of the core prior to its use as a core. A prepared core is similar to a Mesoamerican blade core or a core for

Table 1. Recording system for cores

Columns	Attribute and states
1–2	Site number
	01 RAnL 199B–1
	02 RAnL 199B–3
	03 RAnL 199B–7
	04 RAnL 199B–12
	05 RAnL 200B–1
	06 RAnL 200B–3
3	Tool category
	F Flake
	B Blade
	C Core
	O Obscured or unidentifiable blank
4–6	Individual artifact number
7	Core preparation
	1 Prepared
	2 Partially prepared
	3 Unprepared
	4 Fragment
8–9	Platforms
	01–04 Single
	05–07 Two
	08, 09, 13, More than two
	10–12 Joint
10–11	Shape
	01 Polyhedric
	02, 12 Flat or block
	03, 04 Keeled
	05–09 Pyramidal, conical or tongue-shaped
	10, 11 Discoidal
	13 Fragment
12	Blanks
	1 Flakes
	2 Flakes and blades
	3 Blades
13	State
	1 Whole
	2 Broken
14	Termination
	1 Exhausted
	2 Considerable Use
	3 Minimally used
	4 Broken
15–16	Total number of visible scars
17	Weathering
	1 Unweathered
	2 Weathered
18	Uncore area
	1 Platform
	2 No uncore area
	3 Cortex

Columns	Attribute and states
	4 Unidentifiable or break
	5 Positive bulb, i.e. a core on a flake
	6 Multiple
19	Condition of length
	1 Whole
	2 Broken
20–23	Length
24	Condition of width
	1 Whole
	2 Broken
25–27	Width
28–30	Thickness
33–35	Angle of percussion
44–46	
36–38	Scar length
47–49	
39–41	Scar width
50–52	

removing Levallois flakes. The entire surface of the core has been treated so as to gain perfect blanks. A partially prepared core has had some of the surface irregularities removed, and the flakes or blades removed are more or less of a pattern, but the preparation has not gone as far as in the previous case. Finally, an unprepared core is one at which the people just "hit away," taking for use, or wanting for use, whatever shape of flake came off – the flake shape is not really regulated in any way. Thus, the preparation refers to the preparation on the core of what will be the dorsal surface of the flake to be removed. Obviously, the more a core has been used, the harder it will be to judge the preparation. This is particularly true for the unprepared cores because any core which has been used repeatedly tends to take on an appearance of regularity because it is easier to knap following the lines of weakness already set up on the core than it is to start out in new directions each time one wishes to remove a flake. The state Fragment would seem to explain itself – a piece which has the characteristics of a core, but which has been broken sufficiently to prevent the determination of its likelihood of preparation.

Definite preparation seems more common in 199B than in 200B (Table 2A). This, in combination with a greater prevalence of flakes and blades with cortex in 200B, may be due to the nodules of raw material at 200B being smaller than at 199B. If this is the case one would expect a larger proportion of cortex covered flakes because new nodules must be used more frequently, and one would also expect fewer prepared cores because preparation involves the removal of a fair amount of core to

Table 2.   Basic counts of attribute state distributions among cores (by sites)

A.   Attribute 7: Core Preparation

	1	2	3	4
	Prepared	Partial	Unprepared	Fragment
199B–1	50	36	66	
199B–3	16	27	7	
199B–7	6	14	12	
199B–12	21	17	5	
200B–1	8	18	2	2
200B–3		24	15	
Totals	101	136	107	2

B.   Attribute 8–9: Platforms

	Single	Two	More than two	Joint
199B–1	72	43	10	27
199B–3	18	13	5	14
199B–7	14	7	4	7
199B–12	23	9	3	4
200B–1	9	8	7	6
200B–3	18	11	3	7
Totals	154	91	32	65

C.   Attribute 10–11: Core shape

	Polyhedric	Flat	Keeled	Pyramidal	Discoid	Fragment
199B–1	44	58	17	26	6	1
199B–3	18	16	5	7	4	
199B–7	9	12	5	4		2
199B–12	12	17	1	11	1	1
200B–1	11	10	2	3		4
200B–3	16	11	3	6	1	2
Totals	110	124	33	57	12	10

D.   Attribute 12: Blanks

	Flakes	Flakes & Blades	Blades
199B–1	82	46	24
199B–3	30	15	5
199B–7	20	12	
199B–12	16	19	8
200B–1	16	11	3
200B–3	31	7	1
Totals	195	110	41

E.   Attribute 13: State

	Whole	Broken
199B–1	118	34
199B–3	43	7
199B–7	28	4
199B–12	38	5
200B–1	20	10
200B–3	32	7
Totals	279	67

F.   Attribute 14: Termination

	Exhausted	Considerable	Minimal	Broken
199B–1	63	47	27	15
199B–3	26	16	4	4
199B–7	13	14	3	2
199B–12	28	10	4	1
200B–1	16	8		6
200B–3	14	19	3	3
Totals	165	114	41	31

G.   Attribute 15–16: Number of scars

	1	2	3	4	5	6	7	8–14
199B–1	24	21	26	16	20	8	13	24
199B–3	3	4	11	8	4	7	4	9
199B–7	5	5	3	5	5	3	1	3
199B–12	4	5	6	8	7	6	1	6
200B–1	3	2	4	4	2	6	4	5
200B–3	1	4	4	3	5	6	1	8
Totals	46	41	54	44	43	36	27	55

H.   Attribute 18: Uncore area

	Platform	None	Cortex	Break	Pos. Bulb	Multiple
199B–1	53	37	28	23	7	4
199B–3	12	7	5	7	6	3
199B–7	12	9	7	1	2	1
199B–12	12	14	1	9	6	1
200B–1	13	7	3	1	1	5
200B–3	14	6	14	3		2
Totals	116	80	58	44	22	16

arrive at the desired shape. With small nodules, this preparation would leave no or little core from which to remove blanks.

The number of platforms on a core (A8–9) varied from one to six. This is a two column attribute because these were originally recorded in considerable detail which gave the placement of multiple platforms.

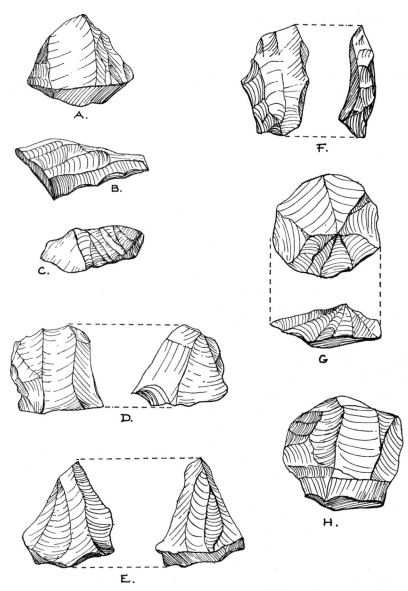

Figure 1. Idealized core shapes
A. Polyhedric; B. Flat; C. Keeled; D. Pyramidal; E. Conical; F. Tongue-shaped; G. Discoidal; and H. Block

After the original tabulation was made it was discovered that many of the states had very few members and that some of the information was redundant, being covered in Attribute 10–11, Core Shape. The final system has four platform designations: Single, Two, More than two, and Joint (Table 2B). A joint platform is one in which flakes going in two directions are removed from the same ridge on the core – one down the front side and one down the back side, so to speak.

Core Shape, Attribute 10–11, was also reduced considerably. This was necessitated both by redundancy and by underrepresentation of states. The original shapes which were defined can be seen in Figure 1. Their number was reduced primarily by combining those which might, through further use, become each other. This resulted in the combination of Flat and Block and of Pyramidal, Conical, and Tongue. Keeled and Discoidal had to remain separate, despite their small numbers, because their shape does not seem likely to change into any of the other shapes (Table 2C). The proportions of various core shapes in the 199B–1 and 12 collections are somewhat different from those in the other four collections.

Attribute 12, Blanks, refers to the nature of the blanks removed from the core. Although blades were defined on dorsal characteristics in addition to length, width, and axis of percussion parameters, the latter are the only ones visible on the core. Therefore, a blade scar is defined as one in which the length, measured along the axis of percussion, is at least twice as great as the width, measured at right angles to the axis of percussion. Any other blank scar is a flake scar. Even though they are few, the presence of pure blade cores seems important enough not to combine them with Flake and Blade cores (Table 2D). This decision was justified as, in clustering the cores, blade core clusters did appear.

Attribute 13 has two states, Whole or Broken (Table 2E). It is not used in the cluster analysis because the same information is provided by a Missing state in one of the measurement parameters.

In Termination (Attribute 14; Table 2F) the major problem lies in the determination of exhausted versus minimal and considerable. A core which has been worked in one direction from one platform until it is exhausted can sometimes resemble a small core which has been minimally used. Similarly, it is difficult to determine whether a core is exhausted or just considerably used. My decision on both of these points was based on my experience as a flint-knapper. When the angles left on the platform or platforms of the core were such that it would be impossible to remove more blanks, I considered the core to be exhausted. When there were still perfectly usable angles, I considered it to be considerably used or minimally used, depending on the number of flakes which appeared to have been removed from it. The minimally used cores usually had only one or two scars coming from only one platform.

The next two attributes are obvious. The only note necessary is to stress that Attribute 15–16 refers only to the total number of VISIBLE scars. It bears no relationship to the total number of flakes which have been removed from the core. Thus, many of the exhausted cores have only one or two visible scars. This is due to the fact that the last one or two flakes to be removed took with them all signs of earlier removals. This presents a problem in the analysis of flakes and cores because it is impossible to estimate the number of flakes which actually came off of any one core. However, the largest remaining scar on many cores was of a size to be considered debitage, which suggests that the cores were quite heavily used and that the large cores necessary to make the majority of the flakes had been totally reduced before being rejected. The most frequent number of scars was three (fifty-four cores), over twenty cores had each number of scars up to seven (Table 2G). In the formation of the similarity matrix, cores having from eight to fourteen scars were treated as having many scars. This cutoff was the lowest value at which some sites had no cores.

Attribute 18, Uncore area, refers to that part of the nucleus which has not been used as a core or core part (Table 2H). The first two states are basically identical in that they both refer to situations in which the whole of the piece shows signs of industrial use. In the first, there are only scars and platform; in the second, the platform is a ridge rather than a surface and, therefore, there are no surfaces but scars.

The measurement attributes which conclude the core recording system were not included in the tabulation since they are continuous variables. I measured the broken cores or fragments but have indicated when the measurements which I made were on whole cores and when they were on broken cores. Width and thickness were determined, except on a few totally prepared cores, by which was larger. The larger became the width and the smaller the thickness. Length was always measured perpendicular to a striking platform. It was measured from that platform, where there were more than one, which gave the greatest length, but, as some of the pieces were quite irregular, the greatest length was not always greater than the width.

The last four measurements were repeated for each platform which was present on the core with the exception of those cores which had more than four platforms. These were only ten cores out of the 346 in all six collections and, rather than use two IBM cards for each of these, I recorded on the cards the information pertaining to the first four plus the angles for the fifth. The information about the rest of the fifth platform and about the sixth is, of course, recorded on the original record sheets which were compiled in Chile. The angles were measured to be the obverse of the angles measured for the flakes and blades. For each platform the maximum and minimum angle present were recorded. If only one flake scar was present from a particular platform, only one angle was recorded. The scar length and width were measured on the largest complete scar left from a particular platform. Note that this was not always the last scar before the platform was abandoned. The last scar was often quite small and didn't obscure an underlying larger scar. In this case, the larger scar was the one measured. Due to many missing values, only information concerning the first two platforms was included in the cluster analysis, with only a single angle measurement for each.

ANALYTIC METHODS

The program used to derive the counts discussed above was written by me in the Fortran IV computer language created by IBM for the 360 operating system. Slight changes in its parameters allow this program to be used for each kind of blank, for the cores, and for the retouched artifacts.

The first mode of multivariate analysis decided upon for this study was Q-mode cluster analysis (Hodson 1970; for an outline of multitivariate methods of analysis see Shephard 1972). This method produces groups of artifacts with similar attributes. Because the tools involved came from quarry sites it was hypothesized that the similarities binding clusters together would be based on technologically significant attributes and that the resultant groups would reflect the techniques which the artificers used in producing blanks and finished tools. The methods used for this analysis and the results given on the core sample are discussed below.

The first large program used in the analysis created the similarity matrix. Named Clus (Rubin and Friedman 1967), it produced an upper half similarity matrix. The lower half was produced and the whole matrix placed on tape by a series of programs written by Steven Butts of the Bureau of Applied Social Research, Columbia University. Clus was used to create the similarity matrix because of its elaborate data manipulating qualities. It was not used to produce the final clusters because I wished to experiment with a graph theoretic program, Complet, which produces polythetic clusters.

In describing data to the Clus program, the programmer can change its form from that which is printed on the computer cards. Thus, after running my program to discover underrepresented states, I could tell the

Clus program to combine a number of states and treat them as one. I could also tell it to ignore attributes that I had decided were uninformative. In addition, the Clus program allows the inclution of bistate variables, multistate variables, and continuous variables.

A major option in matrix formation concerns the similarity coefficient to be used. The Clus program can use either a "fractional match" coefficient, defined below, or the Tanimoto coefficient (Rogers and Tanimoto 1960). The fractional match coefficient, in its basic form, is arrived at by dividing the number of matches by the number of variables, the result being the measure of similarity between two objects. The Tanimoto coefficient divides the number of matches by twice the number of objects minus the number of matches, i.e.

$$\text{Tanimoto } S_{ij} = \frac{M}{2N - M}$$

"This coefficient has the effect of de-emphasizing weak similarities and bringing out only the strong similarities" (Rubin and Friedman 1967: 55–56). Both in Rubin and Friedman's experimentation and in my own, the results, in terms of the order of similarities between objects, are almost identical whichever coefficient is chosen. For my work I decided to use the fractional match coefficient because the coefficients, which are then passed on to the Complet program, are larger.

There are a number of modifications of the fractional match coefficient which Rubin and Friedman introduce in order to have the coefficient mirror more exactly the similarity between the two objects being compared. The first of these, the fractional match (f), allows each pair of continuous measurements to be compared individually as to their similarity. In applying it, the user sets up limits of difference on which to base an assessment of similarity. If two objects are closer in measurement to one another than the lower limit they are considered the same size; if they are farther apart than the upper limit they are considered different; and if they fall within the limits they are considered partially similar. For example, the lower match limit for core length was set to 20 millimeters and the upper to 45 millimeters. This means that cores whose length measurements are within 20 millimeters of each other are treated as the same length; those whose lengths are greater than 45 millimeters apart are treated as totally different in length; and those between 20 and 45 millimeters apart in length are treated as partially different. Three cores might have lengths of 720, 738 and 767 millimeters. Using the limits given above, the first two are considered the same length because they are only

18 millimeters apart; the first and third are different lengths, being 47 millimeters apart; and the second and third would be considered 36 percent different (or 64 percent similar) at 29 millimeters apart. The Clus program also allows you to set up ranges if you wish, although I can see no advantage to be gained from doing so with the fraction of match option available.

A second set of options concerns the missing and "non-applicable" data states. Missing states are handled by not comparing the two objects on any attribute which is missing, due, for example, to breakage, from either one of them. "This approach is based simply on the idea that we have no basis of comparison for a variable whose value is missing on one or both of the objects" (Rubin and Friedman 1967: 81–82). When there are many missing values, as there are in stone tools, two pieces may be compared on very few attributes and therefore erroneously high coefficients can occur because, for example, the pieces are similar on two of the three attributes for which they can be compared. This problem is reduced by creating two dummy variables for each pair of objects being compared. One of these dummy variables is assumed to be a match and the other a mismatch. Thus, the 67 percent match (2 out of 3) reported above would be reduced to 60 percent (3 out of 5). When there are many non-missing variables, the coefficient is changed very little by the use of dummy variables. For example, 5 matches with 15 variables would give 33 percent similarity; with the addition of two dummy variables this would change by only two percentage points, to 35 percent.

A "non-applicable" state differs from a missing state in that the feature does not apply to the object rather than being lost from it. Thus, for example, in discussing projectile points, it is advantageous to separate those with broken butts from those without stems when considering features of stem treatment. Because neither of two points has a stem is no reason automatically to consider them similar to each other, although you DO want to consider them BOTH different from a stemmed point. Rubin and Friedman (1967: 83) handle this problem in the following way (and this sums up the final form of the coefficient). If $n_s =$ the number of matches, and $n_d =$ number of mismatches, then

$$\text{Modified fractional match coefficient} = \frac{n_s}{n_s + n_d}$$

If there is no missing data, and no non-applicable states, this definition is identical with the previously given one, since every variable must produce either a match or a mismatch. We can adopt the following rules when computing a similarity coefficient between two objects:

1. if either object has missing data on a variable, add nothing to either n_s or n_d.
2. if both objects have a non-applicable state for a variable, add nothing to either n_s or n_d (i.e., treat neither as a match nor a mismatch).
3. if one object has the non-applicable state, and the other has an applicable state (for a discrete variable) or value (for a continuous variable) add 1 to n_d, but nothing to n_s (i.e., treat this as a mismatch).
4. for a discrete variable, if both objects have applicable states, then if they match, add 1 to n_s, if they do not match, add one to n_d.
5. for a continuous variable, if both objects have applicable values, compute the fraction of match f, as described above in the paragraph on continuous variables, and add f to n_s, $1-f$ to n_d (i.e., treat as part match, part mismatch).

This procedure appears to result in a similarity coefficient which is a quite accurate measure of the similarity between two objects.

The next program, Complet, is the program used to cluster similar tools together (Alba n.d.). It is still in its experimental stages. It depends on graph theory (see Harary 1969) as the basis of its clustering method. In order to explain the method, I will go through an analysis using a subset of my own data: the first twelve objects of the core analysis. The matrix showing the similarities among the twelve is shown in Table 3.

Table 3.　Similarity matrix for first twelve cores

	1	2	3	4	5	6	7	8	9	10	11	12
1	1000	204	179	179	214	179	257	175	227	169	227	140
2	204	1000	251	237	243	221	200	340	255	310	302	188
3	179	251	1000	200	189	222	189	222	257	246	222	239
4	179	237	200	1000	337	408	278	255	211	188	302	197
5	214	243	189	337	1000	243	293	278	219	188	211	236
6	179	221	222	408	243	1000	394	243	243	188	305	160
7	257	200	189	278	293	394	1000	290	401	169	260	152
8	175	340	222	255	278	243	290	1000	353	267	278	226
9	227	255	257	211	219	243	401	353	1000	500	296	188
10	169	310	246	188	188	188	169	267	500	1000	281	267
11	227	302	222	302	211	305	260	278	296	281	1000	188
12	140	188	239	197	236	160	152	266	188	267	188	1000

"A graph is constructed from the matrix of similarities by setting all similarities above some threshold to 1 and all others to 0, and interpreting the resulting matrix" (Alba n.d.: 2). Table 4 shows the adjacency matrices formed by setting threshold values of .250, .275 and .300 for the sample of 12 cores under consideration. These adjacency matrices form graphs when all points with a cross-entry of 1 are connected. A representation of the three graphs can be seen in Figure 2, A, B, and C. These graphs clearly show the decrease in connectedness which occurs with an increase in the threshold value. A maximal complete subgraph of a graph is one

Table 4.   Adjacency matrices for first twelve cores

A.   250 threshold; B.   275 threshold; C.   300 threshold

A.	1	2	3	4	5	6	7	8	9	10	11	12
1	1	0	0	0	0	0	1	0	0	0	0	0
2	0	1	1	0	0	0	0	1	1	1	1	0
3	0	1	1	0	0	0	0	0	1	0	0	0
4	0	0	0	1	1	1	1	1	0	0	1	0
5	0	0	0	1	1	0	1	1	0	0	0	0
6	0	0	0	1	0	1	1	0	0	0	1	0
7	1	0	0	1	1	1	1	1	1	0	1	0
8	0	1	0	1	1	0	1	1	1	1	1	0
9	0	1	1	0	0	0	1	1	1	1	1	0
10	0	1	0	0	0	0	0	1	1	1	1	1
11	0	1	0	1	0	1	1	1	1	1	1	0
12	0	0	0	0	0	0	0	0	0	1	0	1

B.	1	2	3	4	5	6	7	8	9	10	11	12
1	1	0	0	0	0	0	0	0	0	0	0	0
2	0	1	0	0	0	0	0	1	0	1	1	0
3	0	0	1	0	0	0	0	0	0	0	0	0
4	0	0	0	1	1	1	1	0	0	0	1	0
5	0	0	0	1	1	0	1	1	0	0	0	0
6	0	0	0	1	0	1	1	0	0	0	1	0
7	0	0	0	1	1	1	1	1	1	0	0	0
8	0	1	0	0	1	0	1	1	1	0	1	0
9	0	0	0	0	0	0	1	1	1	1	1	0
10	0	1	0	0	0	0	0	0	1	1	1	0
11	0	1	0	1	0	1	0	1	0	1	1	0
12	0	0	0	0	0	0	0	0	0	0	0	1

C.	1	2	3	4	5	6	7	8	9	10	11	12
1	1	0	0	0	0	0	0	0	0	0	0	0
2	0	1	0	0	0	0	0	1	0	1	1	0
3	0	0	1	0	0	0	0	0	0	0	0	0
4	0	0	0	1	1	1	0	0	0	0	1	0
5	0	0	0	1	1	0	0	0	0	0	0	0
6	0	0	0	1	0	1	1	0	0	0	1	0
7	0	0	0	0	0	1	1	0	1	0	0	0
8	0	1	0	0	0	0	0	1	0	1	0	0
9	0	0	0	0	0	0	1	1	1	0	0	0
10	0	1	0	0	0	0	0	0	1	1	0	0
11	0	1	0	1	0	1	0	0	0	0	1	0
12	0	0	0	0	0	0	0	0	0	0	0	1

within which each point is connected directly to each other with no intervening points. Thus, the 5-member maximal complete subgraph in Figure 2A has points (artifacts) 2, 8, 9, 10, 11 and the 3-member one has points 2, 3, 9. This graph also has two 2-member and four 4-member

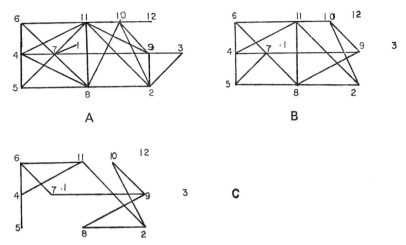

Figure 2.   Aggregated subgraphs, first twelve cores
A.   250 threshold; B. 275 threshold; and C.   300 threshold

maximal complete subgraphs. The second adjacency matrix (Figure 2B and Table 4B) has seven 3-member maximal complete subgraphs and the third (Figure 2C and Table 4C) has eight 2-member and one 3-member maximal complete subgraphs. The threshold to be used in creating the subgraphs can be decided upon in one of two ways. Either it can be preassigned or it can be determined by the program according to the nature of the data.

Once the program has found the subgraphs, it proceeds to reject some as trivial. In graph theory the basic graph with one point and no lines is defined as trivial (Harary 1969: 9). The Complet program allows the user to set a higher trivial value in order to reject small graphs. With a trivial value of 2 (the default for Complet), all but one of the maximum complete subgraphs found in the third graph (Figure 2C) would be rejected. Moving the trivial value up to 3 would leave only the first graph (Figure 2A) with any nontrivial maximal complete subgraphs.

The next step is called the unit merger step. Here any two maximal complete subgraphs are united if either has only one point not in common with the other (they cannot both be required to have only one point not in common because that would preclude uniting different sized subgraphs, such as subgraphs 2, 3, 9 and 2, 8, 10, 11 of Figure 2A). Graph 1 contains only one aggregated subgraph which includes all points (artifacts). With the default trivial value of 2, points 1 and 12 would be left out of this aggregated subgraph. Graph 2 (Figure 2B), on the other hand, produces two aggregated subgraphs, the first with 2, 8,

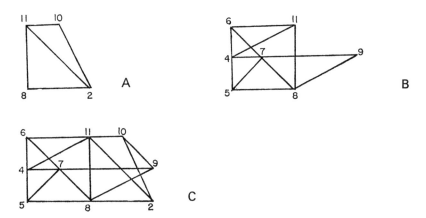

Figure 3.   Aggregated subgraphs of Graph 2 of first 12 cores
A and B.   The two aggregated subgraphs produced after Unit Merger step; and C.
Aggregated subgraph produced after Overlap Merger step

10, 11 (Figure 3A) and the second with 4, 5, 6, 7, 8, 9, 11 (Figure 3B).
These two cannot be joined at this level because the first has two members,
2 and 10, which are different than the second. This shows how Complet
produces polythetic artifact groups.

The final stage in the Complet analysis is the overlap merger step.
"Two subgraphs are merged during the overlap merger step whenever
the size of their overlap (the number of points in their intersection) is
greater than some fixed percentage of the points in the smaller subgraph"
(Alba n.d.: 4). Looking back at Graph 2 (Figure 2B) it can easily be seen
that the overlap of the two aggregated subgraphs is 50 percent. Using
the default value of 33 percent given by the Complet program, these
subgraphs would be joined into one during the overlap merger step
(Figure 3C). This default value can also be changed by the user of the
program.

In addition to a listing of the graphs produced by each step and to
information about which options are in effect during a particular run,
Complet also gives various statistics which aid in the evaluation of the
graphs produced:

These statistics are as follows: the diameter of the subgraphs; the ratio of the
count of lines joining points within the subgraph to the count of all such lines
which are possible (called the completeness statistic); the probability of observing a random, connected subgraph with this completeness or better; the ratio of
the count of lines joining points within the subgraph to points outside the subgraph (called the centrifugal statistic); the probability of observing this centrifu-
gality or worse (Alba n.d.:4).

The diameter of a subgraph is the largest number of lines required to connect any two points within the subgraph (Harary 1969: 14). Thus, by definition, a maximal complete subgraph has a diameter of 1 because every pair of points is connected by a line. The first aggregated subgraphs of Graph 2 (Figures 3A, 3B) each have a diameter of 2; the subgraph produced after the overlap merger step has a diameter of 3 (Figure 3C), three lines being necessary to get from 5 to 10 or from 7 to 10.

The completeness statistic is fairly obvious. Any graph with a diameter of 1 also has a completeness statistic of 1 because all possible lines are present, every pair of points being connected by a line. The first aggregated subgraph of Graph 2 (Figure 3A) has 7 points and can therefore have 21 lines joining them. As it has only 11 lines, its completeness equals 0.52381. The second aggregated subgraph of Graph 2 has 5 of a possible 6 lines for a completeness of 0.83333. These are significantly complete at better than the 0.001 level. The next statistic, the centrifugal statistic is, in a sense, the obverse of the completeness statistic. The completeness statistic looks at the subgraph as an isolate and compares it to an ideal complete subgraph. The centrifugal statistic compares it to its surrounding graph, measuring how strongly it is separated from the whole. The first aggregated subgraph of Graph 2 has 5 lines connecting it to the 5 points not in the subgraph. It could have an additional 15 lines for a total of 20, which gives it a centrifugal statistic of 5/20 or .25000. For the second aggregated subgraph of Graph 2 there are also 5 lines present out of 20 possible lines. These two subgraphs, then, are not significantly centrifugal, which is to be expected as they form a single aggregated subgraph after the overlap merger phase with a significant completeness of 0.5000. The probabilities given by Complet for these statistics are computed according to the hypergeometric probability law.

After giving these statistics for each aggregated subgraph, Complet indicates what other objects are connected to it and how many connections they have. Thus, object 2 has 2 connections with aggregated subgraph 1 of Graph 2 and object 10 has one connection. At the end of the list of aggregated subgraphs for the unit merger and overlap merger steps, Complet lists the proportions of overlap between subgraphs, and lists individual object membership by group. All of these aid in the interpretation of the subgraphs.

This ends the formal, nonarchaeological data manipulation. The final analysis of the Complet output requires a return to the basic data to discover the meaning in technological, functional, or stylistic terms of the graphs Complet has produced.

Table 5. Complete analysis of one-half sample of cores from analyzed sections of RAnL 199B and RAnL 200B (statistics after Unit Merger step)

A. Proportions of overlap between subgraphs; B. Proportions of lines between subgraphs

A.

	2	3	4	5	6	7	8	9	10	11
1	0.00	0.0	0.0	0.0	0.0	0.0	0.0	0.0	0.0	0.0
2		0.846	0.0	0.0	0.0	0.692	0.0	0.0	0.0	0.0
3			0.0	0.0	0.500	0.965	0.0	0.300	0.125	0.143
4				0.0	0.0	0.0	0.0	0.0	0.0	0.0
5					0.0	0.0	0.0	0.250	0.250	0.250
6						0.500	0.0	0.0	0.0	0.0
7							0.0	0.300	0.125	0.143
8								0.0	0.0	0.0
9									0.625	0.714
10										0.714

B.

	2	3	4	5	6	7	8	9	10	11
1	0.058	0.044	0.0	0.0	0.0	0.040	0.050	0.025	0.031	0.0
2		0.022	0.019	0.019	0.0	0.037	0.0	0.015	0.019	0.022
3			0.018	0.013	0.055	0.250	0.007	0.029	0.015	0.033
4				0.063	0.063	0.020	0.050	0.050	0.031	0.036
5					0.0	0.012	0.0	0.037	0.048	0.056
6						0.049	0.0	0.050	0.031	0.036
7							0.006	0.026	0.014	0.030
8								0.0	0.025	0.029
9									0.067	0.200
10										0.167

Table 6. Complete analysis of one-half sample of cores from analyzed sections of RAnL 199B and RAnL 200B (statistics after Overlap Merger step)

A. Proportions of overlap between subgraphs; B. Proportions of lines between subgraphs

A.

	2	3	4	5	6
1	0.0	0.0	0.0	0.0	0.0
2		0.0	0.0	0.0	0.0
3			0.0	0.0	0.250
4				0.0	0.231
5					0.0

B.

	2	3	4	5	6
1	0.0	0.0	0.036	0.050	0.019
2		0.063	0.025	0.050	0.038
3			0.011	0.0	0.028
4				0.006	0.020
5					0.015

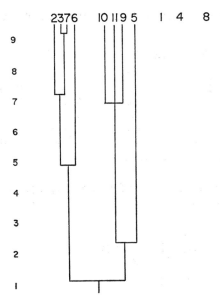

Figure 4.   Dendrograph representation of overlap between subgraphs in analysis of one-half sample of cores from RAnL 199B and RAnL 200B

RESULTS

The average similarity coefficient for the 174 cores in the matrix produced by Clus was .378. The Complet program for the cores was run with a percent level of 5, producing a threshold value of 0.5300, and with a Trivial group size of 3. These parameters led to the formation of 667 maximal complete subgraphs, 500 of which were trivial. Therefore, 167 subgraphs remained to be worked with on the unit merger step. This step produced 11 aggregated subgraphs which then reduced to 6 after the overlap merger step. Ninety-five of the 174 objects were included in these subgraphs, 63 had peripheral memberships, and 16 objects, on the defined levels, had no relationship to any subgraph. The small number of isolated cores serves as an indication of the basic unity of the collection because if we were dealing with a mixed collection of different periods or techniques we would expect more cores which did not relate to the general collection.

The interrelations between the aggregated subgraphs can be seen numerically in Tables 5 and 6 and graphically in Figure 4. These show that the final 6 graphs produced after the overlap merger step are quite well

Table 7.   Completeness and centrifugal statistics for the six subgraphs produced after Overlap Merger step in core analysis

Subgraph	Diameter	Completeness	Probability	Centrifugal	Probability	Number of cores
AGSG 1	1	1	0.0*	0.03382	0.00695	4
AGSG 2	1	1	0.0	0.04853	0.28912	4
AGSG 3	1	1	0.0	0.0250	0.0001	4
AGSG 4	9	0.17093	0.0	0.02391	0.0*	69
AGSG 5	2	0.9000	0.0	0.02130	0.0	5
AGSG 6	4	0.52564	0.0	0.04109	0.01320	13

*   these probabilities are less than 0.00001

Table 8.   Summary of attribute counts for six subgraphs produced after Overlap Merger step in core analysis

A.   Core preparation

AGSG	Prepared		Partially prepared		Unprepared	
	#	%	#	%	#	%
1			4	100		
2			4	100		
3	3	75	1	25		
4	6	9	26	38	36	52
5	5	100				
6	11	85	2	15		
All[a]	101	29	136	39	107	31

B.   Nature of platforms

AGSG	Single		Two		More		Joint	
	#	%	#	%	#	%	#	%
1			4	100				
2	2	50					2	50
3	4	100						
4	31	45	27	41	3	4	6	9
5	2	40	1	20			2	40
6	7	54	5	38				
All[a]	154	45	91	26	32	9	65	19

C.   Core shape

AGSG	Block		Polyhedric		Keeled		Flat		Pyramidal		Conical	
	#	%	#	%	#	%	#	%	#	%	#	%
1	4	100										
2			1	25			1	25	1	25[b]		
3							2	50			1	25[b]
4	2	3	38	57	2	3	24	34			2	3
5											5	100
6							13	100				
All[a]	16	5	110	32	33	10	108	31	11	3	42	12

D. Blanks

AGSG	Flakes		Flakes and Blades		Blades	
	#	%	#	%	#	%
1	4	100				
2			4	100		
3					4	100
4	61	87	6	9		
5			5	100		
6	1	8	12	92		
All[a]	195	57	110	32	41	12

E. Termination

AGSG	Exhausted		Considerable use		Minimal use	
	#	%	#	%	#	%
1			4	100		
2			3	75[b]		
3	3	75[b]				
4	41	57	13	20	9	13[b]
5	3	60	2	40		
6	13	100				
All[a]	165	48	114	33	41	12

F. Uncore area

AGSG	Platform		None		Cortex		Break		Possible bulb		Multiple	
	#	%	#	%	#	%	#	%	#	%	#	%
1			1	25	2	50					1	25
2	3	75									1	25
3			1	25			3	25				
4	47	70	7	10	7	10	2	3			7	10
5			4	80			1	20				
6	1	8	3	23	6	46	2	15				
All[a]	116	34	80	23	58	17	44	13	22	7	16	5

G. Provenience

AGSG	199B-1		199B-3		199B-7		199B-12		200B-1		200B-3	
	#	%	#	%	#	%	#	%	#	%	#	%
1					1	25					3	75
2	1	25	1	25			1	25	1	25		
3	2	50					2	50				
4	24	35	10	14	10	14	9	13	7	10	9	13
5	2	40	1	20	1	20			1	20		
6	7	54	1	8			2	15	2	15	1	8
All[a]	152	44	50	14	32	9	43	12	30	8	39	11

a These numbers and percentages refer to the total 345 core sample.
b The missing members are Missing the attribute.

separated from one another, four of them, in fact, not being combinable on any level other than that of the original maximal complete subgraphs. These 6 graphs are the final output of the program, and my discussion of the results will concentrate on them. Their completeness and centrifugal statistics can be seen in Table 7. Some of these graphs have few members, being infrequently made specialized cores; others, with many members, are frequently manufactured cores which indicate the general nature of the industry.

The first conclusion from the analysis of the cores is that core technology does not differ significantly between RAnL 199B and RAnL 200B. The only exception to this occurs in the case of specialized blade cores which come only from RAnL 199B-1 and 12 (see Table 8 for a summary of the attributes of the subgraphs).

Other conclusions can be drawn concerning the general characteristics of the Aguas Verdes core technology. First, the cores do not tend to be carefully preformed before blanks are removed. The largest group of cores (AGSG 4) consists of flake cores with one or two striking platforms. Those which were minimally or considerably used tend to be polyhedric, those which are exhausted sometimes appear to be flat. Similarly, those which appear to be prepared or partially prepared also are exhausted. Second, this group indicates that the most common use of cores at these two sites was to prepare flakes. Flakes were removed from the nodules until they became exhausted. Those which were abandoned before becoming exhausted show a basic lack of preparation and polyhedric form; those which continued in use sometimes came to have a flat regular outline and an appearance of preparation. Because it is easier to remove flakes along already used faces of a core, a core which has been used extensively tends to take on a regular appearance even though it was not consciously prepared by the workman. The analyst cannot distinquish this fortuitous preparation from purposeful preparation, but the fact that, in this case, a prepared appearance occurs primarily with exhausted cores suggests that the apparent preparation is not purposeful.

In the case of the small groups of cores, however, the reverse situation holds. These seem to be cores which were consciously prepared in order to remove specific blanks. These groups of cores are distinguished from one another mainly by their preparation, blank scars, and overall shape. Two groups, with four members each, contain partially prepared cores. The cores in the first of these (AGSG 1) are block-shaped and have two platforms from which flakes were removed. They have all seen considerable use, but none are exhausted. These are long cores and the flakes removed from them, to judge from the remaining scars, were unusually wide. Thus it would seem that one of the special flake forms desired by the artisans who produced the Aguas Verdes industry was fairly large and very wide. The average core dimensions in this group are 970 by 597 by 448 millimeters, and the average size of the remaining scars is 494 by 485 millimeters. Remember that all of these cores have been used considerably so these dimensions are minimal. A block-shaped core is ideally suited to producing wide flakes because it is characterized by having broad faces.

The second group of partially prepared cores (AGSG 2) is also the first group of cores from which both flakes and blades have been removed. The cores have one platform which is single, with the blanks all going in one direction, or joint: a ridge platform with blanks going in both directions. There is no area of the nodule, except the platform, from which blanks have not been removed.

The first two fully prepared groups of cores also contain flake-blade cores while the third contains blade cores. This strongly indicates that their preparation, which clearly distinguishes them from the majority of the Augas Verdes cores, is due to a desire on the part of the workmen to produce blades. The fact that most of these cores have both flake and blade scars remaining on their surfaces is not surprising if one remembers that these are percussion blades rather than pressure blades. In creating percussion blades it is almost always necessary to take off flakes occasionally in order to clean up a face of the core which contains hinge or step fractures, or to prepare a new area of the core for blade removal. Therefore, one can interpret the flake-blade cores as imperfect blade cores.

The largest group of flake-blade cores (AGSG 6) contains 13 cores from both RAnL 199B and 200B. It is significant to note that the cores from RAnL 199B come from the first collected square surface (199B–1) and excavation (199B–12). These cores are flat with one or two striking platforms and have been used until exhausted. As would be expected from their flat shape and blade core nature, all but one of the cores which have two striking platforms are double-ended, having the striking platforms at opposite ends of the cores. These cores are smaller than the majority of the cores.

The last group of flake-blade cores (AGSG 5) contains conical cores with single or joint platforms. This is definitely a prepared-core type, shaped so as to get the greatest number of blanks from the material. The exhausted state of these cores is indicated both by the remaining angles on the cores and by their small size. About half of these cores have cortex remaining where there are not scars, suggesting that the core was worked around until there was no area remaining that could be worked from the existing platform.

The final group of cores (AGSG 3) is composed of prepared blade cores from 199B–1 and 199B–12. These all have single platforms and are exhausted. Their shapes vary but are regular – conical and flat – rather than irregular. Their measurements are also significantly different from those of the rest of the collection. The cores are long, narrow and thin, and the blade scars are long and narrow. All of these mean measurements except core length and thickness have very small variances. Considering the difficulty of producing percussion blades consistently and the care necessary to prepare the core on which one wishes to produce them, it is natural that blade cores should form clusters distinguishing them from flake cores. It is also good support for the analytic method that they do so. The fact that all of these blade cores, plus many of the flake-blade cores, come from one area of the site, and, in addition, from an area that was previously recognized as a rich area, suggests that this area was the focus of the finer work done at RAnL 199B. It also strengthens the impression given by informal handling of the collections that blades were more important at RAnL 199B than at RAnL 200B. These hypotheses will be tested in the analysis of the remaining artifacts from the sites.

Obviously, from an analysis only of cores, it is impossible to come to any firm conclusions about the nature of the Aguas Verdes industry. However, some suggestions can be put forward for consideration which can then be modified in the light of information provided in the future by the blanks and retouched artifacts. The major conclusion from the above groups is that the division of blanks into flakes and blades is justified in the Aguas Verdes industry because it is paralleled in the core morphology. Secondly, the production of blades was attended to with more care than was the production of flakes. Except when producing particularly wide flakes, the Aguas Verdes artificers seem to have taken very little care with the preparation of their cores, either in producing a particular flake shape or in conserving material. The latter part of this conclusion is not surprising when one remembers that the sites are lo-cated directly at the source of raw material from which the tools were made. The preparation of the blade cores, on the other hand, seems to go considerably beyond that necessary to produce blades in the first place and to indicate a desire on the part of the artificers to produce even, well-formed blades. These blades can function without modification as knives or can be used as blanks in the production of artifacts such as points which require an even blank for their successful manufacture.

Finally, it can be suggested, tentatively, that the finest artisans in the group which worked at RAnL 199B worked in the area of the site tested by square 199B–1 and test pit 199B–12.

SUMMARY AND CONCLUSIONS

This study is a preliminary analysis of lithic materials from northern Chile designed to test the value of flint-knapping experience and multivariate analysis. In discussing the recording system I indicated how the understanding of flint knapping aided both in the formation of the original system and in the decision as to the position of various cores within the system.

A hypothesis upon which the whole study was based was that these sites represented a limited occupation. The outcome of the multivariate analysis supports this hypothesis because so many of the cores did join together with a high level of similarity. It also confirmed the feeling that the area from which sample RAnL 199B–1 was taken was the richest on the site. Not only did it provide this confirmation, but it also led to a further hypothesis that the tools manufactured in this area were better made as well as more numerous than in the other areas.

The value of the Clus program used to produce the similarity matrix was seen to lie primarily in its data manipulation capabilities. This is particularly important because numerous changes in the raw-data cards are usually necessary after a preliminary analysis of the data. The preprocessing facilities of Clus handle these changes easily. The value of Complet is harder to asses because I have not yet tried other analytic methods on my data and therefore cannot evaluate it absolutely. However, it did produce valuable interesting results, confirming some prior hypotheses and suggesting some others to be tested on the rest of the data from the Aguas Verdes collections.

Finally, I wish to stress that the analysis of the collection is not complete. Although the results from the core analysis may seem somewhat meager for an elaborate analysis, the cores are only one segment of the collections, and the analysis of the others, particularly of the retouched artifacts, will provide more information about the technology and should lead to the formation of higher-order hypotheses.

REFERENCES

ALBA, RICHARD D.
  n.d.   "Complet: a graph theoretic sociometric analysis and clustering pro-
          gram." Unpublished manuscript.
BORDAZ, JACQUES
  1970   *Tools of the old and new Stone Age.* New York: Natural History Press.
BORDES, FRANCOIS, DON E. CRABTREE
  1969   The Corbiac blade technique and other experiments. *Tebiwa* 12.
CLARKE, DAVID L.
  1968   *Analytical archaeology.* London: Methuen.
CRABTREE, DON E.
  1966   A stoneworker's approach to analyzing and replicating the Linden-
          meier Folsom. *Tebiwa* 9:3–39.
  1969   "Report to National Science Foundation on lithic technology field
          school." Mimeographed manuscript.
DA VINCI, LEONARDO
  1939   *The literary works of Leonardo da Vinci*, volume one (second edition).
          Edited by Jean Paul Richter and Irma A. Richter. London: Oxford.
DE LUMLEY, HENRY
  1969   A Paleolithic camp at Nice. *Scientific American* 220:42–50.
GOULD, RICHARD A., DOROTHY A. KOSTER., ANN H. L. SONTZ
  1971   The lithic assemblage of the western desert aborigines of Australia.
          American Antiquity 36:149–169.
HARARY, FRANK
  1969   *Graph theory.* Reading, Pennsylvania: Addison-Wesley.
HODSON, F. ROY
  1970   Cluster analysis and archaeology: some new developments and applica-
          tions. *World Archaeology* 1:299–320.
LEROI-GOURHAN, ANDRE, MICHEL BREZILLON
  1966   L'habitation Magdalenienne No. 1. de Pincevent pre Montereau
          (Seine-et-Marne). *Gallia Préhistoire* 9:2.
LEWIS, LUCY
  1966   "Valdivia lithic analysis, part I: typological analysis of flake tools."
          Unpublished manuscript.
MEWHINNEY, H.
  1957   *A manual for Neanderthals.* Austin: University of Texas Press.
NEILL, W. T.
  1952   The manufacture of fluted points. *The Florida Anthropologist* 5:9–16.
OAKLEY, KENNETH P.
  1949   *Man the tool maker.* Chicago: Phoenix.
ROGERS, D. J., T. T. TANIMOTO
  1960   A computer program for classifying plants. *Science* 132:1115–1118.
RUBIN, JERROLD, HERMAN P. FRIEDMAN
  1967   *A cluster analysis and taxonomy system for grouping and classifying data.*
          New York: International Business Machines.
SEMENOV, S. A.
  1964   *Prehistoric technology.* Translated by M. W. Thompson. New York:
          Barnes and Noble.

SHEPHARD, R. N.

1972   "A taxonomy of some principal types of data and of multidimensional methods for their analysis," in *Multidimensional scaling: theory and applications in the behavioral sciences*, volume one: *Theory*. Edited by R. N. Shephard, A. Kimball Romney and Sara Beth Nerlove, 23-51. New York: Seminar Press.

SOKAL, ROBERT R., PETER H. A. SNEATH

1963   *Principles of numeric taxonomy.* San Francisco: W. H. Freeman.

WHITE, ANTA M.

1963   "Analytic description of the chipped-stone industry from Snyders Site, Calhoun County, Illinois," in *Miscellaneous studies in typology and classification.* By A. M. White, L. R. Binford and Mark Papworth, 1–70. Anthropological Papers 19. Museum of Anthropology, University of Michigan.

"Punch Technique" and Upper Paleolithic Blades

M. H. NEWCOMER

This paper has two principal aims: first, to introduce a modification of the terminology used to describe the experimental manufacture of Paleolithic flaked stone artifacts, which will enable the results of these experiments to be more accurately applied to archeological materials. Second, this paper will provide an example of the application of this revised terminology to an archeological problem, the production of blades in the Upper Paleolithic.

TERMINOLOGY

We may recognize three main levels of abstraction in the description of the manufacture of a flaked stone artifact:

1. METHOD   Method refers to the stages used in making a stone artifact. Although this term was not used in this sense until 1967 (Tixier 1967), there are numerous earlier examples of reconstructed methods of manufacture of complex artifacts, for example, Levallois flakes (Bordes 1961a), geometric microliths (Tixier 1963), burins (Bordes 1947), fluted projectile points (Crabtree 1966), etc.

   The method or series of steps used to make a given artifact may be discovered by the examination of finished products and the waste flakes and partially finished pieces found associated on archeological sites, by experiments, or, usually, by a combination of both.

2. MODE   This is a new (and provisional) name for the kind of flaking used within the stage by stage framework implied by method. We may isolate three basic flaking modes: "hard hammer," "soft hammer," and

For Plates and Figures, see pp. ii–iii, between pp. 102–103.

"pressure." The results of the use of each mode are observable both on the finished artifact and on the accompanying waste flakes. Thus the "hard hammer" mode is normally characterized by flake scars with deep negative bulbs of percussion and flakes with prominent bulbs, well-marked cones of percussion, etc. "Soft hammer" flaking produces flatter flake scars, and flakes which are often fairly thin, with flattened, diffuse bulbs, lips between butt and ventral surface, etc. "Pressure" flaking yields flake scars similar to those of the soft hammer mode, but which are often more regularly spaced, and flakes which are often small, with tiny butts, and which have relatively well-marked bulbs – but never cones – of percussion.

The need for MODE to bridge the gap between METHOD and TECHNIQUE (see below) is important; it is only to this level, and no lower, that the results of experiments in making stone artifacts may be safely applied to archeological materials. Thus, while we may confidently define the stages used to prepare a Levallois flake core (METHOD), and observe that the hard hammer MODE is always used in the final stage, detaching the Levallois flake, we cannot tell either from experimentation or examination of Paleolithic Levallois cores and flakes which TECHNIQUE was used to remove this flake. Bordes (1961b:14) points out that either direct percussion with a stone hammer or "direct anvil technique" (Clark in Tixier 1967:817) can produce good Levallois flakes.

3.   TECHNIQUE   Technique may be restricted in meaning and refer to the way in which force is applied to detach a flake, the way the piece is held during flaking, etc. Thus within the hard hammer mode, we may use (or infer) a mobile hammer stone (direct percussion), a stone anvil (direct anvil technique), and the piece being flaked may be held in the hand, on a padded knee, on the ground, by another person, etc. Within the soft hammer mode, a mobile soft hammer of wood, bone, antler, etc. may be used (direct percussion), or a punch may be placed on the edge of the piece being flaked and struck with a mobile hammer (indirect percussion or "punch technique"). Pressure flaking may involve various forms of pressure tools, and the work may be held in the hand, on the ground, etc.

It is asserted here that exact techniques are rarely, if ever, recoverable by examination of stone artifacts, and that experiments will only provide a range of techniques which duplicate the MODE of flaking used on a given artifact. Experimenters often find that several different techniques will produce identical artifacts and waste flakes, and we can be properly skeptical when it is claimed that only one technique will produce the desired results. A well-known case in point here is the use of direct anvil technique to flake Clactonian cores (see Coutier 1929). Baden-Powell (1949), Bordes (1961b:13), and others have pointed out that replicas of Clactonian flakes and cores may be made by another technique – direct percussion with a hammer stone – and although we may infer from the lack of convincing anvils on Clactonian sites that direct percussion is a simpler, safer, and more likely technique (Newcomer 1970), we can only safely say that the hard hammer MODE and the alternate flaking METHOD were used on most Clactonian cores.

Although the method-mode-technique framework as outlined above seems a reasonable approach to use in relating experimental work to archeological data, problems are raised by artifacts, especially bifacially flaked pieces, on which two modes of flaking are mixed (see Tixier 1958-1959:152; Bordes 1947:14). It is also true that the three flaking modes may on occasion produce very similar flakes, and that greater confidence in the definition of each mode's flakes and flake scars could perhaps be provided by measurements of the size of the bulb, etc., on a series of experimentally made pieces.

UPPER PALEOLITHIC BLADES

The utility of this new framework may now be tested in an application to a specific problem, the manufacture of Upper Paleolithic blades. A stage by stage outline of the method of making an Upper Paleolithic blade core has recently been described in papers by Bordes (1967:42–45) and Bordes and Crabtree (1969), based both on experimentation and observations of blades, blade cores, and waste flakes from the French Upper Perigordian site at Corbiac in the Dordogne (see Bordes 1968 for a preliminary excavation report). Three basic stages were described: the preparation of a striking platform at one or both ends of the core, the "cresting" of the front of the core by bifacial flaking to provide a guiding ridge for the removal of the first blade, and the detachment of blades, with platform preparation between blade removals to remove overhangs left by the negative bulbs of previously struck blades.

Within each of these stages, it was noted that different techniques and even different modes could be used. Thus for the creation of striking platforms, both direct percussion with a stone hammer and direct anvil technique were satisfactory (techniques within hard hammer mode), and punch technique could also be used (soft hammer mode). However, examination of waste flakes from Upper Paleolithic sites indicates that the hard hammer mode was generally used for making striking platforms, and that the other two stages of blade making usually correspond to specific modes too, cresting usually being by hard hammer and blade removal usually by soft hammer.

The experiments of Bordes and Crabtree in blade REMOVAL concentrated on indirect percussion or punch technique, and this specific technique has, unfortunately, been singled out by various archeologists as representing the whole method of making Upper Paleolithic blades (see, for example, Binford 1968, McBurney 1972, among many).

Tixier has recently shown that using the blade method outlined by Bordes (1967) and Bordes and Crabtree (1969) the third stage, blade removal, may be accomplished by holding the core under the foot and detaching blades using a "punch" held longitudinally rather than nearly vertically on the core's platform (Tixier 1972). My own experiments, also following the three stages, show that good replicas of Upper Paleolithic blades can be struck by direct percussion with an antler soft hammer, the core being held in the hand as indicated in Figure 1. Plate 2 shows a blade core with its blades replaced, all of which were struck by direct percussion (see Plate 1). In Plate 3 the similarity of the butts of experimental direct percussion (Plate 3b) and punch struck blades (Plate 3a) to a typical Upper Paleolithic blade (Plate 3c) is shown.

From this we may conclude that good duplicates of the type of blades often called "punched blades," with thin, narrow butts, may be detached by several different techniques, all in the soft hammer mode: punch technique (Bordes 1967), modified punch technique with the core held under the foot (Tixier 1972), and now direct percussion with a soft hammer.

It has been claimed that the hard hammer mode, using direct percussion technique, was probably widely used to make Upper Paleolithic blades (Bordaz 1969). This inference was based on the observation of modern Turkish flint-knappers making blades for threshing sleds, and on the lack of punches from Upper Paleolithic sites (but see Combier 1967: Figure 109, Number 6 for an Aurignacian punch from level 2 of Grotte du Figuier). However, these blades, and Brandon gun-flint blades which they closely resemble, are made by direct percussion with a metal hammer, and their proximal ends and butts show all the characteristics of the hard hammer MODE – thick butt, well-marked cone, etc., which are NOT characteristic of most Upper Paleolithic blades. The method of making these Turkish and Brandon blades also differs from the Upper Paleolithic method, because the use of a pointed iron hammer allows precise placement of the blow, and thus the removal of the platform overhangs (part of stage three above) is not necessary because the blow can be placed 7 to 11 millimeters back from the core platform's edge. In summary, these modern blades differ from Upper Paleolithic blades in being hard hammer struck, and in lacking the tiny flake scars on the dorsal surface at the proximal end (Plate 3a-c) which indicate platform preparation between blade removals.

CONCLUSIONS

Since the exact techniques used in the Paleolithic cannot often be re-created experimentally, the use of the short-hand term "punched blade" for Upper Paleolithic blades should disappear, and be replaced by a purely descriptive name such as "blade with small butt." We can however state that in many cases, the METHOD used in the Upper Paleolithic for making blades was that described by Bordes (1967) and Bordes and Crabtree (1969), that the stages of core preparation were usually carried out by the hard hammer MODE, that the detachment of blades was done by the soft hammer MODE, and that within this mode several TECHNIQUES, including punch technique and direct percussion, can successfully repro-duce these blades.

REFERENCES

BADEN-POWELL, D. F. W.
  1949 Experimental Clactonian technique. *Proceedings of the Prehistoric Society* 15:38–41.
BINFORD, S. R.
  1968 Early upper Pleistocene adaptations in the Levant. *American Anthropologist* 70:707–17.
BORDAZ, J.
  1969 Flint flaking in Turkey. *Natural History* 78:73–77.
BORDES, F.
  1947 Etude comparative des différentes techniques de taille du silex et des roches dures. *L'Anthropologie* 51:1–29.
  1961a Mousterian cultures in France. *Science* 134:803–10.
  1961b *Typologie du paléolithique ancien et moyen.* Bordeaux: Delmas.
  1967 Considérations sur la typologie et les techniques dans le paléolithique. *Quartär* 18:25–55.
  1968 Emplacements de tentes du Périgordien supérieur évolué à Corbiac (près Bergerac), Dordogne. *Quartär* 19:251–62.
BORDES, F., D. CRABTREE
  1969 The Corbiac blade technique and other experiments. *Tebiwa* 12:1–21.
COMBIER, J.
  1967 *Le paléolithique de l'Ardèche dans son cadre paléoclimatique.* Bor-deaux: Delmas.

COUTIER, L.

1929   Expériences de taille pour rechercher les anciennes techniques paléolithiques. *Bulletin de la Société Préhistorique Française* 26: 172–74.

CRABTREE, D. E.

1966   A stoneworker's approach to analyzing and replicating the Lindenmeier Folsom. *Tebiwa* 9:3–39.

MC BURNEY, C. B. M.

1972   "Regional differences in the dating of the earliest leptolithic traditions," in *The origin of* Homo Sapiens. Edited by F. Bordes, 237–240. Paris: UNESCO.

NEWCOMER, M. H.

1970   Conjoined flakes from the lower loam, Barnfield Pit, Swanscombe (1970). *Proceedings of the Royal Anthropological Institute* 1970: 51–59.

TIXIER, J.

1958–1959   Les industries lithiques d'Ain Fritissa (Maroc oriental). *Bulletin d'Archéologie Marocaine* 3: 107–244.

1963   *Typologie de l'epipaléolithique du Maghreb.* Paris: Arts et Métiers Graphiques.

1967   "Procédés d'analyse et questions de terminologie concernant l'étude des ensembles industriels du paléolithique récent et de l'épipaléolithique dans l'Afrique du nord-ouest," in *Background to evolution in Africa.* Edited by W. W. Bishop and J. G. D. Clark, 771–820. Chicago: University of Chicago Press.

1972   Obtention de lames par débitage "sous le pied." *Bulletin de la Société PréhistoriqueFrançaise* 69: 134–9.

Plates

M. H. NEWCOMER / ii

HIROAKI KOBAYASHI / iv

BARBARA A. PURDY / xi

JAMES P. GREEN / xix

ANTHONY J. RANERE / xxiii

GEORGE J. MILLER / xxxi

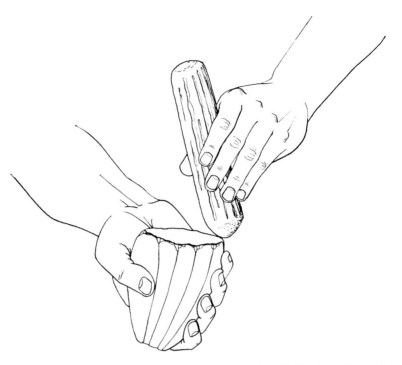

Figure 1.   Sketch showing position of hands and angle of flaking for striking blades by direct percussion with a soft hammer. The author is left-handed. Drawing by J. Newcomer

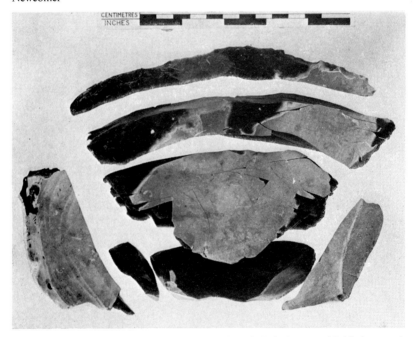

Plate 1.   Exploded view of experimental double-ended blade core with blades struck by direct percussion with a soft hammer. Photo by P. Dorrell

Plate 2.   Experimental blade core with direct percussion blades remounted, showing generally small size of butts. Photo by P. Dorrell

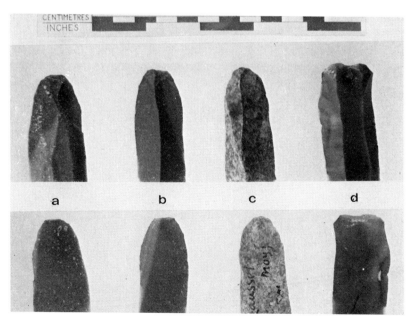

Plate 3.   Dorsal and ventral views of the proximal ends of four flint blades: (a) Experimental punch-struck blade;
(b) Experimental blade struck by direct percussion with a soft hammer; (c) French Upper Paleolithic blade;
(d) Brandon gun-flint blade struck by direct percussion with an iron hammer. Note the small butts and evidence of core preparation between blade removals on the dorsal surfaces of a, b, and c and the wide, thick butt and cone of percussion on d. Photo by P. Dorrell

Plate 1a.   Hammerstone weighing 653 grams and measuring 13.18 centimeters (maximum length) by 6.66 centimeters (maximum width)

Plate 1b.   Hammerstone weighing 2.20 kilograms and measuring 17.89 centimeters (maximum length) by 9.40 centimeters (maximum width)

Plate 2a. Anvil weighing 2.33 kilograms and measuring 18.73 (length) by 15.75 (width) by 4.78 (thickness) centimeters

Plate 2b. Anvil weighing 7.35 kilograms and measuring 15.75 (length) by 13.62 (width) by 4.36 (thickness) centimeters

Plate 2c. Anvil weighing 16.15 kilograms and measuring 21.55 (length) by 16.33 (width) by 11.69 (thickness) centimeters

Plate 3.   Flake in Group A

Plate 4.   Two flakes in Group A

Plate 5.
Flake in Group B

Plate 6a.
Bipolar flake

Plate 6b.
Bipolar flake

Plate 6c.
Bipolar flake
removed from a
bipolar core
(see Plate 6d)

Plate 6d.
Bipolar core

Plate 6e.
Bipolar flake

Plate 6f.
Bipolar flake

Plate 6g.
Bipolar flake

Plate 6h.
Bipolar flake

Plate 7a.   Two flakes classified into Group
D. These flakes were removed from one core
(see Plate 7b) at the same time

Plate 7b.   Core of flakes (see Plate 7a)

Plate 1 (a, b).   (a) Experimental specimen illustrating lateral snap as well as the flake
which caused the unwanted fracture;
(b) Field specimen of lateral snap

Plate 2 (a, b).   (a) Debris resulting when experimental samples were subjected to rapid
elevation of temperature. The rocks exploded at 400 degrees Centgrade
(b) Field samples of blocky angular flakes and potlids similar to experimental samples

Plate 3 (a, b).   (a) Experimental sample of potlid fracture;
(b) Field sample with several potlid fractures

Plate 4 (a, b).   (a) Experimental example of "crenated" fracture;
(b) Field example of "crenated" fracture

Plate 5.   Experimental samples illustrating the typical type of fracture which occurs when specimens are removed from a hot oven

Plate 6 (a, b). (a) Experimental specimen illustrating crazing or shrinkage fractures; (b) Field examples of crazing

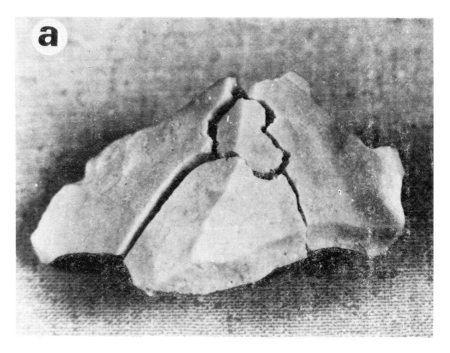

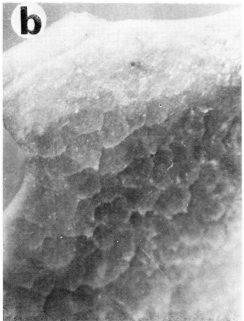

Plate 7 (a, b).   (a) Results of an attempt to "flake" by dripping cold water on a hot stone;
(b) Magnified area illustrating the crazing which occurred

Plate 8.   Nodule of Florida chert that has been destroyed by exposure to heat stresses

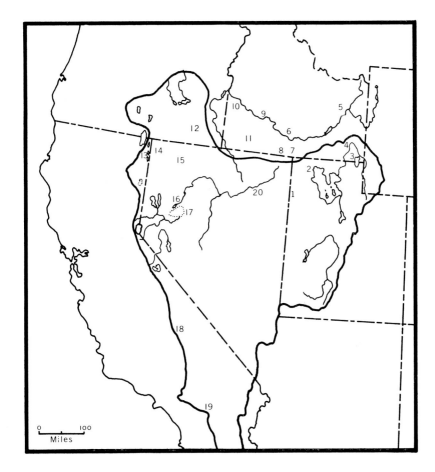

Figure 1.   The Great Basin of Western North America (archeological sites or localities cited in text)

1. Danger Cave	11. Southwestern Idaho Survey
2. Hogup Cave	12. Coyote Flat
3. Weston Canyon Rockshelter	13. Surprise Valley
4. Malad Hill	14. The High Rock Country
5. Pioneer Basin Locality	15. Black Rock Desert
6. Wilson Butte Cave	16. Lovelock Cave and Lakebed Sites
7. The Rock Creek Site	17. Hidden Cave
8. Brown's Bench Locality	18. The Stahl Site
9. Glenns Ferry Locality	19. Pinto Basin
10. Sites 10-OE-128 and 129	20. South Fork Shelter

Plate 1.   McKean projectile points. Row 1 and 2, lanceolate McKean. Row 3, stemmed McKean.

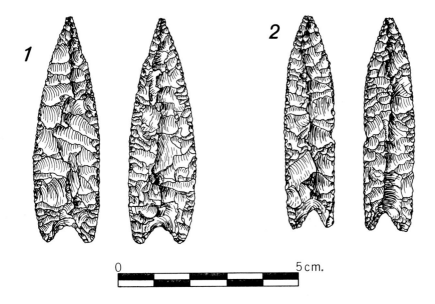

Figure 2. McKean lanceolate projectile points. Specimen numbers 1 and 2 cross-reference with Figure 1.

Key to Plate 1. Measurements of McKean projectile points.*

Artifact	Length (in mm)	Width (in mm)	Thickness (in mm)
1–X	59.0	19.0	4.5
2–149/158	56.5	14.5	4.6
4–24	50.0	17.5	4.8
5–18/52	49.0	18.5	5.5
6–133	47.3	17.5	5.5
7–137	45.2	15.2	4.3
8–138	44.2	18.7	6.0
12–137/red	40.0	15.5	4.5
20–10	43.0	13.5	6.0
23–3	39.3	13.6	4.2
25–156	36.0	10.0	5.1
19–137	46.2	15.2	5.6
28–X2	37.5	17.6	5.3
33–111	53.6	15.3	6.5
37–12	44.0	20.4	6.5
40–23	39.0	17.0	4.7
42–X3	29.0	16.5	4.9

* McKean points are from the McKean type station, 48Ck7, lower level. For identification refer to Figure 4 of the McKean Report (Mulloy 1954). The first number recorded corresponds to the number listed in Mulloy's Figure 4. The second number is the catalogue number on the artifact. This table cross-references with Plate 1 of this article.

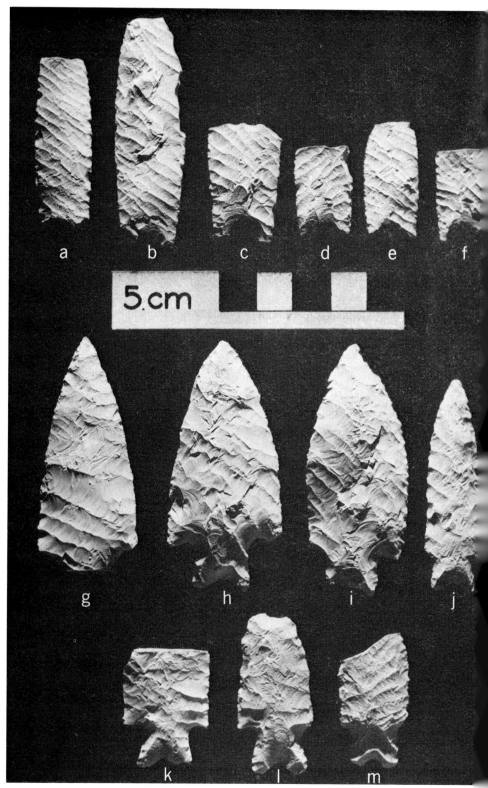

Plate 2. Little Lake projectile points. a-f, Humboldt Concave Base from the South-western Idaho Survey. g-i, Pinto Square Shouldered or Barbed from Weston Canyo Rockshelter. j-m, Pinto Square Shouldered or Barbed from the Rock Creek site.

Plate 1.   A view of the Casita de Piedra during the early stages of excavation

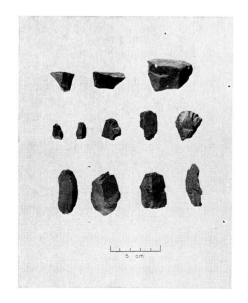

Plate 2.
Top row: conical cores
Middle and bottom rows:
bipolar cores

Plate 3.
The three specimens on the left
are bifacial cores; the three on the
right are irregular cores

Plate 4.
Top row: edge-battered cobbles
Middle row: end-battered
hammers showing the range of
sizes encountered
Bottom row: anvils

Plate 5.
Bifacially flaked celt-like
wedges. Wear polish on
the upper right wedge
appears as smooth, shiny
light facets

Plate 6.
Large irregular wedges

5   cm

Plate 7.
Top three rows: tabular
wedges. Bottom row:
broad-based wedges

5   cm

Plate 8.
Scraper-planes

Plate 9.
Top row: steep scrapers
Second row: concave
scrapers or spokeshaves
Third row: pointed
scrapers or gravers. Bot-
tom row: flake scrapers

5 cm

Plate 10.
Top row: flake knives
Middle row: burins
Bottom row: used quartz
crystals

5 cm

Plate 11.
Top row: bifacial
choppers
Middle row: cobble spall
choppers
Bottom row:
flake choppers

Plate 12.
Ground stone objects
recivered from the
Chiriqui River
excavations
Top left: adze (?) bit
fragment
Top center: chisel bit
Top right: adze (?) bit
fragment from the
disturbed deposits at the
Zarsiadero Shelter (and
therefore quite likely not
preceramic)
Middle row: the two
specimens on the left are
fragments of grooved
stones; the right specimen
is an incised stone bowl
rim section
Bottom: row grooved axe

Plate 13.
Edge-ground cobbles

Plate 14.
Top row: stone mortars
Middle: stone bowl
fragment
Bottom row:
nutting stones

Plate 15.
Top row: "pestles" with
gabled working ends
Middle row: "manos" or
rectangular grinding
stones
Bottom row: grinding
stones with off-set
grinding facets

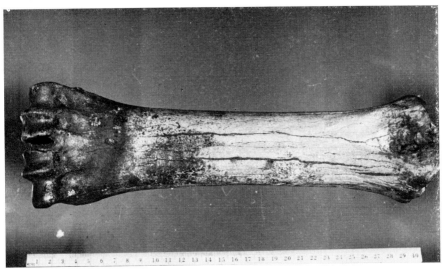

Plate 1 TOP, Recent weathered cow (*Bos taurus*) metapodial from the study area. Note large and small cracks parallel to the longitudinal axis (GJM 913). BOTTOM, Pleistocene bison (*Bison sp.*) metapodial from American Falls, Idaho. The bone was weathered prior to fossilization. Presence of more longitudinal cracks suggest the specimen was subjected to weathering for a longer period of time than the specimen from the cow above (ISUM 6577-17)

Plate 2.   Bone splinters from weathered cow (*Bos taurus*) metapodial *in situ* at study area. Newly produced weathering splinters, when fossilized, sometimes resemble arti- facts. When exposed to the atmosphere for twenty or more years, splinters become so badly weathered that it is highly unlikely that they could be mistaken for artifacts (GJM 910)

Plate 3.   Carcass of Recent cow (*Bos taurus*) *in situ* at study area. Specimen had been dead approximately ten months when photograph was taken. Note presence of large amounts of periosteum adhering to the articulated long bones. Bones have been gnawed and half of the skull has been cleaned by coyotes (*Canis latrans*), other scavengers, and weathering (GJM 909)

Plate 4.   Tibiae of Recent cow (*Bos taurus*) *in situ* at study area. The animal had been dead longer than four years when photograph was taken. Note presence of weathering cracks both parallel and transverse to the longitudinal axis of the bones. Periosteum is no longer present, bones are thoroughly bleached, and exfoliation is taking place on the specimen on the left. The specimens are slightly powdery on the surface (GJM 907)

Plate 5.   Long bones and rib of Recent domestic horse (*Equus caballus*) *in situ* at study area. The animal had been dead longer than eighteen years when the photograph was taken. Note cracks, splinters, and severe exfoliation. Specimens have lost the brilliant white color of younger bleached bones and are becoming a dull gray (GJM 911)

Plate 6.   BOTTOM, surface view of weathering cracks in cow (*Bos taurus*) metapodial froms tudy area. Bone had been exposed to the atmosphere for three years (GJM 913). TOP, surface view of experimentally induced crack in *B. taurus* metapodial. Note the same rough surface texture on both specimens with no distinct cleavage plane on either (ISUM R-155)

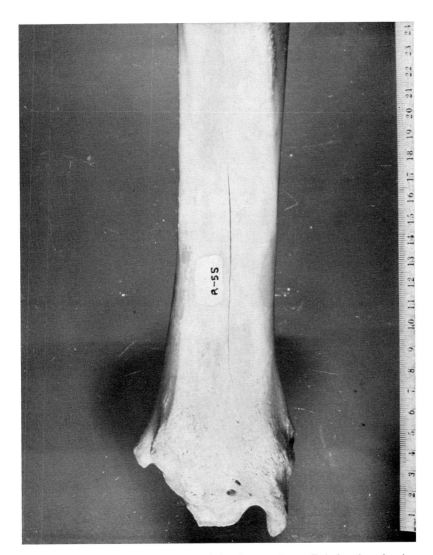

Plate 7.   Tibia of Recent cow (*Bos taurus*) showing experimentally induced crack going through the compact bone and into the marrow cavity. This is the first crack to appear. Other more shallow cracks parallel to this one appeared in a few hours. Many of the shallow cracks deepen with the passage of time (ISUM R–55)

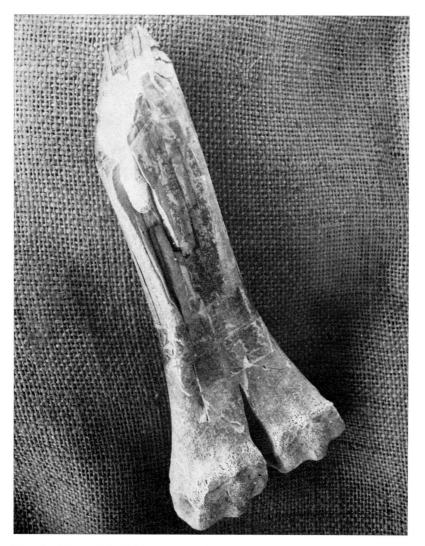

Plate 8.   Metapodial of Pleistocene camel (*Camelops sp.*) with oblique fracture proxi-
mally. Specimen is a suspected artifact; thus no contaminating preservatives have been
used in preparation. Instead, it has been temporarily held together with cellophane tape.
The white color showing in the marrow cavity is cotton gauze. Note the many pre-
fossilization longitudinal and transverse weathering cracks. Microscopic examination
revealed scratches on the surface of the oblique fracture that cross the weathering
cracks (RV 7228/15226, University of California at Riverside, Geological Sciences
Department Collection)

Plate 9.   Weathered bones of domestic horse (*Equus caballus*) and wild coyote (*Canis latrans*) from the study area. The coyote was killed while scavenging on the horse carcass; thus the bones of both animals have been subjected to the same thirty-one years of weathering. Note exfoliation and longitudinal weathering cracks in long bones of both animals. Specimens were rearrarged for the photograph (GJM 908)

Plate 10.   *In situ* photographs of ossified bird tendons at the Rancho La Brea site, Los Angeles, California. Specimens were found of several shapes and sizes: round, oval, flat, and triangular. Shown are one flat and one triangular specimen. Note striking similarity of these specimens to many of the bone "needles and awls" that have been figured in recent literature (LACM Uncatalogued)

PART TWO

Experimental Analysis of Toolmaking

Comments on Lithic Technology and Experimental Archaeology

DON E. CRABTREE

Since the excavations by Dr. L. S. B. Leakey at Olduvai, we now have evidence of the use of stone tools by man for approximately two million years. This gives us pause, when we realize that the Stone Age accounts for at least 99.5 percent of human history. Since artifacts of wood, bone, and other perishable materials had little chance of surviving the ravages of the elements and of time, we must rely primarily on stone tools in attempting to interpret the behavior of prehistoric man during the Stone Age. In brief, 99.5 percent of the history of mankind is represented by the Stone Age, and if we correctly approach an analysis of both his stone tools and the associated manufacturing debitage, we can attempt an interpretation of his behavior patterns and efforts at survival. I think Dr. Leakey summed it up very well when he said, "For the students of lithic technology, the stone tools of man represent fossilized human behavior patterns."

Today, stone tools are still used in only a few remote places in the world, and these societies, too, will probably soon substitute the more versatile metal implements for their stone tools. For this reason it is imperative that any information regarding the manufacture and use of stone implements – whether past or present – be recorded. It is unfortunate that existing Stone Age societies generally lack the sophisticated skill of workmanship of some of the prehistoric lithic industry workers. But we seem to note a degeneration of this skill even at the end of the Stone Age. For this reason, experimental archaeology – by which I mean the replication of prehistoric stone implements – can provide information about the manufacturing methods, techniques, and maybe even the uses of tools of the Stone Age. Certainly experimental replication will help the typologists, and functional experiments can give clues to how and why the tools were used. Through experiment, we will not only be more capable of defining techniques, but will also be able to evaluate the many stages necessary to finish the product, and to consider the significance of broken, malformed, and reworked tools. For those who are doing computer analysis, such evaluation is most important, for we should allow for inferior workmanship, miscalculation, intentional and unintentional fracture, deficient material, interruption of the worker, use by the learner, etc. But experimental archaeology must be related to the specific aboriginal concepts of a particular technology or clusters of techniques and then used to replicate the stages of manufacture from the raw material to completion.

Throughout the Stone Age, man made his stone artifacts by applying force to various lithic materials to detach flakes from the mass and ultimately shape and form a functional tool. He used various types of force and diverse fabricators. The flake or blade (specialized flake) bears the positive features, while the flake scar on the core retains negative features. Both the flake and the core may be formed into more complex tools by the removal of additional flakes, and when complete these are flake and core tools.

To the casual observer, flakes and their counterparts may look much alike, apart from the obvious differences in dimensions. But actually flakes and their scars are very distinctive, and can give clues to the manufacturing technique, direction of force, type of applied force, platform preparation, curvature of the flake, flake termination, stages of manufacture, type of tool used to induce fracture, and the type of artifact being made. An analogy might be if we were to compare fingers by observing shape and tips, rather than by using the sophisticated science of fingerprinting. Flakes detached by the same technique may differ in minor respects, but each will make perfect contact only with its original flake scar. But a drastic change of technique will usually show major differences in characteristics of the flake and scar. Unfortunately, there has been little recovery of pressure flakes except for pressure blades. Most pressure flakes are small and have a tendency to crush during detachment, and consequently to be lost at the workshop area. Therefore, we are generally forced to make our analysis of pressure techniques from the scars retained on the artifact.

Rather than burden the flake analyst with lengthy cumbersome lists of attributes, I would like to call attention to some of the problems of flake analysis and interpretation, based on the manufacture of stone implements. The flake or blade character is influenced by many factors. To name a few – the material, the implements used to apply the force, the applied techniques, the thermal alteration or lack of alteration of the lithic material, and the degree of skill of the artisan.

Force is applied to the stone to induce fracture to detach the flake and leave its corresponding scar on the mass. Both flakes and flake scars retain features which give clues to the aboriginal manufacturing processes. The flake retains more diagnostic features than the flake scar, because the platform usually adheres to the flake, and it bears other characteristics and traits which can indicate the mode of detachment and stage of manufacture. The flake permits the analyst to consider the platform character of the proximal end and to evaluate the termination of the distal end. The flake retains the positive character of the bulb of force; designates the area contacted by the fabricator; sometimes has lips, overhangs, curvature, and undulations; allows inspection of both the dorsal and ventral surface; denotes form and dimensions; and from the flake we can often differentiate between the worker's intent and the error. But the flake scar on the core is not without diagnostic features as well. The scar can indicate the direction of applied force, the depth of the negative bulbar scars, the flaking rhythm, manner of holding, spacing, use of ridges to guide the direction of flake removal, manner of termination, thinning, notching, serrating, etc. In view of the evidence afforded by flakes and flake scars, the experimental manufacture of prehistoric stone artifacts has been useful to replicate, interpret, and record the subtle variations of flakes and scars resulting from different techniques of manufacture. Certainly experimental archaeology is helpful to typology. For example, some artifacts may look morphologically alike but may be made by entirely different techniques. If we have some knowledge of stoneworking, we can more readily define these differences.

Because stone tools have an almost universal distribution covering a vast time span, and because they represent independent developments of multitudes of techniques, it is doubtful whether all of these techniques will ever be fully understood or defined. However, as the science of lithic technology progresses, experimental archaeology will make possible the association of the same or parallel techniques which have features and characteristics in common. Duplicate or parallel techniques will not indicate or prove a direct connection between extinct societies, for no doubt innumerable techniques were developed independently, and some can be outright inventions which have no parallel. Specific flake styles are possible by using diverse approaches to obtain finished products which are similar but not identical.

Many factors must be considered in determining the technique of manufacture. We must first evaluate the vast differences in lithic materials. I cannot stress this too much. I have yet to visit a quarry without evidence of previous aboriginal use giving mute testimony to the workers' discrimination in the choice of materials. Examples of tested and discarded materials are abundant in quarry sites, and I generally concur with the discard reasoning evidenced – e.g. imperfections in the material, cleavage planes, lack of elasticity, wrong size, poor texture, lack of homogeneity, etc.

Let us discuss materials. Obsidian is described geologically as a volcanic glass which is vitreous, isotropic, black in color, having the ability to fracture conchoidally. It was universally preferred by toolmakers for certain tools because under controlled conditions it responded to the workers' intent and gave flakes, blades, and tools with a keen edge. For agriculture and chopping tools, they generally preferred a more resistant material such as basalt, flint, chert, and the like. Yet obsidian varies in workability, depending on its elastic qualities, keenness of edge, mineral constituents, and differences in geological age and formation; all of these qualities can and do influence the workability of the material. Obsidian also comes in a variety of colors and sheens. The worker must appraise the obsidian with respect to the impurities it contains, inherent stresses and strains, temperatures of solidification, flow structures, gas bubbles, and size. All of these good or bad qualities can and do influence control, or restrict the outcome of the end product, whether the desired implement be a flake, a blade, or a multiple-flaked implement. Predominantly siliceous rocks, such as quartzites, flint, chert, and endless varieties of chalcedonies, are even more variable. The worker must either modify or develop techniques which conform and respond to the material being worked. For example, an entirely different cluster of methods and forces would have to be applied to quartzites and basalts than the worker is accustomed to using when he works with more vitreous rock, such as opal, obsidian, or heated siliceous material.

Often lithic material was available in only limited quantity, quality, size, and variety, and this had a direct bearing on the endeavors of the stoneworker. Over large geographical areas ideal lithic material was scarce, and often it had to be obtained from considerable distances. Discriminating stoneworkers who had access to a variety of materials selected their stone according to the intended design and functional purpose. When they intended their tools to be subjected to repeated impact and hard rigorous use, they selected material resistant to shock, to insure a longer lifespan for the implement. When they wanted tools with a keen cutting edge, they selected highly vitreous material. For example, certain obsidians with superior elastic qualities were selected for manufacturing pressure blades, while other less elastic obsidians were more desirable for artifacts which required multiple flaking. In nature, silica is compounded and blended with other elements, giving varieties with diverse qualities, some desirable and some undesirable. The toolmaker appears to have been a good geologist, and to have known how to choose material superior for specific needs.

Now let us consider toolmakers who had access only to inferior material, and yet made adequate tools. When analyzing such tools, one should not indiscriminately write off tools that have random flakes with step or hinge fractures as being the result of inferior workmanship. If you consider the material, you may discover that you have a superior workman who was forced to use inferior material. These tools should not be put aside and labeled "crude". If your evaluation takes into account not only the workmanship but also the material, this may change your opinion of the people who were forced to survive under these conditions.

As some metals are annealed and tempered, so also may siliceous rocks be altered by controlled application of heat. At some early period of time, man found that internal stresses and strains inherent in the rock could be relieved by subjecting the stone to controlled heat. This made the material more homogeneous, changing its texture from coarse to vitreous, and thus improving the flaking quality and enabling the worker to control flake detachment and to produce a tool with a sharper edge. Often lithic material containing impurities will undergo a color change during heat alteration. When this happens, the color change will be more pronounced near the exterior of the altered material. But controlled heating does not change the texture of the exterior or exposed surface. Only when a flake has been removed to expose the interior surface can the texture change be noted. We do not know as yet when prehistoric man discovered this annealing process, but Dr. François Bordes has noted the alteration as far back as Solutrean times.

Often in a collection or at an excavation we will find an aboriginal flake, blade, core, or artifact that will retain a portion of the natural surface of the stone. This will help in determining whether the material has been altered, for the exposed surface does not respond to heat treatment. But if the ventral side of the flake or blade is lustrous in contrast to the dorsal side, then we can safely assume that the material has been subjected to thermal alteration. When we do not have the debris and must rely on only the flaked surface of artifacts such as projectile points, cores, etc., we can look for a facet of the natural material which might still be adhering to the face of the artifact. Then we can compare this facet with the flaked surface to determine whether the material has been altered. If the facet is dull, while the flaked surface is lustrous and of a different texture than the natural facet, then we can be pretty sure the material has been altered. With cores, we can detach a flake to note any difference on the ventral side. If such evidence is not obvious, then we must resort to an experimental approach and conduct a controlled heating process on the same material to ascertain whether the stone has been altered by heating.

Thermal alteration of lithic materials is a sophisticated process involving critical temperatures, correct duration of gradually raised and maintained heat exposure, controlled cooling process, and calculation of time and temperature according to the type, size, and quality of the material being altered. Until one is familar with the stone, each material must be tested individually. When the correct formula has been determined for a given material, then any deviation in control of raising and lowering the temperature will result in the material remaining unchanged, hence worthless for diagnostic purposes. The temperature range for altering siliceous minerals will vary from 450°F to 1,000°F, and only trial and error will determine the ideal temperature index. Basalts and obsidians respond to a much higher temperature without danger of crazing, and they will withstand more rapid temperature changes than siliceous rocks. Archaeological examples of the use of heat treatment are the Hopewell cores and blades from the Flintridge, Ohio material. Analysis reveals that most of these were of treated flint.

The percussors and compressors used to form the stone tool definitely influence the character of the detached flakes and scars, and the toolmaker selects his fabricator to conform to the size and type of material and the desired fracture dimension, choosing one which will perform a specific technique or a group of related techniques. Hammerstones, billets, punches, compressors, and all fabricating tools should be recovered from sites and their wear patterns studied to help determine the technique and type of applied force. For example, the edge-ground cobble technique leaves a consistent wear pattern on the side of the hammerstone rather than on the end, and this can often be mistaken for a rubbing stone. But when the wear patterns on these cobbles are properly interpreted, they can indicate a distinctive type of blade and flake detachment.

There are three major and very general classes of flake detachment: direct percussion, indirect percussion, and pressure. A minor technique is the combined use of pressure and percussion. Flake detachment techniques involve a knowledge of the elastic limits of the materials,

Newton's law of motion, force, gravity, weight, mass, density, friction, levers, moment of force, center of gravity, stability of bodies, projectile motion, and kinetic energy. This is, indeed, a comprehensive list of factors which must be mentally evaluated and calculated to accomplish the controlled fracture of lithic materials. It is highly unlikely that prehistoric man was aware of the scientific laws involved, but as his techniques became more sophisticated, he did take advantage of these principles.

The earliest stone tools were probably natural erosional products selected by man for their sharp cutting edges, and he probably used spheroids as hammers or missiles. Direct percussion was probably man's first approach to intentional fracture to form tools and expose useful cutting edges. This early technique was used to form a wide variety of percussion tools, and involved many and varied percussion techniques. One of the simplest is described by Richard Gould (personal communication), when he observed the Australian aborigines in the process of toolmaking. They threw the lithic material against boulders and then selected flakes with sharp cutting edges to be used "as is," while others were selected to be modified into functional implements. This technique of using a fixed anvil stone is often called "block on block." When further refined, it leads to other, related techniques. But considerably more fracture control is possible when the material is not thrown against the anvil but, rather, is held in the hand and then struck against the anvil stone. This allows the worker to predetermine the point of contact, accurately detach his flake, and expose an edge. It affords the worker more accuracy, and the degree of velocity can be adjusted and proportioned according to the weight of the material being flaked and the desired dimension of the intended fracture. But even better control of the flake or blade detachment may be gained when the worker specially designs the part of the material to be contacted by the fixed percussor. This point of contact is known as the platform. There are many methods of platform preparation, which have diagnostic value and which influence the character of the flake or blade. A few examples of platform preparation are: making the proper angle on a plane surface, isolating the platform area surface, removing the overhang from previous flake scars, grinding the surface, polishing the margin, faceting by the removal of one or more flakes, beveling, and the orientation of the platform with a guiding ridge or ridges. As prehistoric man improved his stone toolmaking, he progressed from simply exposing an edge, to flaking more of the surface. This evolution progressed from the first embryonic attempt, to flaking handaxes with a natural surface butt, then to entirely flaked handaxes, and on to cores, blades, burins, projectiles, etc. During this time he also substituted antler, bone, and hard woods for the stone hammer he used to flake his implements, which enabled him to control his flake detachment better, and make thinner tools. The progression continued to the Solutrean, where we first note the use of pressure flaking. And so on to the New World, where we find sophisticated techniques and combinations of techniques, fluting, and a predominance of pressure work.

There are various other types of percussion and pressure techniques, but all involve proper preparation of the striking or pressing area, correct angle of applied force, control of applied forces, predetermined flake termination, and other factors, too numerous to mention. It is enough to say that both the flakes and their scars must be studied very carefully to arrive at any decision concerning the technique of manufacture. Some of the questions that can often be answered by an evaluation of the lithic debris, broken, and malformed artifacts are:

1. How was an artifact made, and what tools were used to make it?
2. Why was the implement made in this particular form?
3. Why were certain lithic materials selected for certain artifacts?
4. How was the tool intended to be used?
5. What task was it to perform?
6. Was the tool a multipurpose tool?
7. How was the tool held in order to perform a given function?
8. Was the tool hafted?
9. How was the tool hafted?
10. What was the action of the tool on the object material?
11. Was the tool pulled or pushed?
12. Did the tool strike or press the object material?
13. Was the tool used for scraping or cutting?
14. How is the angle of the tool edge related to the resistance of the material formed?
15. How can attrition be distinguished from core polish?
16. What causes the striations on the working edge of the tool?
17. What are the directions of the striations on the working edge of the tool?
18. Was the tool used as a burnisher?
19. Do some softer materials being formed have an abrasive action on the tool?
20. How can use flakes be distinguished from intentional retouch?
21. What are the characteristics of use flakes?
22. What are the implications of a series of use flakes of a given charac-

ter, termination, change of angle, and increased resistance, with respect to improper use, use by beginners or apprentices, or mishandling?

23. Was the tool abandoned upon completion of the task?
24. Was the tool broken by accident, during manufacture, due to imperfections in the material, or during its functional performance?
25. Was the tool exhausted from resharpening?

These are only a few of the problems encountered when evaluating lithic material. Each flake or artifact must be considered independently. Then clusters of like attributes may prove to have diagnostic significance.

You may say, "This is all well and good, but I am not a flintknapper and I have no one to teach me and no access to debris for analysis." It is certainly not my intention to make a flintknapper out of every student, but even making a stab at it will give you a "feel" for controlling fracture, and will help clarify the mechanical problems involved in making stone tools. So for those who are seriously interested in lithic technology, I recommend at least a try in stone fracture. You need not become proficient at the art, but at least try it. If you don't have stone available for experiment, then use building glass, old T.V. tubes, the bottoms of bottles, old porcelain toilet bowls, or anything that will respond like stone. Also, you are fortunate to be studying during a period when information on this art is readily available. Idaho State University has films for rent or sale showing various types of pressure and percussion work, and also has many publications on replication. Tom Hester has published a fine bibliography containing almost everything written on lithic technology. And we now have lithic technology courses available in several universities, with many students teaching actual flintknapping. Many students have attended the Idaho State University Museum summer field school in knapping, and have become quite proficient at toolmaking. Most of these graduates are available to give demonstrations, show actual manufacture, and explain the implications of debitage. Also, in our major universities and museums there are large collections of prehistoric stone tools which we can use as models for replication and analysis. These collections often present a challenge to our ingenuity, inventiveness, and personal resourcefulness in resolving techniques.

Barring these approaches, you can practice experimental replication on your own, as prehistoric man did. François Bordes and I independently learned this way, and it was only by trial and error that we eventually achieved replication of many techniques. But this is slow and laborious, and involves a lot of blood, sweat, and tears, so I would recommend the methods mentioned earlier. And let's not forget Halvar Skavlem, Anders

Kragh, Gene Titmus, and others, who spent many years developing their own approach to replication. Another fine example is Jacques Tixier, of the Museum of Natural History in Paris, France. He learned percussion from François Bordes, and later, when he attended the lithic technology conference in Les Eyzies, he learned the rudiments of pressure flaking from observing demonstrations by François Bordes and me. For years he practiced pressure work on his own, and would send samples of his work to me with questions about removing overhang, obtaining a keen edge, platform preparation, angle of holding tool on the platform, angle of applied pressure, etc. As a result, he became a first-rate flintknapper by experiment and correspondence. Having learned the value of debitage, he was then able to define the Capsian core technique. When he found cores and debitage at an excavation which contained the platform part, he was able to define the Capsian cores and blades as a pressure technique. Since then, he has become one of our most outstanding typologists, and has defined other techniques, including replication of an ancient Ethiopian blade technique.

It is certainly not my intent to infer that only toolmakers are qualified to interpret techniques of manufacture and types of tools. A case in point is Ruthann Knudson. She was intensely interested in paleo-man's tools, and intended to write her thesis on this subject. She was fortunate enough to have the benefit of Marie Wormington's vast knowledge of typology, and to work with her at her excavation in Kersey, Colorado. She was also present on several occasions when I visited Kersey and gave demonstrations in toolmaking. Being a keen observer, she noted each step of manufacture, and later studied the debitage. Then, after examining paleo-man collections throughout the country, she applied what she had observed and came up with an accurate technological description of many tools. When she attended our field school, she brought along her index-card analysis of these tools, and in every instance her analysis was correct. In her case, the school gave her a chance to actually try flintknapping and to verify her conclusions. Thus, experimental archaeology has many approaches, and I recommend them all, or a combination of several, to all students concentrating on lithic technology and typology.

In conclusion, we all owe a vote of thanks to Dr. Earl Swanson and Dr. Marie Wormington for having the wisdom to stress the significance of this experimental approach for a better understanding of the behavior of Stone Age man.

The Experimental Study of Bipolar Flakes

HIROAKI KOBAYASHI

In the Early Paleolithic in Japan, the existence of bipolar flakes and cores has been presumed especially on the Sozudai site in Kyushu island (Chosuke Serizawa 1965: 1–121). Their existence becomes the center of interest when the Early Paleolithic in Japan is studied in relation to the Lower Paleolithic in China.

A paper by C. C. Young (1933:58, 65) about artifacts from Chou-Kou-Tien Loc. 1 illustrates a bipolar core. There are other papers which illustrate the bipolar technique in China (Chia Lan-po 1957: 24–25, 1958: 16–17, 1964: 92).

An experimental study of the bipolar technique may have been done in China (Chia Lan-po 1956: 1–8), but the result of it has not been reported in detail. The necessity for the experimental study and detailed reporting of the bipolar technique has been recognized in Japan.

The term "bipolar technique" refers to the method of flaking bipolar flakes from cores.

I. From June to September 1972 an experiment was performed to investigate the method of making bipolar flakes. Hard hammerstones (andesite) and anvils (andesite) were used to remove bipolar flakes from blocks (rhyolite). Hammerstones (Plates 1a and 1b), anvils (Plates 2a,

I wish to express my thanks to Professor Chosuke Serizawa, Department of Archaeology, Arts and Letters Faculty of Tohoku University, for his kindness in lending me literature on the palaeolithic age in China and in giving me a chance to perform this experiment and for his advice and continued encouragement. Dr. Earl H. Swanson, Jr., Director at Idaho State University Museum, gave me an opportunity to write this paper.

For Plates, see pp. iv–x, between pp. 102–103

2b, and 2c), and blocks were brought from the Hirose River which flows through Sendai, Miyagi prefecture.

The method of flaking bipolar flakes is as follows: A worker sits down or squats on the ground. If he sits down, an anvil is placed between his knees. This method is used when bipolar flakes are removed from small cores. When big bipolar flakes are wanted, then squatting is more useful. A core is held in the left hand (for a right-handed person) and is rested on an anvil. Then direct percussion is applied to the striking platform of the core from right angles, using a hammerstone held in the right hand. In this case, the most important things are as follows:

1.   When direct percussion is applied, the core rested on the anvil should be held firmly in the left hand. If this is not done, the core will slip on the anvil and bipolar flakes cannot be successfully removed.

2.   The direct percussion must be applied vertically on the striking platform of the core. When a core tapers toward the distal end or an anvil with a convex surface is used, it is necessary to tap the platform lightly to see if the force is aligned with the end of the core where it contacts the anvil.

3.   When the direct percussion is applied, the hammerstone must be used as if it were pressed against the striking platform of the core.

4.   The size and weight of a hammerstone are also important. These factors determine the size and thickness of flakes removed from cores. To remove thin, tiny bipolar flakes, a lightweight hammerstone is used (see Plate 1a) and the best result can be expected when the convex head of a hammerstone is used. When large, thick bipolar flakes are to be removed, a heavy hammerstone (see Plate 1b) must be used. It is desirable to have a hammerstone with a straight edge and a U-shaped cross-section.

5.   The surface and thickness of an anvil are also important. A flat surface is much better than a convex one. When the flaking is done, a core resting on a convex surface is apt to slip on the anvil. The more convex the surface of an anvil, the more the shattering at the distal end of a core increases. In general, the thicker the anvil the better. Two anvils (see Plates 2a and 2b) are examples which could not resist the force of the percussion and were broken. It is very interesting that these two anvils broke into three parts from the place where the distal end of a core was in contact with the anvil.

II.   The above-mentioned method was used 300 times to remove bipolar flakes from cores rested on an anvil. The striking platforms and distal ends of the cores were not prepared before flakes were removed. In 300 times, 300 flakes were made. These flakes were classified by their ventral surfaces into four large groups: A, B, C, and D. Group characteristics are as follows:

Group A: Flakes which have one or a twin bulb at only the proximal end on the ventral surface. Flakes which have terminations of distal ends, shattered ends, hinge fractures or feather edges, are included (see Plates 3 and 4).

Group B: Flakes which have one or twin bulb at only the distal end where it was in contact with an anvil, whose striking platforms are shattered or feather edges are included (see Plate 5).

Group C: Bipolar flakes, that is, one or twin bulb is found at both the proximal and distal ends (see Plates 6a, 6b, 6c, 6e, 6f, 6g, and 6h).

Group D: Flakes which are removed from the same core by one percussion blow. Flakes are removed from the striking platform and the distal end which was in contact with the anvil, and two flakes are removed at the same time; therefore, two flaked scars are seen at the surface of the core as if the core were a bidirectional opposed angular one (see Plates 7a and 7b).

Flakes which were classified into the A, B, and D groups were obtained when Group C flakes could not be successfully removed from the cores. By percussion in the first successive 200 times, 200 flakes were removed from cores, with the following results: Group A, 129 flakes; Group B, 29; Group C, 40; and Group D, 2. In Group A, for the termination of the distal end: hinge fracture, 6; shattered 91; feather end 12; and not shattered (except for feather end), 20 flakes. At the striking platform in Group B: edge shattered, 20; feather edge, 5; edge not shattered (bulbs were not recognized at the striking platform), 4 flakes.

By percussion in the next successive 100 times, 100 flakes were removed from cores, made up as follows: Group A, 23; Group B, 2; Group C, 75; and Group D, 0 flakes. Group A: hinge fractures, 3; edge shattered, 12; feather end, 6; and edge not shattered, 2 flakes. At the striking platform in Group B: feather edge, 1; edge shattered, 1 flake.

III. In Group A, flakes which feather at the distal end terminations were removed from cores when distal ends of cores were not successfully on an anvil. Flakes with shattered distal ends were obtained when the force of percussion delivered to the striking platform was too strong and the force of the resistance became much more powerful.

The flaking angles for Group A flakes from the first (200) and second (100) flaking series were measured (Figure 1). The method of measuring the flaking angle of each flake in this paper is shown in Figure 2. There

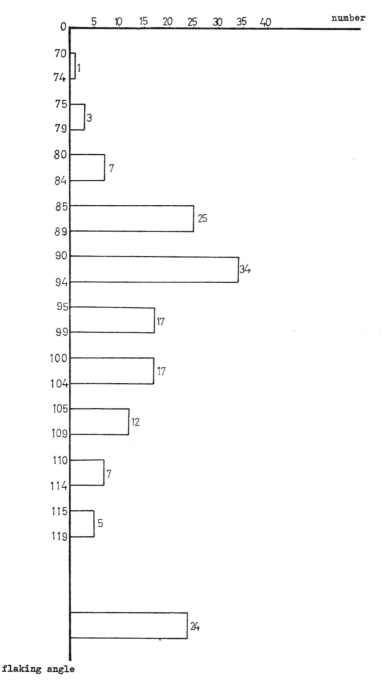

Figure 1.   The relation between the flaking angle and the number of flakes in Group A

were 128 flakes which could be measured and 24 which could not be measured. Thirty-four flakes or 26.6 percent of 128 flakes had flaking angles from 90 to 94 degrees. The next most numerous flaking angle (19.5 percent) is from 85 to 89 degrees.

The flaking angles for Groups B and D were not taken because there were so few flakes.

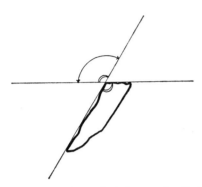

Figure 2.   The method of measuring the flaking angle of a flake

IV.   Group C flaking angles at the striking platform for the first and second flaking series are shown in Figure 3. Measurements were made as for Group A flakes. The most common angles for 31 pieces, 29.0 percent of 107 measurable flakes, are from a right angle to 94 degrees. The next most numerous flaking angle (17.8 percent) is from 80 to 84 degrees.

The relation between the flaking angles of flakes at the striking platforms and at the distal ends which had been in contact with an anvil, on each of the same ventral surfaces, is shown in Figure 4. Seventy-five flakes could be measured. One piece (1.4 percent) had an angle at the platform which was more than twice as much as that at the distal end. Thirtyfour flakes (45.3 percent) have flaking angles at the striking platform which range from twice as great (2:1) as those at the distal ends. Forty (53.3 percent) range from 1:1 to 1:2. The flaking angle at the striking platform is never below half as much as that at the distal end.

The relation between the number of flakes and their flaking angles at the striking platforms is shown at the upper side in Figure 5. The relation between the number of flakes and flaking angles at the distal ends which were in contact with an anvil is shown at the lower side in the same figure. The upper and lower sides are almost symmetrical and it may be said that the ratio of the concentrations of the number of flakes and their flaking angles at the striking platforms and distal ends is almost the same.

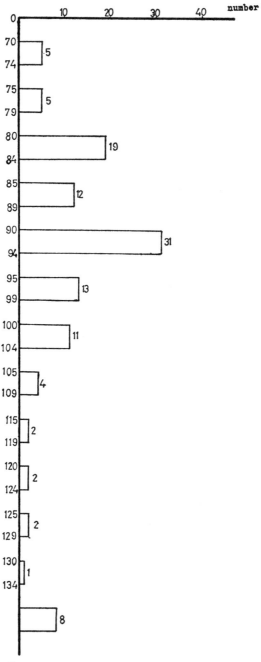

Figure 3.   The relation between flaking angles at platforms of flakes and the number
of flakes in Group C

the flaking angle at

at the striking

platform

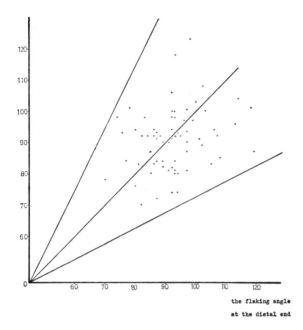

the flaking angle

at the distal end

Figure 4.   The relation between flaking angles at striking platforms and those at distal
ends in Group C

The relation between the number of flakes and shapes of bulbs at
proximal and distal ends is shown next in Figure 6. Many of the bulbs
at proximal or distal ends which were in contact with an anvil were
peculiarly shaped. They are very flat in section and it was recognized
that only fissures concentrate at the proximal or distal ends, so these
are very different from the salient or diffuse bulbs. These bulbs are called
flat bulbs here. They are sometimes produced in the author's other experiment with the block on block technique. The flaking is done when
a block held in the hands is struck at an edge of a rock. Flat bulbs are
seen at the proximal end of the flake at Plate 6b. Twenty-eight flakes,
27.7 percent of 101 measurable flakes, have flat bulbs at the proximal
and distal ends. The second most numerous group (18 pieces or 17.8 percent) has salient bulbs at the proximal and distal ends. The third group
(17 pieces or 16.8 percent) has a salient bulb at the proximal end and a
flat bulb at the distal end. The fourth group (16 pieces or 15.8 percent)
has a flat bulb at the proximal end and the salient bulb at the distal. The
frequency in the emergence of these four groups is very high with the

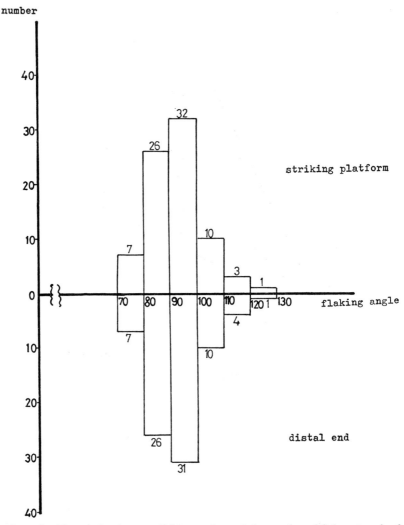

Figure 5.   The relation between flaking angles and the number of flakes at each of platforms and distal ends in Group C

bipolar technique. There are no flakes which have diffuse bulbs at both proximal and distal ends on the same ventral surface.

The number of flakes on which undulations were recognized on ventral surfaces was 58, 53.7 percent of 108 flakes on which ventral surfaces survived well (Figure 7). The number of flakes on which undulations were not recognized is 35 (32.4 percent). The number of flakes on which one or two ridges were recognized from the middle of the bulb at the proximal end to the middle of the flake at the distal end is 15 pieces (13.9

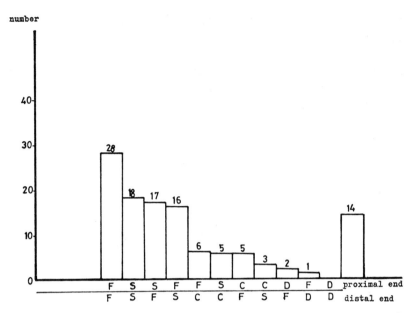

Figure 6. The relation between the number of flakes and shapes of bulbs at both proximal ends and distal ends of the same ventral surfaces in Group C
F – Flat bulb, S-Salient bulb, C– Concave bulb, D–Diffuse bulb

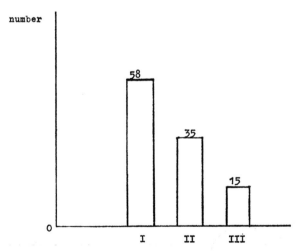

Figure 7. The frequency in the emergence of the undulation in Group C
I   – Undulations are seen on ventral surfaces of flakes
II – Undulations are not seen on ventral surfaces of flakes
III – One or two ridges are seen from the middle of the bulb at the proximal end to that of the bulb at the distal end on the ventral surface of a flake

percent) (see Plates 6c and 6g). In my other experiments, e.g. direct percussion using an andesite hammerstone or a moose antler on rhyolite
blocks, indirect percussion using a moose antler punch and a moose
antler hammer on obsidian cores, and the block on block technique using
rhyolite blocks against a tuff rock, these flakes were not removed. Therefore, it may be said that these flakes are a distinguishing trait of the
bipolar technique.

Direct percussion experiments produce undulations whose frequency
can be compared with those in Group C above. I used an andesite
hammerstone (747 grams) and a moose antler billet (226 grams) giving
the following results: direct percussion with the andesite hammer in 200
successive blows removed 200 flakes. The number of flakes on which
undulations were recognized on ventral surfaces was 157 (78.5 percent).
The number of flakes on which undulations were not recognized was 43
(21.5 percent). Direct percussion with a moose antler, in 200 successive

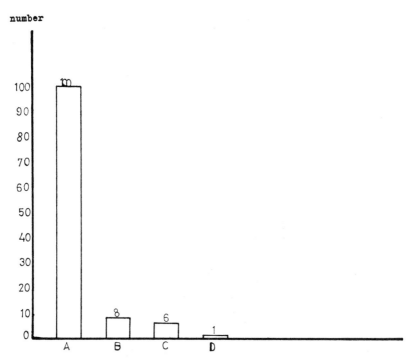

Figure 8.   The frequency in the emergence of the crush or shattering of striking plat-
forms or distal ends of flakes in Group C
A – Both ends are crushed or shattered
B – The striking platform is crushed or shattered
C – The distal end is crushed or shattered
D – Neither end is crushed or shattered

times, removed 200 flakes from rhyolite blocks. The number of flakes on which undulations were recognized was 25 (12.5 percent) and the number on which undulations were not recognized was 175 (87.5 percent). The results can be compared with those from Group C. The frequency in the emergence of undulation in Group C is lower than that in direct percussion with an andesite hammerstone (level of significance is below 2.5 percent) and is higher than that in direct percussion with a moose antler (level of significance is below 0.10 percent).

The word crush is used when damage to the striking platform and the distal end is very slight from percussion. Both ends or either of them has survived well and it is possible to measure the flaking angle on each flake. Crush must be distinguished from the shattering which is used in an

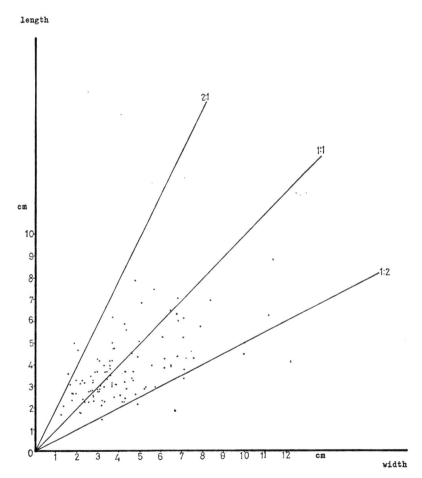

Figure 9. The relation between the length and the width of each flake in Group C

ordinary sense. Figure 8 shows the number of flakes on which crushing or shattering was recognized at both striking platforms and distal ends as 100, 87 percent in 115 flakes. This group is most numerous. The number whose platforms only were shattered or crushed is 8 and 7 percent. The number whose distal ends only were crushed or shattered is 6 and 5 percent. The number of flakes which were not crushed or shattered at both ends is very small.

Crush on the striking platform (including flakes on which crush was recognized at both ends, except for flakes at which crush was recognized at the distal end) in Group C showed in 100 pieces, 80 percent in 115 flakes. With direct percussion using an andesite hammerstone, there were 105 pieces, 52.5 percent in 200 flakes. The frequency in Group C is higher than that of direct percussion with a level of significance below 0.10 percent.

Figure 9 shows that the number of flakes whose length to width relationship is above 2: 1 is 3 pieces (2.8 percent in 108 flakes) which could be measured; from 2: 1 to 1: 1 is 39 (38.9 percent); from 1: 1 to 1: 2 is 57 (52.8 percent); and below 1: 2 is 6 pieces (5.6 percent). The frequency in the appearance of flakes whose width is greater than length is high in this experiment with the bipolar technique.

CONCLUSIONS

1. The bipolar flakes of group C have a most common flaking angle from 90 to 94 degrees. Much the same phenomenon can be seen in Group A.

2. The concentrations of both flaking angles at the striking platform and the distal end were almost the same .

3. In Group C flakes with flat bulbs at both proximal and distal ends on the same ventral surfaces were most numerous. Flakes with salient bulbs at proximal and distal ends and flakes with one salient and one flat bulb at the proximal or distal ends of each of the same ventral surfaces were frequent. Flakes with diffuse bulbs at both proximal and distal ends on the same ventral surfaces do not occur.

4. The frequency of appearance of undulations in Group C was lower than that of direct percussion using an andesite hammerstone on rhyolite blocks and higher than that using a moose antler billet.

5. The crushing or shattering at both striking platform and distal end on the same flake was higher in Group C than in direct percussion using an andesite hammer.

6.   In Group C, the number of flakes in which width is greater than the length was more numerous than that of flakes in which length is greater than the width.

7.   In some Group C flakes one or two ridges were seen from the middle of a bulb at the proximal end to the bulb at the distal end on the ventral surface of a flake. This feature is peculiar to the bipolar technique.

REFERENCES

CHIA LAN-PO

   1956   The new point of view of artifacts of Sinanthropus pekinensis. *Archaeological Journal* 6:1–8. Peking.

   1957   *Palaeolithic culture.* Peking: Youth Express.

   1958   *The Pekinese home.* Peking: Peking Express.

   1964   *Sinanthropus pekinensis and his culture.* Peking: Intellectual Library.

SERIZAWA, CHOSUKE

   1965   A Lower Palaeolithic industry from the Sozudai Site, Oita Prefecture, Japan. *Reports of the Research Institute for Japanese Culture* 1:1–121. Sendai.

YOUNG, C. C.

   1933   *Fossil man and summary of Cenozoic geology in China.* Geological Memoirs, series B, 5:58, 65.

Remarks on Fragments
with Languette *Fractures*

M. LENOIR

In a recent article F. Bordes points out the existence of fragments of blades with a curious kind of fracture, which he calls *pièces a languette* 'fragments with small, tongue-like projections'. Several examples of these are given in the article (1970:105–113, Figure 6, Numbers 5–13).

Pursuant to this article and tp the discussions we have had with Bordes, we were able, like him, to observe the appearance of such fractures during the experimental breaking of blades or flakes of siliceous rocks. We have saved these fragments. It was not always possible, however, for us to retrieve the two fragments resulting from the same fracture (Figure 2, Numbers 4 and 5).

If certain specimens correspond perfectly to Bordes' description and reproduce the examples that he gives in his illustration, others, although capable of being related to the fractures with *languettes*, differ somewhat from the definition and represent variants.

The classic type, as identified by Bordes, can be described as follows: the proximal fragment, which carries the striking platform of the blade, bears a *languette*, the concave side of which is turned toward the observer when the supporting piece is examined from its dorsal face. This *languette* shows impact waves which constitute the negative of those which affect the distal fragment. The latter has a curved end (Figure 1, Number 5[1]; Figure 2, Numbers 4 and 5). This lip curves progressively and has the appearance of being turned upward at the end of the blade, but sometimes it shows as well a small point of rupture at its proximal extremity (Figure

---

[1] For these two examples we were able to preserve only the distal fragment.

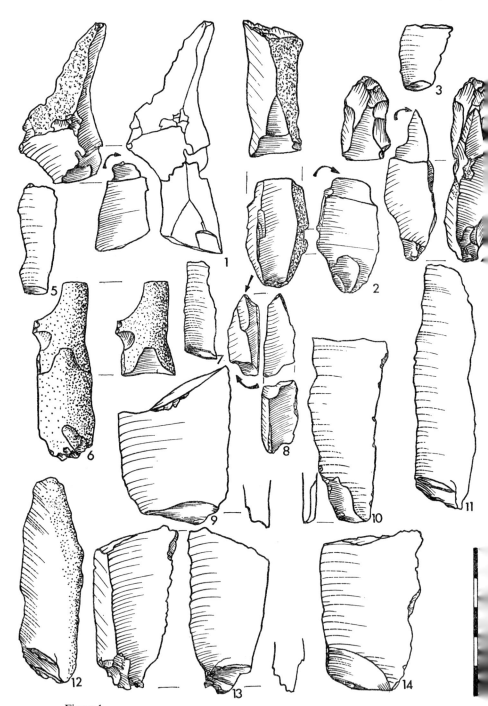

Figure 1

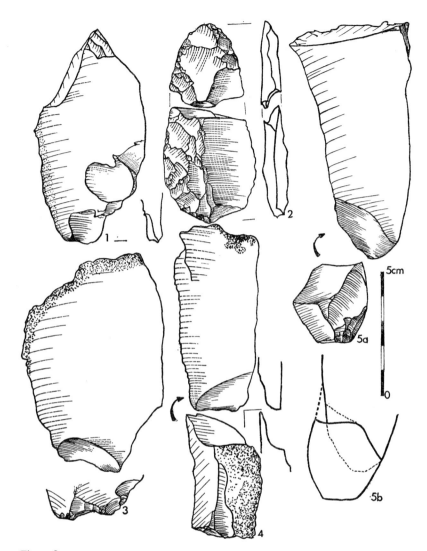

Figure 2

1, No. 9). The impact waves begin at this point and continue toward the distal extremity of the supporting piece.[2]

A variation, which we obtained fortuitously during our experimentation and which we have observed frequently in the course of the study of Paleolithic material, shows an oblique lip the end of which, being at an

---

[2] Bordes points out, however, one or two cases in which the orientation of the undulations is inverse.

angle in relation to the axis of the supporting piece, presents the form of an S (Figure 1, Number 10; Figure 2, Number 1).

We also have obtained, as a result of this type of fracture, fragments of blades without a striking platform the proximal extremity of which presents a hollow splinter on its ventral face (Figure 1, Numbers 11, 12, 13) which curves more or less, producing an up-turned shape. This splinter shows on its distal part a fragment of incompletely detached *languette*, which broke before the total separation from the rest of the supporting piece took place. All these features taken together produce a stepped effect.

Finally, in certain cases (Figure 1, Numbers 1, 2, 4, 6), the *languette* is carried by the distal fragment of the blade affected by this type of fracture, whereas its negative is placed on the proximal fragment; but, again, in this case, the shock waves seem to begin at the heel.

We have obtained these different types of fractures with *languettes* while detaching detaching flakes and blades by direct percussion with a hammerstone in both flint and foundry slag, the nucleus being held in the free hand.

Certain fractures resulted accidentally during the fabrication of tools: blades breaking when one of their extremities was truncated, or a fracture occurring during the pressure flaking of foliated points or during their fluting (Figure 2, Number 2), and finally, fractures of the supporting piece occurring during the removal of a burin spall at one of its extremities (Figure 1, Number 8).

As far as the causes of this type of fracture are concerned, we can only propose several hypotheses: unfavorable spreading action of the impact waves resulting from the heterogeneity of the material, the striking object used being too hard, or the force of the blow being too great; or it could be a matter of a combination of these different factors. Obviously, the possible causes are not limited to the list we have proposed.

REFERENCES

BORDES, FRANÇOIS
  1970   Observations typologiques et techniques sur le Périgordien supérieur de Corbiac. *Bulletin de la Société Préhistorique Française* 67:105–113.

Fractures for the Archaeologist

BARBARA A. PURDY

It has been established that the aboriginal flintknappers of Florida found it advantageous to thermally alter lithic raw materials used to fashion certain chipped stone implements (Purdy and Brooks 1971). While investigations were being conducted to determine the effects of heat on the chipping properties of flint, observations also were made pertaining to the types of fractures that result when flint materials are subjected to various heat stresses. Subsequent recovery and examination of more than sixty-five thousand chipped stone remains from a flint workshop site in Marion County, Florida, provided an opportunity to determine whether the prehistoric inhabitants of Florida always were able to reach and maintain the temperature optimal for alteration without occasionally exceeding this optimum and damaging the stone. Interestingly, I was able to identify, from the field, examples similar to nearly all of the experimental specimens.

The purpose of this paper is to describe the conditions under which various types of fractures occurred in Florida cherts and to illustrate the similarities between experimental and field samples. This comparison should provide additional information pertaining to lithic technology as well as contribute to what is known about man's control of fire before the invention of the thermometer. It should also be an aid to archaeologists in describing flint remains.

Chert (flint) fractures isotropically. It is this property that makes fracture predictable and makes chert or chertlike materials desirable for producing chipped stone tools. Most archaeologists would define chert as a rock composed of microcrystalline quartz that breaks with a conchoidal fracture. This is an adequate general description, but does not suffice

For Plates, see pp. xi–xviii, between pp. 102–103

when specific materials from diverse geographic areas are being considered. Because chert is a rock, it varies greatly in its physical characteristics
even though the basic components, the minute crystals of quartz, are
uniform in character. The factors that determine the physical properties
of cherts are: (1) the size of the quartz crystals; (2) how the anhedral crystals fit together and affect porosity and fracture; (3) the amount of foreign
material, fossil replacements, and other heterogeneities, including flux
compounds, present; (4) void spaces; and (5) crystalline fabric (the crystals are not equidimensional or always randomly oriented).

From the standpoint of this investigation, knowledge of the formation
and composition of the siliceous materials native to the state of Florida
is necessary because stress by heat might not take place at the same temperature in materials whose structure is slightly different. For example,
Crabtree (personal communication) has indicated that thermal alteration
was effected at 400 degrees Fahrenheit in some of his experimental materials. Alteration takes place in Florida cherts at 350–400 degrees centigrade.
Arkansas novaculite is extremely difficult to alter, even though some investigators believe that heat treatment was practiced by native knappers.
I subjected Arkansas novaculite to 600 degrees centigrade for an extended
period, but could detect no change in the material. This could be due to
differences (or percentage differences) in the impurities present compared
to Florida cherts, or it could be because of the low water content of
Arkansas novaculite compared to Florida cherts. In the Florida cherts,
there are different types and even a single nodule is not necessarily
homogeneous throughout its mass. But Florida cherts were all formed under similar conditions and share common characteristics, which distinguish them from other siliceous rocks. They occur as a secondary formation due to the replacement of carbonates with silicas. All of the chert
deposits in Florida are in relationship to relict clay hills in contact with
limestone.

Archaeologists are familiar with the terms "hinge" fracture, "step"
fracture, and "feathered" fracture, which describe the typical ways a flake
terminates when it is detached from the core. Most archaeologists are also
aware of "lateral snap" due to end shock, which results when a substantial
blow is imparted to a rock whose mass is not adequately supported to
absorb the shock. Lateral snap does not occur at the point of impact; thus,
no bulb of force is present on the face of the fracture. Preston describes
the phenomenon as follows:

De Fréminville deals at some length with rupture "par contrecoup," which may
perhaps be translated "by repercussion," that is, with ruptures the "foyer d'ecla-
tement" of which is far away from the point where the blow is struck. When the

blows are mechanical impacts, it is at first sight striking that the explosion should originate in a totally different region, and from a technical point of view the matter is important; but from a physical standpoint it appears to amount to little more than this, that the area of impact is usually a region of compression, whilst the explosion centre will be in the region of maximum tension. Under suitable conditions, a blow delivered at one point will create a great tension in some other region (Preston 1926:250).

Many nearly completed, potentially beautiful projectile points result in failure because of end shock. Plate 1a illustrates lateral snap in an experimental specimen, as well as the flake which was responsible for the unwanted fracture. Plate 1b is a field specimen exhibiting lateral snap. From the workshop site in Marion County, Florida, hundreds of nicely thinned preforms and nearly completed projectile points, which had been rejected because of lateral snap, were recovered. A fossil is generally present on the fractured surface and represented a point of weakness. It is interesting to note that despite the fact that native knappers were extremely talented, they were unable to overcome these heterogeneities or to predict when they might cause trouble. Lateral snap may have occurred more frequently in heated specimens because of the reduction in strength which accompanies thermal alteration. Reduction in strength was about 45 percent in experimental specimens. A correctly executed burin blow often exhibits a fractured surface similar to that of lateral snap. That is, it appears as if the cone has been split. This is true also of nodules that have been cleaved or quartered to be used as blade cores. All of the fracture types mentioned above were plentiful at the Marion County, Florida, workshop site.

I wish to describe, however, fractures which differ from the typical — those which would not be recognized readily even by an experienced flintknapper because the fractures would not occur as a direct result of the knapping process. Crabtree (1964) discusses explosions by expansion and contraction which occur when flint materials are heated or cooled rapidly but he does not illustrate or describe the fractures that result.

The initial experiment conducted to determine the effects of heat on Florida cherts ended in explosion because I mistakenly elevated the temperature by degrees centigrade rather than by degrees Fahrenheit. The specimens were heated more rapidly than anticipated. The rocks exploded at 400 degrees centigrade. Plate 2a illustrates the debris which resulted from this experiment. The picture shows potlid fractures and blocky, angular flakes with no bulbs of force. This kind of debitage does not occur by intentional flaking. It differs markedly from the thinning flakes found on archaeological sites that are suspected of being thermally altered. If these types of remains are found at a site, it might be assumed that the rocks had been subjected rapidly to temperatures such as those produced by forest fires or hearths, or, as in the case cited above, through careless miscalculation. Plate 2b shows similar specimens from the field.

Many subsequent experiments were conducted to determine the reasons for rock failure produced by heating and cooling. The results of these experiments are as follows.

Spalling rarely occurred when the temperature was raised very slowly. Slow temperature elevation should be interpreted as twenty-four hours at each 50 degrees centigrade increment until the testing temperature is reached. No explosion occurred even when the temperature was raised rapidly to 350 degrees centigrade and allowed to remain at that temperature for twenty-four hours before being elevated to 400 degrees centigrade. Rapid temperature elevation should be interpreted as approximately one hour at each 50 degrees centigrade increment until the testing temperature is reached. Explosion occurred on all occasions at 400 degrees centigrade when the material was taken to that temperature without raising it slowly or at least leaving it at 350 degrees centigrade for an extended period. Smaller specimens did not explode as readily. Plate 3a shows an experimental example of potlid fracture. Potlids always occurred during the heating process, never during the cooling process; thus they must be a result of expansion. Explosion occurs when the stress that is causing decrepitation proceeds too rapidly or exceeds the elastic limits of the material. *Webster's New World Dictionary of the American Language* (1970) defines decrepitate: "to roast or calcine (salts, minerals, etc.) until a crackling sound is caused or until this sound stops; to crackle when exposed to heat." Plate 3b illustrates a field sample of potlid fracture. Interestingly, nicely finished, thermally altered projectile points sometimes have potlid fractures. Apparently specimens are preformed prior to thermal alteration. The outer portion of the preform is exposed to stress by heat, first causing differential expansion. Possibly, the surface of the preform is already weakened as a result of the flaking process. The specimen literally "blows its stack" but is able to make a satisfactory adjustment to the stress before permanent damage is done to the inner structure of the rock. Following thermal alteration, the finishing flakes are removed from the specimen but remnants of the potlid remain. It is obvious that this is what happens because the flakes removed subsequent to thermal alteration are very vitreous. This vitreousness in Florida cherts is an indication that thermal alteration has been practiced because unaltered Florida cherts are quite lusterless.

Explosion did not occur at 300 degrees centigrade even when the material was removed from the 300-degree oven immediately. If the temperature was raised rapidly, explosion, or at least some spalling, occurred frequently when the material was removed from the oven at 350 degrees centigrade without allowing it to cool first. Thus it appears that explosion by contraction will occur at a lower temperature than explosion by expansion, which did not take place until 400 degrees centigrade.

The heating required to produce the explosive crack is considerably greater than that needed to allow the formation of the contraction crack on withdrawal of the flame; the contraction crack forms very promptly on such withdrawal (Preston 1926:244).

Even when samples were placed directly into a preheated oven at 350 degrees centigrade, no reaction occurred; but all except one specimen snapped in half when removed from the hot oven and exposed to air temperature. If the temperature was raised rapidly, explosion always occurred whenever the material was removed from the oven at 400 degrees centigrade without allowing it to cool first. Plate 4a illustrates "crenated" fracture, which often occurred when samples were removed from the hot oven without first being allowed to cool. Plate 4b shows a field specimen of "crenated" fracture. This type of fracture also occurred occasionally if a sample was heated to too high a temperature and an attempt made later to flake the specimen. As with lateral snap, fracture did not occur at the point of impact. This situation must result because of shrinkage or residual stresses within the specimen. Another interesting type of fracture occurred when samples were exposed to these same conditions and flaking was attempted later by either percussion or pressure. A half-moon shaped-piece of stone would break off rather than the expected flake. This break occurs at the point of impact, and it looks much like someone had taken a bite out of the stone. Plate 5 illustrates the typical way in which samples fractured when exposed rapidly to a cool environment. I did not search through the debitage from the Marion County workshop site for samples similar to this. It is interesting to note, however, that there are a number of historic references which describe aboriginal flintknappers exposing their lithic material to fire, which caused it to splinter upon removal. These splinters were then used without further modification. They certainly would have served to perform any task requiring an extremely sharp edge or point.

When the temperature was raised rapidly, a crackling noise (decrepitation) was often heard at 350 degrees centigrade and always heard at 400 degrees centigrade when the material was removed from the oven without allowing it to first cool. It was not heard at 300 degrees centigrade nor was it heard when materials were heated for a second time. Explosion never occurred when the material was tested a second time at the same temperature. Explosion rarely occurred at any temperature when the material was removed immediately from the oven if the temperature had been raised slowly and maintained at the testing temperature for a sustained period. Under these conditions, the crackling sound was not heard.

Failure was accompanied by peculiar "clicks." These "clicks" were heard early in the cooling period and never during the heating period, when the rate of temperature change was lower. When the cups were heated to a slightly higher temperature, no higher percentage of failures was observed (Pressler and Shearer 1926:307).

When the rocks are subjected to critical temperatures, there may be a change in the position of oxygen and silicon ions.

...principles of surface chemistry.... When a crystal consists of highly polarizable anions of large size, together with small, highly charged cations, then the anions will be pushed to the surface of the crystal and the cations will be recessed. Thus in a microcrystal of quartz oxygen ions predominate at the surface, while the silicon ions are depressed. It is believed that each microcrystal of quartz then has a negatively charged "skin," and effectively repels adjacent randomly oriented microcrystals... fracture probably takes place between the polyhedral blocks because of the surface repulsion forces (Folk and Weaver 1952:507-508).

If the ions become too excited when temperature is applied rapidly, explosion may take place. This may also explain the clicking sounds which occur and often result in exfoliation when the material is rapidly cooled. Perhaps the reason these clicking sounds aren't heard when the material is removed after a sustained period is that the process is completed and no further change is taking place.

When samples were placed directly into a preheated oven at 400 degrees centigrade explosion commenced after approximately twenty minutes. The oven was turned off immediately; explosion continued intermittently until the oven had cooled to about 375 degrees centigrade. All but one sample had exploded. This exception deserves further comment. Spectrophotometric analysis of material from the same nodule as this specimen revealed a high calcium content. While further experiments should be conducted, it appears that too high a calcium content prevents desirable thermal alteration. Ceramists are faced with this same problem.

Plate 6a illustrates shrinkage cracks or crazing, which occurred when experimental samples of Florida chert were exposed to temperatures exceeding 500 degrees centigrade. This crazing occurred even though the temperature was elevated very slowly. Plate 6b shows crazing in field specimens. These flakes appear to have been exposed to direct heat. That they did not explode is probably due to the fact that they are small and thin. Small experimental specimens seldom exploded as readily as large specimens.

Plate 7 illustrates the results of an experiment which has already been reported upon in the literature (Purdy and Brooks 1971). It bears repeating here because it is applicable to this investigation. A dental syringe was used to drip cold water along the edge of a sample of Florida chert that had been heated for an extended period at 400 degrees centigrade and had not been allowed to cool. The sample was then placed directly under the tap and cold water allowed to flow over the entire sample. This resulted in an audible hissing sound but no "flakes" or even spalling occurred. The material became crazed, and subsequent attempts to flake the material caused it to crumble. It was impossible to pressure flake this material because the flakes could not be removed in a predictable way. The specimen literally fell apart.

Failure on quenching was shown by irregular cracks differing in appearance from the smooth conchoidal fractures... (Pressler and Shearer 1926:308).

Plate 8 illustrates one of many nodules found in the field, all of which appear to have been subjected to intense and prolonged heat. The entire inner structure of the nodule is "dead" and seems to consist of literally hundreds of potlids superimposed upon each other. Why specimens of this kind did not explode is difficult to determine unless the limestone cortex served to insulate or prevent explosion while the stresses were being relieved internally. I have no experimental examples but I suspect this extreme type of destruction might occur by constant or repeated exposure to heat — perhaps near a hearth.

CONCLUSIONS

This study is significant because it describes and illustrates types of fracture which will occur under various stresses associated with heat. In regions where investigators suspect that thermal alteration was practiced by aboriginal flintknappers, recognition of these types of remains may provide the proof needed to demonstrate conclusively that thermal alteration represented one step in the manufacturing process of chipped stone tools. Even if doubt still exists because one might argue that most of these fractures could occur by accidental exposure to heat, nevertheless a knowledge of these fractures is valuable to explain "anomalies" that may be present in the stone material recovered from archaeological sites.

More importantly, this investigation is valuable because it demonstrates that on a prethermometer level, man was able to control temperatures within a very narrow range. My first impression, resulting from the many and diverse conditions to which I subjected Florida cherts to heat, was that while early flintknappers were successfully altering lithic materials prior to final retouch, they had only to be concerned with slowly reaching and maintaining the critical temperature (350–400 degrees centigrade). I did not think it mattered if the rock was exposed to temperatures greater than 400 degrees centigrade as long as this exposure was gradual. It is apparent, however, that failure occurs if the rock is subjected to temperatures much higher than that necessary for alteration. This is probably because the impurities, serving as fluxes within the interstitial spaces to cement the microcrystals, begin to shrink. This would be a logical explanation for "crenated" fracture described previously and for crazing. There is very definitely an increased reduction of point tensile strength with increased temperatures. Material that had been heated slowly to 350–400 degrees centigrade and maintained for a sustained period had approximately a 45 percent reduction in point tensile strength. Material that was removed immediately from the hot oven after exposure to this temperature range, or material that was exposed to higher temperatures, had a reduction in point tensile strength as great as 65 percent.

Because the use of fire and the use of stone were two of the earliest and most important items in the inventory of early man, it should come as no surprise that he gradually acquired an intimate knowledge of their attributes. Prior to written records, however, we have very little proof of just how exact man had to be in order to accomplish certain tasks. This investigation has demonstrated that man needed to be very precise in his utilization of fire to alter lithic materials. Not only that, it appears that this precision differed from region to region and depended upon the type of flint materials available. In Florida, man was successfully subjecting his lithic raw materials to heat at least by the Early Archaic and continued this practice until sometime around A.D. 1000 when he, for reasons unknown, began to tip his arrows and spears with points other than stone.

REFERENCES

CRABTREE, DON E., B. ROBERT BUTLER
  1964   Notes on experiments in flint knapping, I: Heat treatments of silica minerals. *Tebiwa* 7:1–6.
FOLK, R. L., C. E. WEAVER
  1952   A study of the texture and composition of chert. *American Journal of Science* 250:498–510.

PRESSLER, E. E., W. L. SHEARER
  1926 Properties of potters' flints and their effects in white ware bodies. *Bureau of Standards Technologic Papers* 20:289–315.
PRESTON, F. W.
  1926 A study of the rupture of glass. *Society of Glass Technology Journal* 10: 234–269.
PURDY, BARBARA A., H. K. BROOKS
  1971 Thermal alteration of silica minerals: an archeological approach. *Science* 173:322–325.
Webster's Dictionary
  1970 *Webster's new world dictionary of the American language.*

PART THREE

Application of Analysis to Archaeology

The Trimmed-Core Tradition
in Asiatic-American Contacts

DON W. DRAGOO

The antiquity and origin of man in the New World has been of concern to many archaeologists for years, but within the past fifteen years interest in this phase of New World prehistory has increased greatly. Many newly discovered early sites have been investigated with the application of new methods and techniques. Increasing emphasis has been placed on the study of tools others than projectile points with a view to understanding the technology employed as well as establishing a typology. Sites have been studied for clues to settlement patterns and subsistence activities of the people who inhabited then. Radiocarbon dates were obtained for several sites and new methods of dating, such as obsidian hydration and archaeomagnetic determination, were applied to early cultural manifestations by some archaeologists. Invaluable insights into the environment affecting man over the past several thousand years have been given to the archaeologists by geologists, paleontologists and palynologists who have turned their attention increasingly to Pleistocene problems. It has been a period of great advancement but many questions remain unanswered.

In 1970, a symposium on "Early Man in North America, New Developments: 1960–1970" was held at the American Anthropological Association Annual Meeting in San Diego, California and the papers resulting from this meeting were published in *Arctic Anthropology* (1971). Their authors presented a survey of the then current status of knowledge on early cultures of the New World, but the obvious conclusion that can be drawn from these papers is that there is much disagreement as to the age and origin of these cultures. Wormington's comment (1971:88) that "there remain many points to be argued" was an apt summary to the symposium and to the status of our knowledge in general. In this paper it is my intention to discuss some of the major problems confronting students of Early Man in the New World and to suggest some lines for further research.

One of the crucial questions evading an answer pertains to man's first appearance in the New World and the kind(s) of culture he brought with him. As Wormington (1971:84) has noted no one really knows when man first came and all efforts to place certain time limits on the event by some workers are probably incorrect. We do know that man was well established in the New World by 12,000–11,000 B.C. and some radiocarbon dates extend the range to much earlier times. To many workers, however, these early dates are to be seriously questioned on various grounds and some individuals have discounted them completely.

Some of our arguments and disagreements seem to stem from historical events. The first indisputable evidence of man's association with extinct Pleistocene fauna was found at the Lindenmeier site in Colorado and the Blackwater Draw site in New Mexico beginning in 1927. Since these early discoveries several other localities have yielded similar remains in other areas of the Southwest United States. The oldest culture found at these sites seems to be the Clovis which is associated with extinct fauna such as mammoth at "kill sites" where the animal was slain and butchered. The tool assemblage found at such locations tended to be limited to projectile points and occasionally a few knives and scrapers. The distinctive fluted projectile points, however, became the trademark for Early Man and the Southwest his center of occupation.

The Southwestern homeland bias seems to have been postulated by some workers on the bland assumption that once man crossed the Bering Straits he first made a mad dash for that region with only the briefest of stops in between. Once there, man increased in number and eventually began to push outward to other areas of North America and eventually southward to Mexico and South America. This simple idea of the Southwest as the seedbed of New World cultural development has led many workers to view finds in these other areas as later than and derived from the Southwest. Although this position recently has suffered many blows, it is still maintained by some influential workers.

A prime example of the belief that man arrived in the New World near the end of the last glacial advance, about 12,000 years ago, is a recent article by Martin (1973:969). He presents the thesis that man made his appearance about that time and within 1,000 years he had raced to the tip of South America. In this brief period there was a population explosion of sufficient magnitude to exterminate the Pleistocene megafauna. By 11,000 years ago man had been forced into a major cultural readaptation from big game hunting to a diversified economy in most of the hemisphere.

With this change, Martin (1973:973) also thinks there was a sharp drop in human population.

Perhaps there were population declines in some marginal areas such as the Southwest, but the evidence for eastern North America indicates quite a contrary situation. The East, and particularly the Southeast, was intensively occupied during the Early Lithic period as typified by the users of fluted points. More Clovis-type fluted points have been found in such states as Tennessee and Alabama than have been recorded for the entire western United States. In the East there were many subtypes of fluted points developed over a considerable period of time. The work of Coe (1964), Broyles (1966), and others clearly indicates that there was a continuous occupation of the East from the Early Lithic Period into the succeeding Archaic period. Judging from the size and number of sites and the amount of cultural debris on them, there was also a steady increase in population that began late in the Early Lithic period and continued throughout the Archaic period. The Southeast was certainly the most densely populated area in North America at the end of the Early Lithic period and in the millennia that immediately followed it. Thus, I find it exceedingly difficult to understand how Martin, or anyone else, can reconstruct the Early Lithic Period and the extinction of the Pleistocene megafauna based only on information from the Southwest and with the exclusion of the Southeast from any serious consideration as part of the picture.

It is not my intention here to go into the causes of megafauna extinction and to discuss fully the development of Early Lithic culture during its later phases, but it has beeen necessary to draw attention to this southwestern bias, as it is clearly expressed by Martin, since this bias has had an enormous influence on the study of New World cultural beginnings. It is a view which I believe to be unfounded in fact and a detriment to enlightened research on the complex problems of the Early Lithic period.

All too often the fluted point complex has been looked upon as the starting point for tracing New World contacts to the Old World. Since the fluted point was considered to be the earliest well-documented and datable artifact, it was assumed that man probably had this tool when he made the crossing from Asia. However, the search for cultures having fluted points, or possible ancestral forms, in northeastern Asia and Alaska has met with little success. Haynes (1964, 1969) and Humphrey (1966) have advocated the thesis that specialized mammoth hunters from Siberia were isolated in Alaska until an ice-free corridor opened, when they became the hunters represented by the early fluted point horizon of about 10,000 B.C. Wormington (1971) has stated her reluctance to accept this idea on the basis that there are few points in Alaska and none in a firmly datable context. In accord with Wormington, I would agree that "we are not yet in a position to say where, or even when, the tradition of fluting developed." There are no established prototypes for Clovis and other early fluted points, but it is certain that unfluted points must have preceded fluted points somewhere in North America. The transition from unfluted points to fluted points could have occurred in the Southeast where many fluted types were developed rather than in the west where only a limited number of forms have been found.

If we consider the fluted point as a New World innovation, then it is necessary to discover and isolate a prior complex, or complexes, from which the fluted point and associated tools could have developed. It seems quite unlikely that man began the making of fluted points soon after his arrival in the New World and a considerable period of time must have elapsed during their evolution. Wormington (1971:84) has stated her belief that man has been here for a far longer time than the period for which we have absolutely convincing proof, and she has suggested that this time will probably be prior to 25,000 years ago when acceptable evidence is found. I have stated (Dragoo 1968:176) that on the basis of typological uniqueness, geographic distribution, high degree of patination of tool surfaces, and the similarity of tool types to those of the Upper Paleolithic of the Old World that there are complexes that have been found in the New World which possibly date as early as 40,000 years ago. Similar views of the time involved have been presented by Willey (1966:37), Müller-Beck (1966), Krieger (1964), MacNeish (1971), and others who have attacked the problem of early cultures from different perspectives and have worked in various areas of the New World.

In recent years there have been a number of finds for which considerable antiquity has been indicated by radiocarbon dates. Irving (1971:69) has reported a bone scraper found at the Old Crow Flats in the Yukon dated at 27,000 years ago. Bison and mammoth bones, apparently cracked by man, from the same locality were dated 25,750 to 29,100 years ago. Similar finds of mammoth with indications of possible human associations have been found at Santa Rosa Island, California with dates of 30,000–37,000 years ago (Orr 1968), the Cooperton site in Oklahoma dated at about 20,000 years ago (Andersen 1962), and several localities in the Valsequillo area near Puebla, Mexico where a date of 21,800 years ago was obtained at one site, Caulapau, from a stratum containing a simple uniface scraper (Irwin-Williams 1967, 1969). Malde (1967) has studied the stratigraphy of these Mexican sites and suggests that some of the tool bearing deposits may be as much as 35,000 years old. All of these sites with mammoth and other Pleistocene fauna are of great importance as indicators of man's early presence, but the scarcity of tools at most of them gives us little evidence for the cultures involved.

Several sites for which early dates in excess of 20,000 years have been obtained by radiocarbon analysis, geological placement, or other means, have questionable human associations with the dates. Among the more important of these sites that have drawn serious attention in recent years are Lewisville, Texas (Crook and Harris 1957, 1958; Krieger 1964; Willey 1966), Tule Springs, Nevada (Harrington and Simpson 1961; Shutler 1965) and the Calico Mountains site in California (Leakey, Simpson, et al. 1972). At both the Lewisville and Tule Springs sites there has been doubt as to the association of the cultural remains with the materials being dated. In the case of the Calico Mountains site excavated under the direction of Leakey and Simpson, a date of about 70,000 years ago has been suggested by the project geologist Thomas Clements. Wormington (1971: 84), with whom I agree, has presented the majority opinion of those of us who have studied the site which is that the so-called artifacts are doubtful works of man and that they could have been produced by natural forces during the building of the alluvial fan in which they were found. The supposed tools from Calico also lack any patterning to types and the edges appear to be fractured and crushed rather than deliberately chipped. Some geologists who studied the site would date the alluvial fan deposit from 500,000 to as much as a million years old. Thus, in spite of the tremendous effort, time, and care by the excavators of Calico, the results are still inconclusive and subject to future verification.

Although studies of man's presence in the New World earlier than the bearers of fluted points have met with many difficulties in dating precise associations, and sample size, the evidence for such cultures is now too great to ignore and to sweep under the carpet even though dating does remain a crucial problem. More than one complex seems to be present among the possible candidates for early honors. We will now take a look at these complexes and their possible connections with the Old World.

In recent years there have been a number of finds of pebble tools in North America (Dragoo 1965; Lively 1965; Borden 1968). The greatest concentration of these tools have been found in the Southeast, but similar tools also occur in the West. In the Southeast crude pebble tools were reported from many sites in Alabama by Matthew Lively (1965) working in conjunction with the late Daniel Josselyn (1967) of the Alabama Archaeological Society. The classic tools of this complex consist of chert pebbles that were chipped by percussion. From a simple platform at the end of the pebble, one or more flakes were removed to produce a sharp cutting edge in several variations to form choppers, planes, and scrapers. Several thousand tools have been found at more than 70 sites in northern Alabama. Several distinct and basic tool types seem to be present at all the sites, but there is evidence of change and development in that some tool types, such as pebble drills, seem to be present at some sites and absent at others.

Prior to Josselyn's death in 1971 I had worked with him and Matthew Lively on the collections from many of these classic pebble tool sites and from several other sites having similar tools fashioned from materials other than chert pebbles. Crude tools of the same types were found to have been made on tabular cherts and quartzites in areas where chert pebbles were not available. Some of the sites where these tools are found seem to be single component with only crude tools while others are multicomponent with cultures of various time periods represented. The location of these sites varies from isolated hilltops to river terraces and rock shelters. When these crude tools occur on multicomponent sites, the location usually is one that would have been favorable for man at any time or cultural level.

The exact cultural provenience and age of the pebble tools and similar tools in other materials found at the sites in northern Alabama and in adjacent areas of Georgia, Tennessee, and Mississippi is a difficult problem to solve. Attempts to assign a specific age to them is not easy since they may span a long period of time. In an attempt to answer the problem of time and context, DeJarnette (1967) excavated the Stutz Bluff shelter site and the Crump site in northern Alabama. At the open air Crump site located in an area above a river flood plain, pebble tools were found scattered through a deposit nearly four feet in depth with no noticeable concentration and in association with late Early Lithic Dalton points in the lowest levels and Early Archaic projectile points in the upper levels. At the Stutz Bluff shelter there was a similar random distribution through the upper levels of the deposit ranging in time from Archaic to Woodland, but in the lower levels which represented a late Early Lithic transition to Early Archaic there was a marked increase in pebble tools with the lowest level containing mostly pebble tools. Thus, DeJarnette concluded that pebble tools were present from late Early Lithic times, but that they also persisted through much later cultures.

It has been my observation that nearly all the rock shelters in eastern North America have occupation zones that begin only near the end of the Early Lithic period. Prior to that time most rock shelters seem to have been wet and uninhabitable and there is a layer of water deposited sand representing this period directly below the late Early Lithic deposit. This unfortunate situation has generally precluded the finding of pebble tools with earlier Early Lithic remains in a datable stratified deposit. However, pebble tools, or crude tools similar in type but of different raw material, have been found at two Early Lithic sites assignable to earlier times than the deposit excavated by DeJarnette at the Stutz Bluff site. These sites are the Wells Creek site in Stewart County, Tennessee (Dragoo 1965; 1973) and the Debert site in Nova Scotia (MacDonald 1968) where early to middle eastern Clovis points have been found in association. Thus, pebble tools are at least as old in the eastern United States as the Early Lithic Clovis culture. Whether or not they are older is neither proven nor disproven.

Since pebble tools have been found in association with several cultures spanning several thousand years, it has been suggested that they do not represent a complete and distinct industry or cultural complex but they are a technological tradition employed in certain areas where pebbles provided a convenient source for manufacturing large, crude, disposable tools possibly associated with the exploitation of certain resources. MacDonald (1971:35) has expressed this view in his study of pebble tools in British Columbia and Wormington (1971:87) has expressed a similar position on the pebble tools reported by Borden (1968) in that same area but apparently of a more recent date than those found in the East. This is a possibility that François Bordes and I also entertained during our extensive study of the Alabama pebble tools in April 1971. Their apparent association with several cultures through time certainly indicates that pebble tools were a persistent technological tradition, but it is now impossible to answer the question of whether or not they ever represented at an earlier time a separate complex. There is increasing evidence that pebble tools have a wide distribution in the New World and I believe we are far from having the last word on this intriguing subject.

When we turn to the Old World we find pebble tools as a very important element in the development of man's technology beginning in Africa with the dawn of man. In Asia, pebble tools were very important in the earliest cultures and they persisted as an important element in cultures as far north as Siberia where sites in the Baikal area such as Mal'ta and Afontova Gora have produced radiocarbon dates ranging from 21,000 to 12,800 years ago (Cherdyntsev, et al. 1968). Along with the pebble tools at these sites there are core bifaces, flakes, and blades struck from polyhedral cores. At a site in the Zeya River area, Okladnikov found pebble tools which he believes to be older than other Siberian complexes and which he assigns to a pre-Mousterian complex (Derevianko 1968). Thus, it would seem that pebble tools were an old and persistent element in several complexes of both the Old and New Worlds, but until they can be isolated as a distinct complex in the New World with adequate early dates to indicate their priority over complexes containing core, flake, and blade tools their relationship culturally and temporally with the Old World will remain obscure. We certainly cannot postulate a pebble tool stage of cultural development in the New World on the basis of the crude technology involved in their manufacture.

Perhaps a more useful and significant indicator of early Old and New World contacts is the study of those complexes containing trimmed cores of a generally polyhedral form. These cores not only served as primary tools but also often as a source of blades and flakes from which a variety of cutting and scraping tools were fashioned. In the New World there is increasing evidence to indicate that the trimmed core was an important element in the Clovis complex and that there may be some sites where this lithic tradition precedes fluted points by several thousand years.

The most extensive evidence of trimmed polyhedral cores in the Clovis complex comes from the Wells Creek site in Tennessee (Dragoo 1965; 1973). At this site many trimmed cores were found which had been fashioned into denticulates, scrapers, spokeshaves, and planes. In most examples, the cores were chipped primarily as a tool and not necessarily as the source for flakes and blades. The total lithic assemblage at Wells Creek is exceedingly rich and varied and contains in addition to the trimmed polyhedral cores many unifacially and bifacially chipped tools such as large "handaxes," knives, scrapers, perforators, cleavers, choppers, spokeshaves, picks, and denticulates in association with typologically early Clovis fluted points in all stages of manufacture.

Of all the known Clovis sites, the tool assemblage at Wells Creek seems to give the most complete and illuminating insight into the cultural foundation upon which the making of fluted points developed. Unlike the western Clovis sites with their limited tool inventory consisting of a few fluted points and scrapers, Wells Creek and other eastern Clovis sites, on a more limited scale, such as Debert (MacDonald 1968), Williamson (McCary 1951), Shoop (Witthoft 1952), Holcombe (Fitting et al. 1966) and several smaller sites all present a picture of a well-developed tool assemblage with fluted points constituting only one important element in the complete tool kit. If we are to find the complete foundation upon which the fluted point cultures developed, the best approach would seem to be the study of the core, blade, and flake tools. The large and often crude polyhedral core tools of Wells Creek would seem to be an important clue to the possible antiquity and origin of these early cultures. Because of problems in dating it is currently impossible to place a date on these tools much earlier than 12,000 years ago in Eastern North America, but surface collections made at several high terrace sites in Alabama, Tennessee, and the Ohio Valley indicate that there may be sites containing these crude tools without the association of fluted points. Only the finding of datable, stratified sites will answer this question.

Recent work by MacNeish (1973) in Peru has uncovered an assemblage of crude tools similar to those found at Wells Creek. In the bottom two zones of Flea Cave in the Ayacucho Valley tool types including sidescrapers, choppers, cleavers, spokeshaves, and denticulates were dated between 19,600 and 14,150 B.C. MacNeish has divided these tools into a lower complex, Paccaicasa, and an upper complex, Ayacucho. No projectile points were found in the lower zone but bone points were present in the upper or Ayacucho complex. Similar tools have been found recently at several other sites in Peru by James Richardson (of the University of Pittsburgh) who has stated to me their near identity to those found at Wells Creek. Prominent in these assemblages are the same crude polyhedral and bifacial core tools which MacNeish (1973:77) suggests may represent in the Paccaicasa complex the earliest stage of man's appearance in South America between 25,000 to 15,000 years ago. MacNeish (1973:77) has called this earliest complex the "core tool tradition" and the slightly later Ayacucho complex the "flake and bone tool tradition." The "trimmed-core tradition" as used in this paper would encompass both of MacNeish's traditions since at this point in time I can not fully separate the two complexes over a wide range except for MacNeish's evidence at Flea Cave. Such a division may exist at that site, but the evidence for separation of core and flake tools at other sites is not conclusive since the samples are extremely limited in number and kinds of items.

When MacNeish looked for possible origins of his "core tool tradition" he suggested it would be derived from the chopper and chopping tool tradition of Asia which is well over 50,000 years old in that area. He (MacNeish 1973:79) further suggests that the "core tool tradition" may possibly have arrived in the New World from 40,000 to as much as 100,000 years ago. Since our discovery of the Wells Creek site in 1963, I have been searching the Asiatic scene for possible clues to the origin of the New World core tool complexes with the hope that some hint of the time when contact began could be found. As MacNeish and others have suggested there are typological similarities between the New World core tool complexes and those in various areas of East Asia, but since such tools persisted over a very long period of time they are of little use in dating their introduction to the New World. However, I have been impressed with the growing accumulation of evidence for the spread of core tools from the Asiatic mainland to various adjacent island land masses such as Japan, the Philippine Islands, and Australia. The great similarities between the tools that I have examined from these areas and those from Wells Creek, Flea Cave, and other sites in the New World lead me to believe that all these areas were recipients of Asian immigrants possessing a basic core tool complex at about the same time.

In Japan the Hoshino and Iwajuku complexes seem to be the earliest cultural manifestations (Serizawa 1968; Ikawa 1968). On the basis of radiocarbon dated geological horizons the Hoshino complex is at least 30,000 years old and may extent back in time to as much as 50,000 years ago. The Iwajuku complex probably dates to about 25,000 years ago. In 1968 I examined many specimens from the Hoshino and Iwajuku complexes and I agree with Ikawa (1968:198) that the Hoshino complex has rather close affinities with the Ting Ts'un and Chiao-Ch'eng of the Fenho Valley of northern China. Many of these early tools also are similar to those found by MacNeish (1973: 79) at Flea Cave in Peru and the crude core tools at Wells Creek in Tennessee. The later Iwajuku complex contains many more blade tools than the Hoshino but it is probably a descendant of that culture just as later flake and blade tools were added to a basic core tool complex in the New World.

The picture of early complexes now emerging from Australia presents an interesting parallel to that of Japan and the New World (Mulvaney 1969). In 1971 I had the opportunity to visit many of the early sites in Australia and to study the artifacts found at them. I was impressed with the marked similarity of these early core tools with the trimmed cores at Wells Creek and other New World sites. The radiocarbon dates now available for these earliest sites appear to be about 30,000 years old with some sites believed to be even older (40,000 years) based upon geological evidence (Thorne, Gallus, and Mulvaney — personal communications).

In the Philippines radiocarbon dates indicate that man was well established there 30,000 years ago, and on the basis of geological evidence Fox (1968, personal communication) has suggested that man may have been there as much as 50,000 years ago. Both core and flake tools are present in these early assemblages. Mulvaney (1969:58) has suggested that man may have made his way into Australia from Asia by way of south China, through Taiwan, the Philippines and Borneo to the Celebes, and thence south through New Guinea to Australia because during the Pleistocene there was more dry land in this direction than through the more direct route by way of Java and Timor. If this is so, we should expect the similarities that seem to exist between the early tools of the Philippines and Australia.

Although there are many gaps in the picture, I find it more than mere coincidence that man seems to have moved outward from the Asiatic mainland at about the same time to the New World, Japan, the Philippines, and Australia. All the present radiocarbon dates indicate that he was well established in all these areas by 30,000 years ago and we can probably add a few thousand more years for his establishment. However, on the basis of the present evidence, I would not expect this time to be much more than 40,000 years ago. The similarities of the early tool assemblages in all these areas suggest that they were derived from a basic core tool tradition that was widespread on the Asiatic mainland. This tradition probably had as its foundation a complex like that discovered in the Fenho Valley of northern China. Because flake tools are also prominent in most of these foreign complexes, the outward migrations probably came at a time when the Fenho tradition was being modified and subjected to new influences from western Europe which included the introduction of the Levallois technique and certain tool types reminiscent of the Mousterian. This blending probably occurred between 50,000 to 40,000 years ago. By the time man began his spread to the New World and the outlying areas of Asia he possessed a basic technology that included a variety of techniques for working stone. Time and isolation eventually saw the differential development of certain techniques and tool types in each area.

It has not been my intention to suggest that there were any direct contacts between the New World and such distant areas as Australia, the Philippines, or Japan, but I do believe that all these areas were influenced from a common Asiatic source and at about the same time. It is of interest to note that these now unattached and distant areas were at times during the Pleistocene part of an almost continuous land mass that formed the outer margins of Asia and North America. It would have been almost possible to walk on dry land from Australia to the New World during the advance stages of the last glacial period (Würm or Wisconsin).

It is not possible at this time to understand the major factors that may have led to the spread of peoples from the Asiatic mainland to these distant and previously unoccupied areas. However, we may conjecture that during the interstadial period (Gottweig) between 50,000 to 40,000 years ago man extended his range and increased in number throughout Asia and Europe. It was during this period that European lithic traditions spread into Asia and mixed with the core tool tradition. As the ice again advanced between 40,000 to 30,000 years ago large areas of mainland Asia came under its influence, but new lands also became available along the continental shelf, because of the drop in sea level, linking it with the New World, Japan, the Philippines, and the large islands leading to Australia. Human groups living in central and northeastern Asia slowly drifted into these new territories during this time carrying with them their basic core and flake tool assemblage. By 30,000 years ago the descendants of these wandering hunters had penetrated the most distant of these new lands and the last major land areas of the world had fallen under the influence of man.

REFERENCES

ANDERSEN, ADRIAN
   1962   The Cooperton mammoth: a preliminary report. *Plains Anthropologist: Journal of the Plains Conference* 7:110.
Arctic Anthropology
   1971   *Arctic Anthropology* 8 (2). Entire issue.
BORDEN, CHARLES E.
   1968   New evidence of early cultural relations between Eurasia and Western North America. *Proceedings of the Eighth International Congress of Anthropological and Ethnological Sciences* 3:331–337.
BROYLES, BETTYE J.
   1966   Preliminary report: the St. Albans site (46 Ka 27), Kanawha County, West Virginia. *West Virginia Archaeologist* 19:1–43. Moundsville.
CHERDYNTSEV, V. V., et. al.
   1968   Geological Institute radiocarbon dates, II. *Radiocarbon* 10 (2):426.
COE, JOFFRE L.
   1964   The formative cultures of the Carolina Piedmont. *American Philosophical Society Transactions*, n.s. 54 (5). Philadelphia.
CROOK, W. W., JR., R. K. HARRIS
   1957   Hearths and artifacts of Early Man near Lewisville, Texas, and associated faunal material. *Texas Archaeological and Paleontological Socciety Bulletin* 28:7–97. Abilene.
   1958   A Pleistocene campsite near Lewisville, Texas. *American Antiquity* 23: 233–246.
DE JARNETTE, DAVID L.
   1967   Alabama pebble tools: the Lively complex. *Eastern States Archeological Federation Bulletin* 26:11–12.
DEREVIANKO, A. P.
   1968   The history of the ancient settlement of man in the Far East. *Proceedings of the Eighth International Congress of Anthropological and Ethnological Sciences.*
DRAGOO, DON W.
   1965   Investigations at a Paleo-Indian site in Stewart County, Tennessee. *Eastern States Archaeological Federation Bulletin* 24:12–13.
   1968   Early Lithic cultures of the New World. *Proceedings of the Eighth International Congress of Anthropological and Ethnological Sciences* 3: 175–176.
   1973   "The Wells Creek site, Stewart County, Tennessee," in *Archaeology of Eastern North America.* Eastern States Archeological Federation 1.
FITTING, JAMES E., J. DE VISSCHER, E. WAHLA
   1966   *The Paleo-Indian occupation of Holcombe Beach.* Anthropological Papers, Museum of Anthropology, 27. University of Michigan.

HARRINGTON, M. R., R. D. SIMPSON
1961 *Tule Springs, Nevada, with other evidences of Pleistocene Man in North America.* Southwest Museum Paper 18. Los Angeles.

HAYNES, C. VANCE
1964 Fluted projectile points: their age and dispersion. *Science* 145:1408–1413.
1969 The earliest Americans. *Science* 166:703–715.
1971 Time, environment, and Early Man. *Arctic Anthropology* 8 (2):3–14. Madison.

HUMPHREY, R. L.
1966 The prehistory of the Utokok River region, Arctic Alaska: early fluted point tradition with Old World relationships. *Current Anthropology* 7:586–588.

IKAWA, FUMIKO
1968 The Japanese Palaeolithic in the context of prehistoric cultural relationships between northern Eurasia and the New World. *Proceedings of the Eighth International Congress of Anthropological and Ethnological Sciences.*

IRVING, W. N.
1971 Recent Early Man research in the North. *Arctic Anthropology* 8 (2): 68–82. Madison.

IRWIN-WILLIAMS, CYNTHIA
1967 "Associations of Early Man with horse, camel, and mastodon at Hueyatlaco, Valsequillo (Puebla, Mexico)," in *Pleistocene Extinctions.* Edited by P. S. Martin and H. E. Wright, Jr. New Haven: Yale University Press.
1969 Comments on the association of archaeological materials and extinct fauna in the Valsequillo region. Puebla, Mexico. *American Antiquity* 34 (1):82.

JOSSELYN, D. W.
1967 The pebble tool explosion in Alabama. *Anthropological Journal of Canada* 5 (3):9–12.

KRIEGER, ALEX D.
1964 "Early Man in the New World," in *Prehistoric Man in the New World.* Edited by Jennings and Norbeck. Chicago: University of Chicago Press.

LEAKEY, L. S. B., RUTH D. SIMPSON, *et al.*
1972 *Pleistocene men at Calico.* San Bernardino County Museum.

LIVELY, MATTHEW
1965 The Lively complex: announcing a pebble tool industry in Alabama. *Journal of Alabama Archaeology* 11 (2):103–122.

MAC DONALD, GEORGE F.
1968 Debert: a Paleo-Indian site in central Nova Scotia. *Anthropology Papers, No. 16.* National Museum of Canada.
1971 A review of research on Paleo-Indian in Eastern North America, 1960–1970. *Arctic Anthropology* 8 (2):32–41.

MAC NEISH, RICHARD S.
1971 Early Man in the Andes. *Scientific American* 224 (4):36–46.
1973 "Early Man in the Andes," in *Early Man in America,* 69–79. Readings

from Scientific American. San Francisco: W. H. Freeman and Company.

MALDE, HAROLD E.
1967 "Volcanic-ash chronology, with examples from the Valsequillo archaeologic sites Puebla, Mexico." Paper given at Valsequillo Symposium Arizona State University, Tempe, October 27, 1967.

MARTIN, PAUL S.
1973 The discovery of America. *Science* 179:969–974.

MC CARY, BEN C.
1951 A workshop site of Early Man in Dinwiddie County, Virginia. *American Antiquity* 17 (1):9–17.

MÜLLER-BECK, H.
1966 Paleohunters in America: Origins and diffusion. *Science* 152:1191–1210.

MULVANEY, D. J.
1969 *The prehistory of Australia.* New York: Frederick A. Praeger.

ORR, PHIL C.
1968 *Prehistory of Santo Rosa Island.* Santa Barbara Museum of Natural History.

SERIZAWA, CHOSUKE
1968 The chronological sequence of the Palaeolithic cultures of Japan and the relationship with mainland Asia. *Proceedings Eighth International Congress of Anthropological and Ethnological Sciences* 3:353–357.

SHUTLER, RICHARD
1965 Tule Springs expedition. *Current Anthropology* 6:110–111.

WILLEY, GORDON R.
1966 *An introduction to American archaeology: North and Middle America.* Englewood Cliffs, New Jersey: Prentice-Hall.

WITTHOFT, JOHN
1952 A Paleo-Indian site in eastern Pennsylvania: an early hunting culture. *Proceedings of the American Philosophical Society* 96:464–495.

WORMINGTON, H. M.
1971 Comments on Early Man in North America, 1960–1970. *Arctic Anthropology* 8:83–91.

McKean and Little Lake Technology: A Problem in Projectile Point Typology in the Great Basin of North America

JAMES P. GREEN

While analyzing lithic material from the Rock Creek site, located in the South Hills of Idaho (Figure 1), I found that past and present projectile point identification was inadequate, if not misleading. This was particularly true in the identification of lanceolate and stemmed indented-base projectile points found in this portion of the northern Great Basin. Without the use of lithic technology in typological problems, misidentifications continue to be made. Errors committed and published were compounded, with wide-ranging cultural relationships the outcome. Once errors are perpetuated in the literature they become difficult to dislodge.

Before undertaking archeological research in Idaho, I had previously worked in the California and Nevada sections of the Great Basin. I was thus familiar with what can be called the Little Lake series of projectile points which includes Humboldt Concave Base and the Pinto subvarieties. Lanceolate and stemmed indented-base projectile points recovered in southern Idaho and contiguous areas have for many years been assigned to the McKean type. My analysis of the Rock Creek and other Great Basin collections suggests that this assignment is incorrect. A reevaluation of McKean and Little Lake indicates that projectile points formerly ascribed to the McKean type in the northern Great Basin are technologically equivalent to members of the Little Lake series found elsewhere in the Great Basin.

I am indebted to William Mulloy for allowing me to inspect and photograph the the McKean type site material. I would also like to thank Robert F. Heizer, Jesse D. Jennings, Roderick Sprague and Earl H. Swanson, Jr. for permitting me to inspect archaeological collections stored at their respective institutions. This paper is a revised version of a presentation entitled "McKean in the northern Great Basin," given at the 1972 Northwest Anthropological Conference.

For Plates and figures see pp. xix–xxii. between pp. 102–103

A short history is necessary to understand properly the McKean problem in the Great Basin, and southern Idaho in particular. McKean lanceolate points were first identified in Idaho by Thomas Kehoe in 1955. These projectile points were recovered from two surface sites near the town of Glenns Ferry in southwestern Idaho. The reference cited by Kehoe for the identification of these points is the article by Wheeler (1952) on the McKean Lanceolate Point. Projectile point descriptions are important as they provide the basis of comparison when the specimens are not in hand. Description of the two so-called McKean lanceolates are as follows (Kehoe 1955:14–15):

The first McKean is a simple lanceolate shape with a notched base, bilaterally symmetrical, sides incurve toward the tip and tapered toward the base. The blade is fully flaked and flat-lenticular in longitudinal and cross section. Faces of the blade bear irregularly orientated conchoidal flake scars of varying widths and depths. Lateral edges are slightly sinuous, somewhat uneven but sharp, base to tip. The base has a symmetrical, broad, shallow notch which was produced by the removal of several short longitudinal flakes from each face toward the tip. The basal edge is sharp. Material is basalt.

The second is simple lanceolate shape with notched base bilaterally symmetrical, sides incurve toward the tip and tapered toward the base. The blade is fully flaked and is flat-lenticular in longitudinal section, and lozenge-shaped near the tip and flat-lenticular near the base. Both of the faces of the blade bear shallow parallel flake scars directed downward from the sides to the midline at the tip two-thirds of the specimen, thus producing a low median ridge, and irregularly orientated conchoidal flake scars of varying widths and depths at the basal one-third of the specimen. The lateral edges are sinuous, somewhat uneven, but sharp tip to base. The base has a symmetrical, broad, very shallow notch resulting from the removal of a few short longitudinal flakes from each face toward the tip. Basal edge is sharp. Material is grey chalcedonic chert.

In 1958 and the following year Earl H. Swanson, Jr. directed archeological reconnaissance in the southwestern section of Idaho. The survey was restricted to the three counties of this area: Cassia, Twin Falls and Owyhee. This survey produced twenty-nine so-called McKean lanceolate projectile points. These appear to be associated with a grassland setting. Swanson, et al. (1964:4) describe their finds as:

narrow points with nearly parallel or slightly excurvate sides. Maximum width is near the center of the blade and the base is concave. They are well flaked, 17 examples exhibiting parallel oblique flaking. Materials are ignimbrite, obsidian and cryptocrystallines.

Primary sources were not used in the identification of the so-called

McKean material recovered in this survey. The source utilized is an article by Ruth Gruhn (1964), "Test excavations at sites 10-OE-128 and 129, southwest Idaho." These two sites are located about fifteen miles southwest of Boise, Idaho. The sites produced thirty-one concave base-lanceolate projectile points. The majority of these were in the possession of the property owner. These projectile points are described by Gruhn (1964:29):

Lanceolate outline is characteristic, blades of 23 specimens are narrow, 7 others are relatively broad, edges are excurvate, converging toward the concave base. Basal concavity is relatively deep and 10 specimens have pronounced ears. Cross-sections are lenticular, however, 3 are very thick. Flaking in most cases is well-controlled with several specimens exhibiting fine oblique ribbon flaking.

The range in size and general form in this group of points, form what appears to be a single-component site [which] is of interest: it is obvious from the illustration that while individual extremes in size and form can be selected out, the entire group forms an intergrading series; and all specimens appear to represent one basic type in the component.

A number of these specimens can be assigned to the McKean lanceolate point type well-known in the Northwest Plains area in the Middle Prehistoric Period. I have elsewhere discussed the fact that such medium-sized lanceolate points are also very common at sites in the Northern Great Basin, where the type appears to have considerable time depth. Present evidence suggests that the appearance of these points on the Plains may represent a diffusion out of the northern Great Basin area.

Gruhn, following Bryan (1965:50), views the development of classic parallel flaking as a western Cordillera development, which diffuses eastward through Oregon and Idaho, and climaxes technologically on the Central High Plains during Anathermal times. This hypothesis would support an Anathermal date for the so-called McKeans recovered in southern Idaho.

McKean projectile points are also reported from Wilson Butte Cave in southcentral Idaho. Four type 3 (McKean) projectile points, are restricted to the Wilson Butte V Assemblage placed between 4,000 and 2,500 years ago. Gruhn feels that Wilson Butte V shows great affinities with sites of the Northwestern Plains of the Early and Late Middle Prehistoric Periods (Gruhn 1961:131). The so-called McKeans at Wilson Butte Cave are described as follows (Gruhn 1961:54–55):

They are slender, lanceolate in outline with excurvate sides converging toward the concave base. Cross-sections are lenticular to plano-convex. Pressure flaking is well controlled, one specimen has oblique (up to left) parallel flaking. The remaining three have horizontal collateral flaking. All specimens are basally thinned. Materials are ignimbrite and obsidian.

The sources used to identify the so-called McKean points at Wilson Butte Cave are Wheeler (1952), "A note on the McKean lanceolate point" and Mulloy (1954), "The McKean site." Inspection of the four so-called McKean lanceolates indicates that a number of flake patterns are present in the collection; however, collateral flaking is not one of them. An additional comment made by Gruhn (1961:131) is of importance: "McKean Lanceolate Points appear to be restricted in distribution to the Snake River Plain and the foothills to the south where they are quite numerous." This distribution coincides with that of the stemmed indented-base and lanceolate points of the Little Lake series found in southern Idaho. Projectile points of the Little Lake series are also present in the Wilson Butte III Assemblage, dated to 6,850±300 years ago, and occur in Wilson Butte IV which is placed at about 6,500 years ago (Gruhn 1961:27, 149).

The most recent article which identifies and discusses McKean projectile points in the northern Great Basin is that by Butler (1970a). Although located outside of Idaho, this material and the statements expressed within the article warrant its discussion. Analysis of this collection prompted Butler to propose a new point series, the McKean-Humboldt Concave Base A-Pinto series. Humboldt and Pinto points (Little Lake series) are common in the northern Great Basin and have been the subject of study for a number of years. Clewlow (1967:144) has previously stated that Humboldt Concave Base A points may be a developmental variant of the Pinto series rather than a distinct type. They have been kept separate, however, until more is known about their technological and cultural affinities.

The association of the two types, Humboldt-Pinto and McKean, is based upon the range of variation in outline shape present within the McKean type site and Coyote Flat collections. The only technological difference recognized between the two types is that of edge grinding modification (Butler 1970a:37). A modal tendency of the Humboldt-Pinto series is that they are edge ground or dulled. Lower-level McKean projectile points show no intentional dulling or edge grinding (Mulloy 1954:445). The two types are otherwise identical (Butler 1970a:37).

As can be seen, the identification and spatial limits of McKean in the Great Basin has grown, climaxing with the coalescence of the Humboldt-Pinto series.

What becomes obvious about the proposed McKean-Humboldt-Pinto series is that it connotes a specific kind of cultural system that is either displaced upon or genetically related to the prehistoric cultures of the northern Great Plains. It also functions to give legitimacy to the notion that Great Basin culture develops out of, or is the progenitor of, the Plano Cultures of the Great Plains (Bryan 1965:50; Kehoe 1955:17).

In an effort to avoid perpetuating what was viewed as a misidentification of McKean in the Great Basin, I set about personally to inspect a number of archaeological collections which were said to contain McKean or McKean-Humboldt-Pinto projectile points. As a base of comparison, I secured from William Mulloy seventeen McKean projectile points from the lower level of the McKean site. These were said to be representative of the collection and included points illustrated in the McKean report. As photographs of the McKean collection have not been published, a plate of the McKean points received from Mulloy is included (Plate 1).

Utilizing Mulloy's report, and with the McKean points in hand, a comprehensive description was constructed. This description includes what was previously lacking and is the deciding factor between the two point types in question, that of a suite of technological attributes. Analysis provided the description that follows (see Plate 1, 1–25; Figure 2; 1–2):

McKean lanceolates have blade elements which in plan view range from excurvate to parallel ovate.

Longitudinal sections are biconvex to asymmetrically biconvex.

Blade cross-sections range from biconvex to asymmetrically biconvex and exhibit a hollow-ground effect produced by prominent negative bulbs of pressure, characteristic of collateral flaking.

Flake scar pattern is defined as collateral expanding. Collateral expanding flakes are produced by the removal of broad, expanding flakes which are initiated at the lateral edge margin and extend to the mid-section where they terminate and form a dorsal ridge. Termination is not well controlled, thus a sinuous ridge is produced. Flake scars lie at right angles to the long axis of the point. On edge, negative bulb scars alternate from face to face.

When present, edge retouch is imposed at the intersection of flake ridges and the lateral edge margin. Retouch is clustered about these sites, although it occurs randomly along the edge. Edges are even and regular when retouched and sinuous when no retouch is present.

Basal concavities are of the notched variety. The concavity is produced by a series of bifacial notches, directed in toward the tip of the specimen. The semilunar notches are rather steep, indicating a downward pressure rather than a longitudinal force. The concavity is thus notched and not "thinned." No intentional grinding or dulling is present on the lateral edges of the haft. Retouch is present and extends inward and over the semilunar notches in the basal concavity. Crushing is present within the basal notch produced as a product of the notching technique. The inner edge of the concavity is occasionally retouched.

Points appear to be made on bladelike flakes which are thin and slender. Large expanding flakes with one or more dorsal ridges may be a better description.

Dimensions of the lanceolate McKeans are (after Wheeler 1952:47):
Length: Range 33.00 to 60.00 millimeters Mode 46.3   millimeters
Width: Range 13.75 to 20.50 millimeters Mode 15.7   millimeters
Thickness: Range 3.25 to 6.00 millimeters Mode 4.75 millimeters
Weight: Range 2.10 to 7.4 grams   Mode 4.6 grams

The stemmed McKeans have blade elements essentially identical to the lanceolate form (Plate 1, 19–42). Flake pattern on the blade of several specimens is collaterally expanding; however, in others it often tends to be more unpatterned. Retouch is all but nonexistent. Stems and shoulders are well formed. The stem is produced by initiating a number of successive flake removals in toward the long axis of the point. At the juncture of the stem and blade, flakes of a semilunar type are present. The point tends to be thickest at the juncture of the stem and blade. Lateral haft edges of the stem appear not to be ground, although crushing and dulling are present. Basal concavity ranges from notched to slightly concave. When notched, they are produced as they are in the lanceolate form. When concave, the basal edge is bifacially beveled. Edges in the concavity also appear to be crushed. According to Mulloy (1954:445), these also are made on bladelike or large ridged flakes.

The dimensions of the six stemmed McKean points are:
Length   Range 29.00 to 53.60 millimeters Mean 41.55 millimeters
Width: Range 15.20 to 20.40 millimeters Mean 17.00 millimeters
Thickness: Range 4.70 to 6.50 millimeters Mean 5.58 millimeters

The age of McKean points has led many to speculate about their antiquity. William Mulloy, however, states in a written communication September 21, 1971:

As closely as I can read the evidence, and some of our colleagues would disagree here, the lanceolate and stemmed McKean points and some of the things loosely called Hanna and Duncan belong to the same time period. This time period lies between 4000 and 5000 B.P. more or less.

Armed with this technological information on McKean points, I inspected the following Great Basin and Idaho collections: Danger Cave, Hogup Cave, Weston Canyon Rockshelter, Malad Hill, Pioneer Basin, Wilson Butte Cave, Rock Creek, Brown's Bench (archaeological and private), the 1959 Southwestern Idaho Survey, Sites 10-OE-128 and 129, the Coyote Flat Collection, South Fork Shelter, Lovelock Cave and Lake Bed sites, Black Rock Desert Survey material, and the Surprise Valley material (see Figure 1).

I found NO projectile points technologically equivalent to McKean in ANY of these collections. Projectile points assigned to McKean at Danger

Cave were technologically divergent from the McKean type of material, as were the points in other collections inspected. Recently the collections from Danger and Hogup Caves have undergone reanalysis. Those points previously ascribed to the McKean type are now classified as Humboldt or Pinto of the Little Lake series. The primary distinction between McKean and the Little Lake series lies in the different technological systems employed in their production and the vast differences in time depth between the two types.

An additional problem that has obscured projectile point identification in the Great Basin is our ignorance of the production stages leading toward a particular point type. Only rarely do archaeological sites provide this kind of record. Inspection of a large number of collections and a growing knowledge of lithic technology has permitted a clearer picture of the McKean-Humboldt-Pinto problem.

As I stated above, McKean is technologically divergent from Humboldt and Pinto, members of the Little Lake series. To demonstrate this distinction, a type description must now be given for these projectile points. Humboldt and Pinto points recovered from Great Basin archeological sites are not well described. This is partly owing to their frequencies, but is also due to the cursory manner of description used in the past. If one were to combine the descriptions of all the so-called McKeans from the northern Great Basin, we might fabricate a fairly comprehensive picture of the Humboldt and Pinto types.

Humboldt points derive their name from the Lovelock Lake Bed site (Nv-Ch-15) which is situated on the eastern edge of Humboldt Sink in central Nevada. They are common here, but have a wide distribution in the Great Basin. Three Humboldt subvarieties were defined at the Lovelock Lake Bed site: Humboldt Concave Base A and B, and Basal-Notched (Heizer and Clewlow 1968:68). Humboldt A's are lanceolate in outline, longer than three centimeters, and weigh more than three grams. Humboldt B falls below these limits. The basal-notched form is triangular in outline with a V-shaped basal-notch (Clewlow 1968a:90). At present I believe there are two distinct size and weight modes within the Humboldt Basal-Notched form. There is little information on Humboldt Basal-Notched, so I will not attempt to include them in this study.

Humboldt Concave Base projectile points appear to have a wide range of variation. However, closer inspection of a large number of specimens aided in the formulation of a type description. Please note that the Little Lake projectile points pictured in Plate 2 have been coated with a white chemical smoke to enhance surface morphology. Humboldt Concave Base projectile points may be described as follows (Plate 2, a–f):

Humboldt Concave Base A is lanceolate in outline with a blade element that is parallel-ovate to expanding-ovate in plan view. When expanding-ovate, the widest distance between lateral edges is approximately half-way between the tip and base. Humboldt B's are usually excurvate in plan view. Except for the lower length and width modes, the following techological description also applies to Humboldt concave base B.

Longitudinal sections range from biconvex to asymmetrically biconvex.

Blade cross-sections range from biconvex through lenticular to asymmetrically biconvex. Cross-sections are usually smooth and without irregularities.

Flake scar pattern is defined as parallel oblique. This type of flake character is produced by the removal of narrow flakes which usually begin at the upper left and are overlapped by narrow flake scars coming from the lower right. This pattern gives the impression that the flake scar is a single continuous flake removal. The flake scars lie diagonally to the long axis of the specimen. Flake scars on finished pieces average two millimeters in width. Negative bulbs of pressure are shallow and often obscured by the small platform area used. On edge, one face will exhibit a bulb scar while the opposite face exhibits a ridge. This is characteristic of oblique and transverse flaking. Blanks may exhibit a rather random flaking pattern, but the general lanceolate outline must be established and the edges made regular. Between the blank and preform stage, ridges must be established in a diagonal orientation. These need not terminate over the mid-line. During the preform stage, flakes are directed diagonally over the face of the point utilizing ridges established in the previous stage. Flakes imposed on a diagonal reduce the gradient over the face of the preform, thus the flake carries farther, over the mid-line and on occasion to the opposite edge of the piece. Diagonal flaking may also be seen as a thinning technique, as the area along the long axis of the point is reduced by flakes carrying over the mid-line. It is proposed that distinctive flaking techniques produce definite types of blade cross-sections. During the preforming stage, flake character becomes progressively more refined, better controlled and evenly spaced. Edge retouch is not needed, as platform areas are relatively small and leave the edge sharp and even.

Bases are of the concave variety. The concavity is established during the blank stage. It is produced by the removal of several steep flakes from both faces of the piece. This remains unchanged until flaking has been completed on the face of the point. The last phases of the preform stage involve further thinning of the basal concavity. A number of small longitudinal flakes are removed from one or both faces of the concavity. These may terminate evenly or in a number of step fractures. These longitudinal flakes carry over the final flake scars on the face of the point. The concavity may be lightly crushed with lateral haft margins ground or crushed.

Humboldt Concave Base A points are usually made on large expanding ridged flakes. In some cases, dorsal ridges may be prominent. Humboldt B points can be made on smaller flakes.

Humboldt Concave Base A points range in length from 3 to 9 centimeters, width between 1.2 and 2.5 centimeters. Thickness ranges from .40

to .70 centimeters, weight ranges are from 3 to 12 grams. Humboldt B points have measurement ranges below those given above.

Pinto, or the Little Lake series, was redefined by Harrington (1957) at the Stahl site in Owens Valley, southern California. Projectile points of the Pinto type have been found in increasing numbers in the northern Great Basin. These points are stemmed indented-base in form with triangular excurvate blade elements (Plate 2, g–m). The Pinto subvarieties are defined on the appearance of the shoulder: square-shouldered, single shouldered, sloping-shouldered, or barbed-shouldered. Little Lake points recovered in Idaho and the northern Great Basin are usually lenticular to plano-convex in cross-section. Longitudinal sections vary between plano-convex to asymmetrically biconvex. Some may exhibit a rather curved longitudinal section. Flake scar pattern on finished pieces is parallel oblique, as with the Humboldt Concave Base points.

Flakes are imposed from the upper left and carry over the mid-line of the point. They are overlapped by flake scars coming from the lower right, giving the impression of a continuous flake scar across the face of the point. On several specimens a bi-directional flake pattern is present. Setting up the flake pattern in the blank and preform stages is identical to that of Humboldt, with the exception of the shoulder and stem formation. While the stemmed indented-base forms do not appear to be as well flaked as the Humboldt lanceolates, the oblique flake pattern is well established. Flake scars average four millimeters in width. Lateral edges of the stem are crushed or ground to facilitate hafting. The basal concavity is further thinned by a number of small flakes or a single longitudinal flake which usually terminates near the juncture of the blade and stem. This may be present on only one face. Basal thinning is a final step in the production of the point. The longitudinal thinning flakes overlap final flake scars on the point blade. No grinding is present within the basal concavity, although some crushing is usually evident. Except for outline, the technology of Humboldt and Little Lake projectile points is identical.

Little Lake points are made on large expanding ridged flakes which can be reduced to the desired shape and size. They range in length from 2.5 to 7.2 centimeters, widths from 1.5 to 3.3 centimeters with thickness between .45 and .70 centimeters. Weight ranges between 1.5 and 12.5 grams. Weight and size modes may be affected by site function.

The age of Humboldt and Little Lake series points has been debated for many years. In a recent compilation of Great Basin archeological data, Pinto material is seen as occupying a time range from 5,000 to about 2,700 years ago (Hester 1973:28). Humboldt Concave Base A material is thought to possess a similar time range (Thomas 1971:91), although others believe that Humboldt first appeared during late Anathermal times (Layton 1970:314, Roust and Clewlow 1968:108). I am of the opinion that both Humboldt and Little Lake series projectile points possess great time depth in the Great Basin. I must reiterate that my assignment of projectile points to either the Humboldt or Little Lake types is not based solely on outline morphology but on flaking technology as well.

Based on present evidence, Humboldt and Little Lake series projectile points appear to occur earlier in the northern Great Basin. A time gradient from the northeast Great Basin to the western Basin is also supported by the data (see Green 1972:120–140). An understanding of the time depth of Humboldt and Little Lake series may be realized with a review of the following archaeological data. Humboldt and Little Lake series points first occur in Danger Cave II, dated to about 9,500 years ago (Jennings 1957:93; Aikens 1970:47; Hester 1973:136). At Hogup Cave these projectile points occur together in Stratum 5, dated to about 7,500 years ago (Aikens 1970:28). At Weston Canyon Rockshelter in southeastern Idaho, barbed or square-shouldered Little Lake points date before 7,200 years ago (Miller 1972:36, Table 3, 10). Humboldt and Little Lake points were also recovered from the Rock Creek site in southcentral Idaho, where they occur together in Occupation II, placed between 7,900 and 7,000 years ago (Green 1972:26, 29, Figure 10). In northwestern Nevada, Humboldt Concave Base points become prominent in the Calico Phase, placed between 8,000 and 7,000 years ago (Layton 1970:314). Little Lake series points come into florescence during the Silent Snake Phase, dated to between 6,000 and 3,500 years ago, although they first occur in the earlier Calico Phase (Layton 1970:316, Table 22).

I would place the upper time boundary for Humboldt and Little Lake material at about 2,200 years ago. This is somewhat later in time than other students of Great Basin prehistory would cite, but is consistent with present evidence. Based on the foregoing data, Humboldt and Little Lake material can be seen as possessing considerable time depth and persistence in Great Basin. In addition to the longevity of these projectile points, the technology employed in their production also remains intact. Only during the latter phases of their popularity does their characteristic flaking technology begin to deteriorate.

McKean and Little Lake projectile points have been described and an analysis of their technological attributes made. It is evident from the data presented that McKean and Little Lake points are technologically divergent and represent two distinct point types. This is further supported by distributional and time depth studies. It is feasible on technological grounds and time depth to remove McKean from the McKean Humboldt Concave Base A-Pinto series proposed for the northern Great Basin. We may also remove McKean, with its cultural overtones, from consideration in developing Great Basin culture history. The data provided here are intended to provide a technological corpus for Great Basin archaeologists, but should be of aid to prehistorians working in contiguous areas as well.

REFERENCES

AIKENS, MELVIN C.
   1970   *Hogup Cave.* University of Utah Anthropological Papers 93. Salt Lake City.
BARNES, PAUL L.
   1964   *Archaeology of the Dean site: Twin Falls County, Idaho.* Laboratory of Anthropology Reports of Investigations 25. Pullman, Washington: Washington State University.
BINFORD, LEWIS
   1963   "A proposed attribute list for the description and classification of projectile points," in *Miscellaneous studies in typology and classification.* Anthropological Papers 19:193–221. Ann Arbor: Museum of Anthropology, University of Michigan.
BOWERS, ALFRED W., C. N. SAVAGE
   1962   *Primitive man on Brown's Bench.* Idaho Bureau of Mines and Geology Information Circular 14. Moscow, Idaho.
BRYAN, ALAN LYLE
   1965   *Paleo-American prehistory.* Occasional Papers of the Idaho State University Museum 16. Pocatello.
BUTLER, B. ROBERT
   1970a A surface collection from Coyote Flat, Southeastern Oregon. *Tebiwa* 13(1):34–58.
   1970b A report on the 1967–69 archaeological survey of the National Reactor Testing Station, Idaho. *Tebiwa* 13(1):58–75.
CAMPBELL, E. W. C., W. H. CAMPBELL
   1935   *The Pinto Basin site.* Southwest Museum Papers 9. Los Angeles.
CLEWLOW, C. W., JR.
   1967   Time and space relationships of some Great Basin point types. *University of California Archaeological Survey Reports* 70:141–149. Berkeley.
   1968a Projectile Points from Lovelock Cave, Nevada. *University of California Archaeological Survey Reports* 71:89–101. Berkeley.
   1968b Surface archaeology of the Black Rock Desert, Nevada. *University of California Archaeological Survey Reports* 73:1–93. Berkeley.
DELISIO, MARIO
   1970   "The Natural and Cultural Stratigraphy of the Weston Canyon

Rockshelter, Southeastern Idaho." Unpublished master's thesis, Idaho State University. Pocatello.

1971 "Preliminary report on the Weston Canyon Rockshelter, Southeastern Idaho: a big game hunting site in the northern Great Basin," in *Great Basin Anthropological Conference 1970, Selected Papers.* Edited by C. Melvin Aikens. University of Oregon Anthropological Papers 1.

GREEN, JAMES P.

1972 "Archaeology of the Rock Creek site, 10-CA-33, Sawtooth National Forest, Cassia County, Idaho." Unpublished master's thesis, Idaho State University. Pocatello.

GRUHN, RUTH

1961 *The archaeology of Wilson Butte Cave, south central Idaho.* Occasional Papers of the Idaho State College Museum 6.

1964 Test excavations at sites 10-OE-128 and 10-OE-129, Southwest Idaho. *Tebiwa* 7(2):28–36.

HARRINGTON, MARK R.

1957 *A Pinto site at Little Lake, California.* Southwest Museum Papers 17. Los Angeles.

HEIZER, R. F., M. A. BAUMHOFF, C. W. CLEWLOW, JR.

1968 Archaeology of South Fork Shelter (NV-EL-11), Elko County, Nevada *University of California Archaeological Survey Reports* 71:1–58. Berkeley.

HEIZER, R. F., C. W. CLEWLOW, JR.

1968 Projectile points from site NV-CH-15, Churchill County, Nevada. *Univity of California Archaeological Survey Reports* 71:58–88. Berkeley.

HESTER, THOMAS R.

1973 *Chronological ordering of Great Basin prehistory.* Contributions of the University of California Archaeological Research Facility 17. Berkeley.

JENNINGS, JESSE D.

1957 *Danger Cave.* Society for American Archaeology Memoir 14.

KEHOE, THOMAS F.

1955 Some chipped stone artifacts from southwest Idaho. *Plains Anthropologist* 3:13–18. Lincoln.

LAYTON, THOMAS N.

1970 "High rock archaeology, an interpretation of the prehistory of the northwestern Great Basin." Unpublished doctoral dissertation, Harvard University.

1972 A 12,000 year obsidian hydration record of occupation, abandonment and lithic change from the northwestern Great Basin. *Tebiwa* 15(2):22–28.

MILLER, SUSANNE J.

1972 "Weston Canyon Rockshelter: big-game hunting in southeastern Idaho." Unpublished master's thesis, Idaho State University. Pocatello.

MULLOY, WILLIAM

1954 The McKean site in northeastern Wyoming. *Southwestern Journal of Anthropology* 10(4):432–460.

O'CONNELL, JAMES F.
  1971 "The archaeology and cultural ecology of Surprise Valley, northeast California." Unpublished doctoral dissertation, University of California. Berkeley.

O'CONNELL J. F., R. D. AMBRO
  1968 A preliminary report on the archaeology of the Rodriguez site (CA-LAS-194), Lassin County, California. *University of California Archaeological Survey Reports* 73:95–193. Berkeley.

ROUST, NORMAN L., C. W. CLEWLOW, JR.
  1968 Projectile points from Hidden Cave (NV-CH-16), Churchill County, Nevada. *University of California Archaeological Survey Reports* 71:103–115. Berkeley.

SWANSON, E. H. JR., ROGER POWERS, ALAN LYLE BRYAN
  1964 The material culture of the 1959 southwestern Idaho survey. *Tebiwa* 7(2):1–27.

SWANSON, E. H., JR.
  1965 Archaeological explorations in southwestern Idaho. *American Antiquity* 31(1):24–37.

SWANSON, E. H. JR., JON DAYLEY
  1968 Hunting at Malad Hill in southeastern Idaho. *Tebiwa* 11(2):59–69.

THOMAS, DAVID H.
  1971 "Prehistoric subsistence-settlement patterns of the Reese River Valley, central Nevada." Unpublished doctoral dissertation, University of California. Davis.

WHEELER, RICHARD P.
  1952 A note on the "McKean lanceolate point." *Plains Archaeological Conference News Letter* 4(4):45–50. Lincoln.

WORMINGTON, H. M.
  1957 *Ancient man in North America.* Denver Museum of Natural History (popular series) 4. Denver.

Toolmaking and Tool Use Among the Preceramic Peoples of Panama

ANTHONY J. RANERE

We present here an initial attempt to make some sense out of preceramic lithic assemblages recently discovered in western Panama. The analysis of these assemblages has been heavily dependent on experiments in replicating stone tools and on experiments in using these replicated tools to perform various tasks. The technological characteristics (of both the tools and the chipping waste) and wear patterns resulting from these experiments have been compared with those of the archaeological specimens with the aid of a binocular microscope. Although this analysis is far from being completed, it seems worthwhile to present the results obtained thus far for two reasons. First, a general characterization of the lithic assemblages can be made now with some confidence that further research will enlarge upon, but not force a revision of this characterization. Second, it seems valuable to make available for comparative pur-

The excavations of the Chiriquí River sites were financed by a National Science Foundation Grant (2846) awarded to Olga F. Linares, a National Science Foundation dissertation improvement grant, and Ford Foundation traineeships awarded to me for three field seasons. The work was done with the permission and cooperation of the Dirección de Património Histórico, Panamá. Much of the analysis and the writing of this paper were done during my tenure as a postdoctoral fellow at the Smithsonian Tropical Research Institute, Balboa, Canal Zone. A Sigma Xi grant-in-aid helped defray the costs of producing the illustrations. I gratefully acknowledge the support provided by these institutions. I am indebted to Olga Linares for aiding me in innumerable ways throughout the duration of the project. I wish to thank my wife, Joan, and Richard McCarty for reading and commenting on parts of the manuscript. Richard McCarty also did the drawings in Figures 1, 4–7, 10–12, and 18–21, and spent long hours working with me on various aspects of the analysis. I also thank Robert McNealy for drawing Figures 2, 3, 8, 9, and 13–17, which originally appeared in my dissertation.

For Plates, see pp. xxiii–xxx, between pp. 102–103

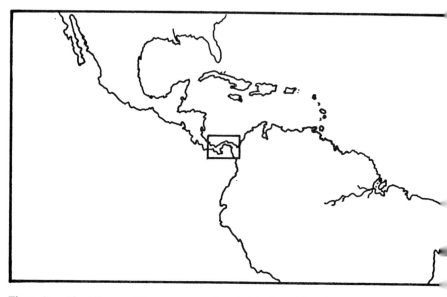

Figure 1a.   The Isthmus of Panama connecting the North and South American continents

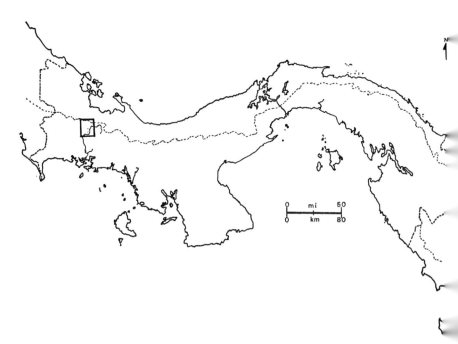

Figure 1b.   The location of the Chiriquí River study region is marked by the small rectangle
map of Panama

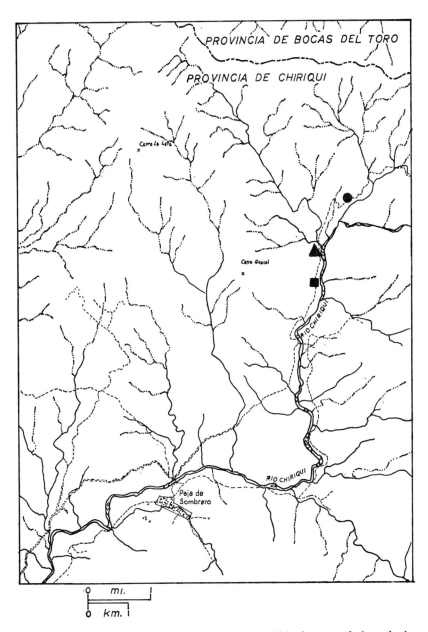

Figure 1c. The locations of the Chiriquí River sites within the upper drainage basin of the Chiriqui River. The Trapische Shelter and the Horacio Gonzales Shelter (■ square), the Casita de Piedra and the Schoolyard site (▲ triangle), and the Zarsiadero Shelter (● circle)

poses a description of one of the few preceramic lithic assemblages known from tropical contexts in the New World.

THE ARCHAEOLOGICAL AND ECOLOGICAL BACKGROUND

Recent excavations in the tropical forests of western Panama have yielded evidence of human occupation beginning over 6500 years ago and continuing into modern times (Ranere 1972; i.p.). The first 4500 years of occupation predate the introduction of pottery into the region, and it is on two related assemblages from this preceramic period that this study is based. Four rock-shelters and one open campsite, all within five kilometers of each other, were examined in the province of Chiriquí (Figure 1). The sites are within eight kilometers of the Continental Divide, which is roughly 2,000 meters in height, but they themselves are located at elevations varying from 645 to 900 meters above sea level in the bottom of the Chiriquí River canyon. Located less then nine degrees north of the equator, the region has a decidedly humid tropical climate. Mean annual temperature exceeds 20 degrees centigrade and annual rainfall measures more than 2,000 millimeters, falling primarily during the wet season from May-to-December (CATAPAN 1970). This climate supports a vegetation which could be classified as semi-evergreen seasonal forest (see Beard [1944, 1955] for definitions of American tropical vegetation formations); that is, some trees shed their leaves during the dry season and others don't. A substantial portion of the study area along the Chiriquí River has been cleared for pasture within the last twenty years, but for the moment, large tracts of forest still remain on this frontier of expanding agricultural activity in western Panama.

Two stratified rock-shelters, with cultural deposits 1.0 to 1.5 meters deep, produced the bulk of the 45,000 stone flakes and artifacts recovered from the Chiriquí River sites. Ten and twelve square meters were excavated in the Casita de Piedra and Trapiche Shelter, respectively, representing about a third of the total available living space in each shelter. Excavation was carried out by natural, or cultural layers; those layers thicker than 10 centimeters were subdivided and excavated in arbitrary 10-centimeter levels. In both sites, the major break in deposition coincided with a change in cultural assemblages. Thus, the lowest layers in both the Casita de Piedra and Trapiche Shelter contained lithic assemblages which have been assigned to the Talamanca phase. Three radiocarbon dates from the Casita de Piedra, 4610 ± 120 B.C. (I-6278), 3845 ± 105 B.C. (I-5765), and 3730 ± 105 B.C. (I-5764), came from Talamanca-phase contexts as does one date, 3900 ± 110 B.C. (I–5613), from the Trapiche Shelter. The uppermost deposits attributed to this phase have not yet been dated, but by extrapolation should fall around 3,000 B.C.

The later of the two preceramic phases, termed Boquete, has a single carbon-14 determination of 2125 ± 105 B.C. (I–5614) on deposits in the Casita de Piedra. The phase is thought to span the time between 3000 and 500 to 100 B.C., at which time cultural assemblages containing ceramics appear in western Panama. The Casita de Piedra (Plate 1), except for surface materials, is a completely preceramic site, while the Trapiche Shelter has a shallow (less than 15 centimeters thick) upper ceramic component. More substantial ceramic phase deposits overlie Boquete materials in a third rock-shelter, the Horacio Gonzales site, and the open Schoolyard site. The fifth site tested, the Zarsiadero Shelter, contained materials from the Talamanca and Boquete phases as well as from a late ceramic phase, but the deposits are somewhat mixed and for this reason, difficult to work with. The analysis presented here is almost entirely based on the lithic assemblages from the two well-stratified shelters, the Casita de Piedra and Trapiche Shelter.

Preservation in the sites was exceedingly poor, as is so often the case in the humid tropics. Only charcoal and stone were recovered, and even some of the stone was badly weathered. In some instances it is impossible to characterize stone flakes beyond suggesting that they were produced by man. Any retouch or use-flakes that these specimens might have had are simply unrecognizable. Less extreme weathering permitted identifications of use-flakes, but not wear-polish and striations. Andesite and the granitic cobbles used for grinding and pounding were the most heavily eroded materials. Chalcedony, obsidian, and quartz were altered very little if at all by weathering.

Sources for all raw material used in the chipped and ground stone industries can be found in the immediate vicinity of the sites. Outcrops of andesite occur all along the canyon. In addition, andesite cobbles and boulders occur in terrace sediments and river gravels as do smaller nodules of chalcedony (a cover term which is being used here to include chert, jasper, agate, etc. as well as chalcedony) and quartz crystals. Obsidian may also occur here (although I have not seen any). If not, a source has been reported which lies near the rim of the canyon directly behind the Casita de Piedra and the Trapiche Shelter. The variety of pebbles, cobbles, and boulders utilized in the sites for hammering, mashing, and grinding can be found in stream gravels not more than 200 meters away from any of the sites. Thus, raw material was not only local, but present in abundance. In fact, the amount of chipping debris found in the sites suggests that stone tool manufacturing was an important activity, and that the availability of raw material may have been a factor in attracting people into the area.

For a variety of reasons, it is much easier to state what is absent from the Chiriquí River chipped stone assemblages than to state what is present. Besides being easily accomplished, this somewhat negative approach to lithic analysis also serves to set the Chiriquí assemblages apart from most other New World assemblages. Absent from the western Panama preceramic are stone projectile points, bifacially flaked knives, drills, and blades. Aside from some specialized woodworking tools, the assemblages consist of simply made cutting, scraping, and chopping tools. These come in a variety of shapes and sizes and occur throughout the preceramic record with some changes in frequencies.

On viewing the preceramic assemblage as a whole, one is left with the distinct impression that stone working was not a particularly important aspect of material culture. Both the simplicity of the technology and the conservative nature of the stone industry — only slight changes are recorded over long periods of time — strengthen this feeling. In view of what we know about modern and historical tropical forest groups, the general neglect of the lithic arts should not come as a surprise. Other materials are usually substituted for stone in making a variety of tools: hardwood projectile points, shell gouges, bamboo knives, rodent incisor chisels, etc. (see Steward [1948] for numerous examples). Only heavy-duty woodworking tools of stone (axes and adzes) are consistently encountered among ethnographic tropical forest groups, although stone-flake knives and stone chips set in manioc grater boards are occasionally reported. This lack of emphasis on stone working noted historically for tropical forest peoples seems to hold true for a period of time going back at least as early as 4600 B.C., or to the first occupation of the Chiriquí River shelters.

Clearly, the use of stone depends to a large extent on its availability, so that in the middle Amazon, where suitable stone for tool manufacture is exceedingly rare, so are archaeological and ethnographic examples of stone tools. In the Chiriquí River canyon, where suitable materials are plentiful, we would expect to find maximum usage of stone in a tropical forest context. This seems to be true, judging from comparisons made between the Chiriquí assemblages and other tropical forest preceramic assemblages reported in an admittedly scanty literature (e.g. McGimsey 1956; Reichel-Dolmatoff 1965; Hurt, Van der Hammen, and Correal 1972). Yet even so, stone is not important even under what we might call optimum conditions in the Chiriquí River sites.

Although it is probably true, then, that stone industries are poor reflections of the complexity of tropical forest cultural patterns, it does not follow that archaeologists can afford to pay them little attention, if for no other reason than the fact that stone tools and manufacturing debris are often the only cultural material found in tropical forest (preceramic) sites. If exhaustive analysis of these assemblages appears to be nothing more than making the best out of a bad situation, at least the predicament has parallels in other archaeological settings—for instance, in many of the reputed preprojectile-point assemblages in the New World and lower Paleolithic assemblages in the Old. With its relative abundance of stone, the Chiriquí River canyon seems a good place to begin an examination of tropical forest stone industries in the Americas.

THE METHOD OF ANALYSIS

The analysis of the Chiriquí River assemblages was carried out with as little reference to other New World assemblages as possible. This approach seemed preferable to one in which the Panama specimens were forced into tool categories originally defined for entirely different kinds of artifact inventories. However, it goes without saying that all tools hold certain general features in common regardless of their specific cultural contexts. That is to say, all stone tools have a working area (edge, tip, facet, surface, etc.) which is used in some task (cutting, scraping, pounding, grinding, etc.) on some other object (wood, stone, meat, seeds, etc.). These tools are also shaped by one process or another (flaking, grinding, pecking, etc.), either intentionally or simply through use. The analysis of the Chiriquí River assemblages was undertaken with this general understanding of tool characteristics serving as a sort of base line.

My first concern was to gain some familiarity with the kinds of flakes and tools recovered from the Chiriquí excavations. Accordingly, the entire collection of 45,000 specimens was examined piece by piece. Unmodified, unused flakes (i.e. chipping waste) were separated from all other specimens. In this "other" category were included all possible tools, tool fragments, used flakes, and flakes which provided information on toolmaking processes whether or not they themselves were tools. A hand lens ($7\times$) and binocular microscope ($6\times$–$50\times$) were used in the sorting procedure. When patterns began to emerge in the form of recurring technological, functional, or stylistic attributes, I initiated a series of experiments in manufacturing and using stone tools in an attempt to reproduce these patterns. This set in motion a feedback cycle of sorts whereby the information provided by the experiments led to new insights in the examination of archaeological materials, which in turn suggested other experiments. By the time the collections had been sorted through once, a number of experiments had been completed. I then had a much better grasp of stoneworking techniques and tool functions represented in the Chiriquí River assemblages. The entire collections were reexamined from this relatively knowledgeable position, and flakes were moved into or out of the unmodified, unused group where necessary.

Finally, all specimens from one site which were considered to be tools or tool fragments (i.e. all specimens not classified as unmodified, unused flakes) were placed on a laboratory table and similar specimens were grouped together. What should be clear from the previous discussion is that the resulting tool categories were not invented during this final sorting operation, but gradually emerged during the course of the experiments and the two examinations of all specimens in the collections. Although no attention was paid to artifact provenience in the analysis (indeed, it was purposely avoided in favor of a technological-functional approach), most tools have a discrete time dimension. Several types were restricted primarily or entirely to just one of the preceramic phases. Others were found in both preceramic phases but not in the later ceramic phases. Only such broad categories as flake scrapers and flake knives are found in both ceramic and preceramic contexts.

Although numbering less than half a dozen specimens, the appearance of ground-stone axes, adzes, and chisels in the late preceramic phase documents an important addition to the stone-working repertoire of the Chiriquí River inhabitants. These few tools were analyzed primarily by looking for evidence of use and for indications of manufacturing techniques. Some replicative experiments were also conducted in order to to help differentiate striations produced through use from those produced during the manufacturing process.

A number of rounded cobbles, pebbles, and boulders were recovered from the preceramic layers which had been used for hammering, pounding, mashing, and grinding. The analysis of these tools proceeded in much the same manner as the analysis of chipped-stone tools. First, tool and tool fragments were separated from unmodified, unused cobbles and pebbles. Secondly, all tools from a single site were set out on a laboratory table and grouped into tool types. Replicative and functional experiments, here a single process (i.e. hammerstones are "made" by using them), were carried out in conjunction with the sorting.

EXPERIMENTAL PROCEDURES

The bulk of the raw material used in my knapping experiments was collected from central Panama and was quite similar to the andesite and chalcedony which together accounted for over 90 percent of the chipped stone recovered from the Chiriquí River shelters. The very little quartz used in the experiments came from a local source, but the obsidian did not. The river cobbles and pebbles used by me came from either the Chiriquí River canyon or from central Panama. Although it would have been preferable to experiment with materials from exactly the same sources used by the rock shelter inhabitants, the flaking characteristics of my experimental materials can be considered similar enough to those of the original materials so that the possibility of erroneous interpretations resulting from dissimilar experimental and archaeological raw materials is slight. The matching of flaking characteristics between experimental and archaeological raw materials is not to be taken lightly, for different materials react differently to the same flint-knapping techniques. Likewise, tools made from different materials often display different wear attributes even when used for the same task. Some of these differences will be brought out later in the paper.

In my flint-knapping experiments, all flakes were recovered and kept together with the implement or core from which they were struck. The kind of hammer used, core support (if any), platform preparation and other observations were recorded for each experiment. Before tabulating various attributes of the experimentally produced waste flakes, they were screened through a quarter-inch mesh in order to obtain a sample more compatible to the ones provided by the site excavations. The smaller flakes were, however, kept and examined as well, even though they were not tabulated in the strictly comparative analysis. Small flakes were recovered from several excavation units in the Casita de Piedra and Trapiche Shelter, where small-mesh window screen was used in sifting the sediments. In making comparisons with these units, the small, experimentally produced flakes could be included in the analysis.

Thus far, functional experiments using chipped-stone tools have been almost entirely confined to woodworking (although a few attempts to work bone and antler have also been made). I have made no particular attempt to fashion specific wood tools (e.g. spear shafts, cooking implements, beverage troughs) or to carry out specific tasks (e.g. chopping down trees, stripping bark). Pieces of wood brought into the laboratory (both native and exotic varieties) have simply been scraped, planed, chiseled, chopped, and split in order to produce wear patterns on replicated tools. Details of these experiments are provided under the descriptions of the various tool types found below. Results of experiments in making and using ground-stone tools and cobble tools are also incorporated in the description of tool types.

THE TECHNIQUES AND TOOLS USED IN MANUFACTURING CHIPPED-STONE IMPLEMENTS

By far the most important manufacturing technique used for making chipped stone tools in the Chiriquí River collections was simple percussion with a hammer stone, often used in conjunction with an anvil stone. In fact, with the exception of pressure retouch on a few very small tools, it is fair to say that all chipped-stone tools and all flake attributes from the preceramic assemblages could have been produced by hammer stone percussion flaking (both with and without an anvil) alone. I do not mean to insist that other techniques were not also used — for example, the attributes shown on a number of flakes are as compatible with the use of a hardwood billet as with a soft hammer stone — but they need not have been.

Treatment of the core and platform for flake removal was at best minimal. There is no indication that the platforms were either abraded or polished in an attempt to strengthen them. Even the extensive crushing of leading platform edges observable on some flakes and core remnants seems accidental. One gets the distinct impression that the core was bashed repeatedly until a flake was driven off without too much consideration of platform preparation, platform isolation, or core preparation. The occurrence in the collections of numerous flakes with multiple bulbs of percussion, and the high frequency of hinge fractures and battering of the platform edge give evidence for a fairly casual approach to flint-knapping. The few exceptions to this pattern will be discussed later.

Cores

A considerable number of chalcedony and quartz core remnants have negative bulbs of force at opposite ends accompanied by various degrees of crushing (see Figure 2 and Plate 2). These characteristics result from what is called the bipolar flaking technique, because force is, in effect, applied to both ends or poles of the core at the same time (through the hammer stone and anvil). With the bottom of the core firmly supported

Figure 2. A bipolar core, length 4.4 cm (see Plate 2, lower left specimen for a photograph of this specimen from a slightly different angle)

on an anvil stone, force directed straight downwards is reflected upwards, causing the detached flakes to have almost straight ventral surfaces. In contrast, when the bottom of the core is not rigidly supported, the force of the detaching blow "curves under" the core, producing a flake with a curved ventral surface. Andesite flakes from the Chiriquí River shelters almost invariably have these curved ventral surfaces, whereas straight or flat ventral surfaces are common among flakes of chalcedony and quartz. Because chalcedony and quartz normally occur in this region as small nodules and crystals, respectively, an anvil is a great aid in breaking them up. Small obsidian nodules were percussion-flaked with the aid of an anvil as well.

Andesite, on the other hand, occurs in large angular blocks throughout the study area and is easily fractured by using a hammer stone alone. In laboratory experiments, large blocks of andesite (or large blocks of chalcedony, for that matter) were easily fractured using a hammer stone without supporting the core on an anvil. Small rounded chalcedony nodules proved difficult to fracture in this manner unless small, hard, pointed hammer stones were used (a type extremely rare in the archaeological collections). The task was made easy when the nodules were supported on an anvil.

A few of the andesite cores recovered were bipolar; however, most have to be classified as irregular or multidirectional (see Plate 3). That is to say, more than one area of the core served as a platform for flake detachment. The flaking strategy used here might best be described as opportunistic;

Figure 3. A side and bottom view of a conical core, length 2.2 cm (see Plate 2, upper left specimen for a photograph of this core)

flakes were detached wherever a suitable platform for their detachment could be found. Not all andesite cores conformed to this pattern. A few cores from the base of the cultural deposits had single striking platforms and were conical in shape (see Plate 2 and Figure 3). Fewer still in number were bifacial cores (see Plate 3), specimens which tended to be discoidal in shape, and which had flakes removed from the periphery (which served as the striking platform).

Neither the bifacial nor conical cores seem to be associated with the production of blades. Out of context, roughly eighty flakes in the Chiriquí River preceramic collections could pass for blades. That is, they are more than twice as long as they are wide, the direction of force was applied parallel to their long axis, and negative flake scars running parallel to the long axis occur on the dorsal surface. In context, eighty blades among 45,000 flakes seem less than significant. In fact, in my experiments in replicating tools from the Chiriquí River sites, I accidentally produced a higher blade-flake ratio than that found in either preceramic assemblage.

Hammer Stones and Anvil Stones

These tool types were recovered in both Talamanca and Boquete phase contexts. Hammer stones come in two distinct varieties. One type is subspherical to oval in shape and has battering either completely around the periphery or along a substantial portion of it (see Figure 4 and Plate 4). The second type is more oblong in shape and has battering on the ends (one or both) only (see Plate 4). The "edge-battered" hammer stones

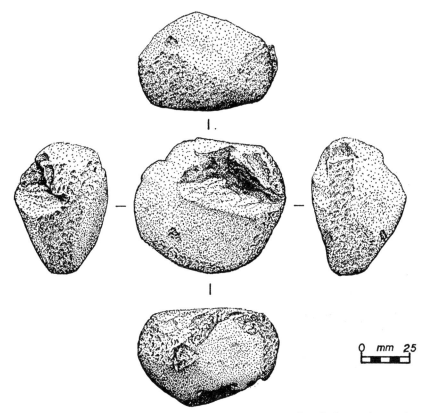

Figure 4.   An edge-battered cobble. This specimen has been heavily battered around its entire circumference

consistently show heavier use than the "end-battered" hammer stones. In most cases, the hammering facet on the edge-battered cobbles was broad and smooth, although clearly this is the end product of considerable use. New hammer stones would have much narrower facets or impact zones.

Examination of striking platform remnants on flakes showed that both hard-stone hammers and soft-stone hammers were used in the preceramic industries. It should, however, be noted that a hammer stone, as it becomes more and more battered, has its hard cortex striking area removed and replaced with a smoother, softer facet. Thus, the same hammer stone can initially produce flakes exhibiting hard-hammer characteristics (e.g. crushing at a small impact point, prominent but confined bulb of force, eraillure scar), and later, flakes with soft-hammer characteristics (e.g. relatively broad impact zone, diffuse bulb of force, slight projection or lip on the ventral edge of platform). Indeed, changing the character of striking platforms on flakes can be simply accomplished by shifting the hammer stone in your hand so that first a battered soft facet strikes the core, then a fresh surface with cortex intact strikes the core. This somewhat tortuous consideration of hammer stone and platform characteristics provides some background for what is intuitively obvious: that hammer stones change character as they are used and that these changes (from hard, small impact zones on the hammer to softer, broader impact zones) are reflected in the character of the flakes being detached.

As we discussed earlier, anvils were used in flaking chalcedony nodules and quartz crystals, to judge from the attributes seen on what have been called bipolar core remnants. Several anvil stones were recovered from both the Casita de Piedra and Trapiche Shelter in preceramic contexts (see Figure 5 and Plate 4). The pitted surfaces of the stones have been duplicated in laboratory experiments where chalcedony nodules were fractured by the bipolar flaking technique.

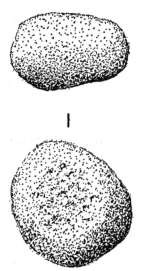

Figure 5.   A small anvil, maximum diameter 5.3 cm (see Plate 4, lower right specimen for a photograph of this anvil)

CHIPPED STONE TOOLS

Bifacial Wedges

Found only in the early Talamanca phase are large bifacially flaked splitting wedges which, without the benefit of microscopic analysis, would

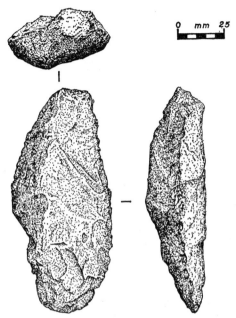

6.   A bifacially flaked celt-like wedge (see Plate 5, upper right specimen for a photograph of this wedge)

probably be classified as celts (Figure 6 and Plate 5). Careful attention to wear-polish and striations found on the implements, however, makes it quite clear that they were not hafted. Wear-polish is particularly heavy on the bit, but traces also exist on most of the specimens in an area extending from the bit back two-thirds or three-fourths of the length of the tool. This polish is more pronounced on the more convex side of the tool. The heavy battering on the butt end of these tools provides further evidence that they were used as wedges. Lateral edges are often dulled by crushing, undoubtedly to save wear and tear on the hand holding the tool while in use.

A few of the wedges have parallel striations visible on polished surfaces extending backwards from the bit at about a 30° angle to the long axis of the tool. Consistent with the orientation of these striations are the facts that the bit edge itself is worn more heavily along one corner, and that the battered spot on the butt is offset directly opposite the worn corner of the bit.

I have manufactured several celt-like wedges, using a hard hammer stone to shape the blank which was held unsupported in one hand. These replicated wedges were used to split wood by holding them at an angle of approximately 30° to the surface of the wood and driving them with a

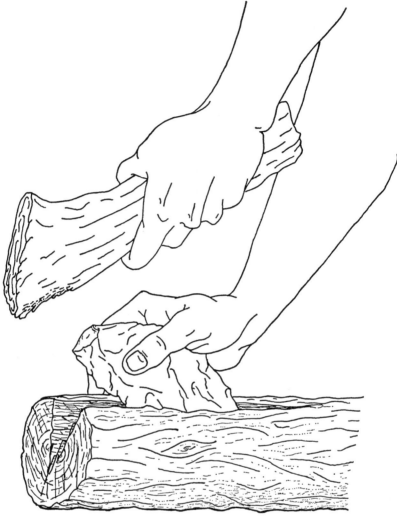

Figure 7. A reconstruction of the manner in which celt-like wedges were probably used

heavy wooden mallet (Figure 7). Used in this manner, the replicated tools developed the same wear patterns as observed on the archaeological specimens.

In the manufacturing of over half of the celt-like wedges from the Chiriquí River shelters, a small section of cortex was retained on that part of the butt end which received the heaviest pounding. This was undoubtedly done because the cortex is capable of withstanding heavier battering than is a freshly flaked surface. In some of my experiments I was not as careful to leave this cortex as I should have been and consequently had some problems with the butt end accidentally flaking while I was driving the wedge into the wood. In fact, I had systematically to crush the butt end of one specimen to produce what was in effect a poor replica of the cortex in order to make the tool serviceable. A similar solution to this problem was arrived at by my predecessors, to judge from a few of the wedges in the collections.

Andesite was almost invariably the raw material chosen for these wedges, and with good reason. Andesite is a "tough" material which takes considerably more force to fracture than most chalcedony. The advantages of this characteristic were obvious after attempting to use chalcedony replicas to split wood. Besides the greater tendency for spalls to be driven off the hammered end of chalcedony wedges, the bits were more easily damaged. Thus the life-span of an andesite wedge would far exceed that of a chalcedony specimen.

Although only hard-hammer percussion is used in shaping the celt-like wedges, a certain amount of skill is involved in making the tool. The quality which makes andesite ideal for holding up under the battering it receives as a wedge is a quality which makes it difficult to flake initially. Considerable force is necessary to drive off flakes while shaping an andesite wedge. In addition, some planning must be done to retain the cortex at the proper place on the butt end of the tool. Attention must also be paid to the smoothness and taper of the bit end.

The angle of the working edge on the Chiriquí River wedges averages between 45° and 50° with little deviation. This may represent the initial manufactured angle and thus the one preferred on the tools, or it may represent a maximum usable angle. Some of the smaller wedges have working edge angles closer to 30°, and by extending older slopes past resharpening scars on other wedges, I reconstructed initial edge angles closer to 30° than to 45°. In my experiments the replicated wedges had edge angles of slightly under 30° to slightly over 50° (measured at the center of the bit). I had more success using the more acute angled bits in splitting wood, but hesitate to make the same claim for the Chiriquí River woodworkers.

It should be noted here that several specimens (Plate 6) which functioned as splitting wedges were not as carefully shaped by bifacial flaking as the ones I have been discussing. Similar to the celt-like wedges, these specimens had wear-polish on the bits and back along both faces (but more strongly developed on the more convex side). Most also had a battered area at the butt end. The major difference in the two wedge categories is that the irregular wedges were made on cobbles and large flakes which needed little retouch to convert them into usable tools. Although irregular wedges are technologically distinct from celt-like wedges, the two types were probably functionally interchangeable. Both share the same time dimension, being restricted to the Talamanca phase.

Tabular and Broad-based Wedges

The most diagnostic tool from Boquete phase contexts is a small wedge very unlike the bifacial wedges from the earlier Talamanca phase. Whereas the bifacial wedges average nearly 10 centimeters in length and 150 grams in weight, these small wedges average little more than 2 centimeters in length and 2 grams in weight. The small wedges were made on flakes and core remnants which are for the most part products of bipolar flaking. Two varieties can be distinguished: one in which the tool tapers to a chisel-like bit from a broad base, thus being truly "wedge-shaped" (see Plate 7 and Figure 8); and a second more common variety which,

Figure 8.   A small broad-based wedge, length 2.3 cm

Figure 9.   Two opposite faces of a small tabular wedge, length 2.0 cm

from a maximum width around midpoint, tapers in both directions to opposing bits, thus being tabular in form (see Plate 7 and Figure 9). The bits of these wedges are generally crushed and polished through use. Tabular wedges often have wear-polish on both ends, indicating that these tools were reversed in use (that is, the bit and butt ends were interchangeable). Numerous use-flakes have been removed from both faces of the bits. On some of the tabular specimens large flake scars extend nearly the entire length of the wedge, giving them a fluted appearance. Wear-polish occurs on high spots on both faces of the tools. Striations visible in the polished areas run parallel to the bit-butt axis of the tool showing that it was driven straight into the wood.

In experimental use of replicated small wedges, I was able to split relatively large pieces of wood, using several wedges together to open the split. Often parts of the bit broke off while it was embedded in the wood, and with further hammering on the butt end, these tiny chips acted as small anvils, causing even larger flakes to be driven off (occasionally

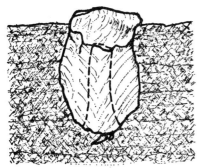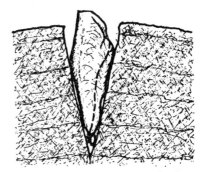

Figure 10. Two views of a small wedge embedded in wood. Tiny flakes broken off the bit act as anvils and when the wedge is struck again, the flake outlined by the dotted line will be detached, "fluting" the wedge

fluting the wedge), or causing the wedge to be broken (Figure 10). Commonly, in the accidental breakage of specimens in my experiments, the wedges were "cleaved" by the pounding, leaving two or more pieces which resemble nothing so much as burins and burin spalls. Similar burin-like pieces occur in the archaeological collections which are obviously damaged tabular wedges.

Most small wedges were made from chalcedony or quartz crystals, materials most often worked with bipolar flaking techniques. Bipolar core remnants and flakes are ideally suited to function as wedges without modification, although a bipolar retouch technique might also be used for final shaping. Heavily used small wedges are so distinctively shaped by use-flakes and battering of the butt end that it is not possible to determine if specimens started out already retouched into tabular forms or if they were just straight flakes.

In my experiments I used hammers of hardwood and stone to drive the wedges. Both were successfully employed, but the stone hammers did shatter the wedges more rapidly than the wooden ones. Final appearance of the used replicas was heavily influenced by the character of the raw materials from which they were made. Wide variances were noted even within what I have been calling chalcedony (but which includes chert, jasper, agate, etc.). Some of the more "brittle" pieces snapped at the point where the bit entered the wood rather than having flakes peeled back from the bit end. Nonetheless, the replicated specimens which I used in splitting wood developed all of the wear characteristics (polish, crushing, use-flakes, removal of channel flakes and burin-like breaks) seen on the archaeological specimens. A word of caution should be inserted here about naming these tools wedges rather than chisels or something else. All that can be said with any certainty is that these are tools which are driven deeply into wood (the depth of penetration can be inferred by the wear-polish running the length of the faces). I can only suggest that the purpose for doing so was to split wood.

Because the distributions of the large bifacial wedges and the small wedges are complementary, it is tempting to suggest that the latter are in some way functional replacements for the former. The extreme difference in size could easily be accounted for if the small wedges were socketed in a wood, bone, or antler haft and thus functioned as bits for large composite splitting wedges. I have used a tabular wedge socketed in an antler haft to split wood and found it superior to the bifacial wedges. Unfortunately, there is no evidence that the tabular wedges were ever hafted. To the contrary, the battered butt end and the extension of wear-polish the length of the tool argues that they were not. Therefore, unless the wedges were reversed in their haft, we must conclude that the small wedges, like their large predecessors, were used unhafted.

Scraper-planes

Large unifacially flaked scraper-planes formed an important part of the Talamanca tool assemblage (Figure 11 and Plate 8). These tools were characteristically made on large andesite flakes by using the ventral surface as a striking platform and removing flakes around the entire perimeter of the platform with a hammer stone. As a result, some of these implements look very much like conical cores, and indeed, may have served this purpose before being used as planes. The outlines of the working edges are variable; some are almost straight, others are "toothed" and still others contain large concavities. The edge angles on these tools varied from 45° to 95°, with most falling within a range of 60° to 70°.

On specimens whose surfaces have remained relatively unweathered, wear-polish is observable on the tools' edges and occasionally on the

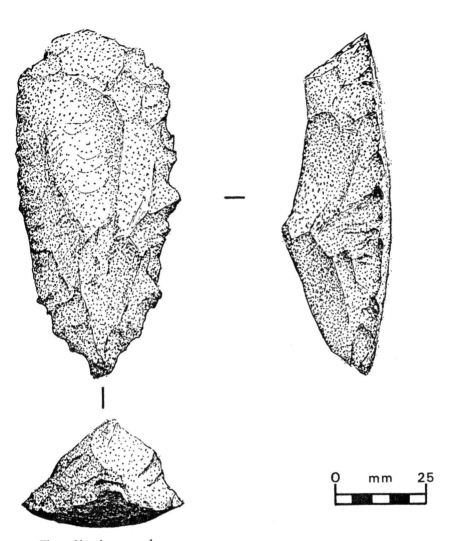

Figure 11.   A scraper-plane

ventral surface. Striations in the polished areas reflect the orientations of
the tools while in use. Short use-flakes can also be detected on the ventral
surfaces of some specimens. Taken together, the wear patterns indicate
that the tools were pushed or drawn, flat surface facing downward, along
the surface of wood (and perhaps bone and/or antler) in order to remove
shavings.

Scraper-planes are large enough tools to be used effectively without
being hafted. A number of replicated specimens made from different
kinds of stone were used to plane wood in my laboratory experiments.

Some differences in wear patterns resulted. Andesite scraper-planes developed a heavy polish on the ventral side of the bit edge, but no use-flakes were removed in the planing process. Various kinds of chalcedony planes developed an identical wear polish on the bits, but in addition had a number of small use-flakes taken off the flat underside of the bit. The removal of use-flakes seems dependent on a combination of factors, the toughness of the material used in making the scraper-plane perhaps being most important. In addition, the force employed in using the plane, the manner in which force is applied (i.e. smooth pushing or pulling versus a chopping or hacking motion) and the material being worked are all contributing factors to the production of use-flakes. I produced use-flakes on one tool only when it slipped and hit against another stone. Thus, improper use of a tool might be considered still another factor in the production of use-flakes.

Most planes cannot be used by pushing them along their ventral surface. They must be tilted slightly in order to allow the bit to penetrate the surface of the wood. However, some planes, or portions of planes,

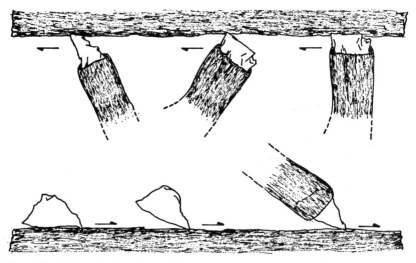

Figure 12.   Schematic drawings of how scraper-planes (upper) and steep scrapers (lower) could have been used (not drawn to scale). The upper left scraper-plane could have been pushed along its ventral surface because it is slightly concave and therefore allows the bit edge to dig into the wood. The upper center and hafted upper right scraper-planes have slightly convex ventral surfaces and must be tilted in order to get the bits to dig into the wood. The two hafted steep scrapers in the lower left and lower center drawings illustrate working positions with the ventral surface facing downwards, as is the case with the scraper-planes. The lower right specimen, however, has the dorsal face against the wood and the ventral surface facing in the direction that the tool is moved in scraping. Each position produces distinctive wear patterns (see text).

have concave ventral surfaces which allow the bit to penetrate the wood while the tool rides on the higher sections of the ventral surface (see Figure 12). In these cases, the high points also show signs of wear-polish from sliding over the wood and in effect, burnishing it. As I mentioned earlier, a few archaeological specimens have such wear-polish, and I was able to replicate the tools and wear-polish in the laboratory.

Although large enough to be used unhafted, a number of these scraper-planes would have been more effective tools if they were hafted in the same manner as the Australian adze flakes which they somewhat resemble (Gould, et al. 1971). In my experiments, I hafted replicas in split sticks wrapped with cord (see Figure 12), and while not the most suitable haft for this kind of tool, it did increase the speed at which I could plane wood two- to three-fold. Examination of the archaeological specimens does not reveal whether they were hafted or not, and so the question must remain open.

Scrapers

Small scraping tools numerically dominated the Talamanca phase assemblage and remained important in the succeeding Boquete phase. Some were carefully shaped, but more often, flakes with suitable edges were used without retouch. Perhaps all, or at least most, of these scrapers began simply as unretouched flakes, and only through resharpening were tools produced which are recognizable as being purposely manufactured. Scrapers from the two preceramic assemblages can be somewhat arbitrari-

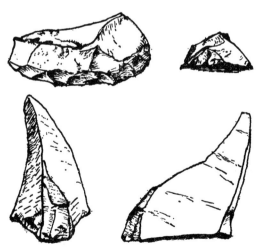

Figure 13.   Two steep scrapers. Length of upper left figure, 2.6 cm

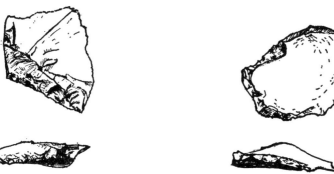

Figure 14. Two flake scrapers. Length of upper right figure, 3.0 cm

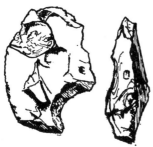

Figure 15. A concave scraper or spokeshave, length 3.5 cm

Figure 16. A pointed scraper or graver, length 2.7 cm

ly separated into three groups on the basis of the outline of their working
edges: most numerous are scrapers with straight to convex working
edges (Figures 13 and 14 and Plate 9); less numerous, but still abundant,
are scrapers with concave working edges (spokeshaves — see Figure 15
and Plate 9), and occurring infrequently are pointed scrapers (gravers —
see Figure 16 and Plate 9). Two, or even all three, of these working edge
outlines can be found on the same tool, which underscores the arbitrari-
ness of the division.

Scraping edges, whether they are straight, convex, concave or pointed, can be used in two different ways: they can be pushed or drawn with the flat unflaked surface downward as with a modern plane, or they can be drawn with the flaked dorsal surface downward and the flat ventral surface roughly perpendicular to the surface being worked (see Figure 12). The former is much like using a potato peeler, the latter like scraping the skin from a carrot.

Wear patterns on scrapers with steep working-edge angles (around 70° to 95°) indicate that this kind of tool was generally used with the unflaked flat surface down, that is, they were used as planes. Wear-polish extends back from the bit on the underside of the tool, sometimes occurring on high spots on the ventral surface. In using replicas of these steep scrapers to plane wood, it was only possible to do relatively light work by holding the tools unhafted between my fingers. Yet, the very heavy wear-polish and use-flakes on some of the archaeological specimens would have been difficult if not impossible to produce by using the tools in this fashion. Thus it seems reasonable, if not demonstrable, to suppose that these tools were hafted in some manner. I have used numerous scrapers and unmodified flakes hafted in a simple socket to plane wood. A small scraper hafted in this manner (see Figure 12) is at least as efficient in shaving wood as an unhafted scraper-plane.

Not all wear patterns on steep scrapers were produced by a planing motion. Some specimens were used for scraping with the dorsal face toward the surface being worked. In this position, the ventral surface is facing the worker, and the scraper is drawn toward him. Here again, the use of a haft greatly improves the efficiency of the tool.

The pointed scrapers or gravers were used in the same fashion as the majority of the steep scrapers; in fact the gravers are simply miniature steep scrapers. They are pushed along the surface being engraved so that the underside of the bit becomes heavily polished, and has an occasional use-flake removed. Some of these tools have more than one engraving spur isolated by fine unifacial pressure flaking on either side. In such cases the concavities between the spurs look like concave scraping edges. However, on the specimens where wear-polish is preserved, it is clear that the short engraving point was the part of the tool used and not the concavities on either side.

In contrast to pointed and steep scrapers, concave scrapers (spokeshaves) were usually drawn along the shaft being scraped, with the dorsal side next to the wood. Wear-polish on spokeshaves is most heavily developed on ridges demarcating flake scars in the dorsal side of the concavity. Most use-flakes come off the dorsal surface. Nonetheless, use-flakes also occur on the ventral surface of some tools, and it may well be that such tools were used in a bi-directional fashion.

In my experimental work I have used scrapers of various descriptions, both hafted and unhafted, to work wood and, to a lesser extent, bone and antler. Needless to say, other possible uses for these small scrapers need to be explored. At this stage in the analysis I cannot identify the function of these tools beyond pointing out that wear patterns which have survived for study are compatible with planing and/or scraping wood or other hard materials and are not compatible with scraping such soft materials as animal skins.

Knives

Found throughout the archaeological sequence in the Chiriquí River canyon were flakes with wear-polish and/or use-flakes along one edge (see Figure 17 and Plate 10). These flakes appeared to have served as cutting tools. They are characterized by small working-edge angles (generally less then 45°) and the occurrence of small use flakes on both sides of the working edge. They have been called "knives" in order to distinguish them from the more steeply angled unifacially use-retouched flakes described above as "scrapers."

Knives vary widely in shape and size. A reasonable conclusion is that the principal consideration for selecting a flake for use as a knife was whether or not it had a suitable cutting edge. We might speculate that a second consideration would be whether or not the flake could be comfortably used in the hand or could be hafted for comfortable use. With the possible exception of two knives which may have had the side opposite the working edge blunted (backed), flakes were not purposely modified for ease of use or ease of hafting. Such characteristics were apparently

Figure 17.   A flake knife, length 4.1 cm

included in the original selection of the flake. For example, a number of specimens are naturally backed by platform remnants, negative flake scars, or sections of cortex. Others seem ideal for hafting in a slotted or split handle.

I have used a number of flakes as knives, both hafted and unhafted. Wear patterns on the archaeological specimens were most satisfactorily replicated when hafted flakes were used to whittle wood. Without hafting the specimens, I could not apply enough force on andesite and most chalcedony flakes to remove use-flakes similar to those found on heavily used archaeological knives. Much work is yet to be done on the identification and interpretation of knives from the Chiriquí River assemblages. It is unlikely that I was able to identify all of those flakes from the collections which had been used as knives. Tough material like andesite can be used for indefinite periods of time for cutting soft materials (for example, meat or plant foodstuff) without ever having use-flakes removed, although the cutting edge and part of either face do become polished. Unfortunately, much of the andesite from the Chiriquí River shelters was weathered to the point where only the heaviest wear-polish can be confidently identified. For this reason, only a few knives having wear-polish alone (without use flakes) have been identified in the collections. Such knives were presumably used to cut materials softer than wood, bone, or antler.

Choppers

Large implements with heavily battered edges were recovered from cultural layers dating to both the Talamanca and Boquete phases. A few of these chopping tools were bifacially flaked (see Figure 18 and Plate 11). Most were simply large flakes struck from cobbles or large cores which had battering around the periphery or a portion of it (see Figure 19 and Plate 11). These choppers were roughly disc-shaped (around 6 to 8 centimeters in diameter and 2 centimeters thick) with edge angles of approximately 45°. Sizable use-flakes ending in hinges occur on both sides of the working edge. In the single attempt I made to use a replicated chopper to cut wood, I found that I needed to haft the implement in order to penetrate the wood and remove large use-flakes similar to those on the archaeological specimens. This is not to say that these choppers were necessarily used as hafted woodworking tools. The experiment does indicate that these choppers were used with some force on a material at least as hard as wood.

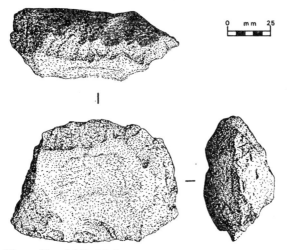

Figure 18.   A bifacial chopper

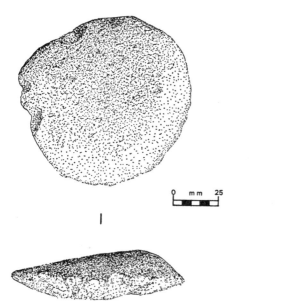

Figure 19.   A cobble spall chopper

Quartz Crystals

Sharing the same distribution as the small tabular wedges (i.e. limited to the Boquete phase), the same size range, and perhaps the same function, were used quartz crystals (see Plate 10). The chisel-shaped end of these crystals have use-flakes peeled back along both faces, and the opposite end often shows the effects of battering.

Burins

Among the numbers of burin-like pieces resulting from bipolar flaking and accidental breakage of small tabular wedges were a few specimens which appear to be purposely manufactured burins (see Plate 10). The majority of these came from Talamanca-phase contexts. The burin bits are formed either by two intersecting burin facets or by a single burin facet and a natural truncation (the edge of a snapped flake, part of the platform, etc.). Small use-flakes are present on these bits, and one specimen has been resharpened by the removal of two burin spalls, one on each side of the bit (one of these spalls was recovered and matched with the burin). All of the Chiriquí River burins are small (averaging less than 3 centimeters in length) and therefore probably used in fine engraving tasks. The function of these tools has not yet been explored experimentally.

Ground-stone Tools

Ground-stone tools first make their appearance in the Chiriquí River sequence during the Boquete phase (Plate 12). Because the specimens are few in number, often fragmentary and badly eroded, one cannot characterize the manufacturing and use of the ground-stone tools from the Chiriquí River shelters with as much precision as one would like. Still, the very fact that the technique of shaping tools by grinding was present during the late preceramic phase is important.

Grooved Stone Axe

A single example was recovered from the Casita de Piedra (see Plate 12). The relatively broad (2.0 centimeters) and shallow (0.2 to 0.6 centimeters) groove completely encircles the axe near the flattened butt end. The bit is convex and asymmetrical as if one edge (possibly the lower section) had been worn down and resharpened. Unfortunately, I cannot demonstrate that such was actually the case because the surface of the tool has been completely eroded away.

Adze

A ground-stone fragment, apparently from an adze, was also recovered from the Casita de Piedra (see Plate 12). Its surface was reasonably well preserved. Shaping of the stone by grinding has left heavy, regular striations running parallel to the long axis of the tool along its sides and parallel to the bit edge (and therefore perpendicular to the other striations) on the two beveled facets which meet to form the bit. As is the case with all ground-stone fragments from the Chiriquí River sites, the steps in the manufacturing process before the final grinding cannot be determined because the grinding had removed all evidence of these earlier shaping operations. Presumably the adze was chipped and/or pecked into nearly finished form before the final grinding of the tool began.

Chisel

The upper layers of the Casita de Piedra yielded a third ground-stone specimen (see Plate 12), the bit end of a small chisel (3.3 by 1.8 by 0.5 centimeters). The chisel was snapped at the point where it was hafted by pressure exerted perpendicular to the face of the tool. Two incised lines encircle the tool at the point where it snapped, and seem to have been made by the tool rubbing against its hafting. Two sets of parallel striations running diagonally across the face of the tool (and crossing each other at nearly right angles) indicate the directions in which the tool was abraded during its manufacture.

Sets of long parallel striations observed on ground-stone tools from the Chiriquí River sites are clearly the results of the manufacturing process rather than use of the tools. I produced very similar marks on two replicated specimens using a sandstone abrader. In contrast, the striations resulting from use of one of these tools to dress wood were concentrated near the bit edge, and were shallower, shorter, and more irregular than manufacturing striations. No use-striations could be identified on the archaeological specimens because of the poor preservation of their surfaces.

GRINDING, POUNDING AND MASHING TOOLS

Edge-ground Cobbles

These were the most common grinding or mashing tools used in both

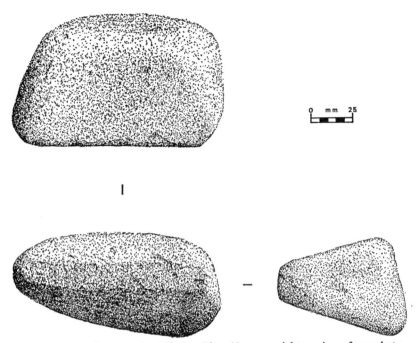

Figure 20. An edge-ground cobble (see Plate 13, upper right specimen for a photograph of this artifact)

preceramic phases. The grinding facet on these tools is located along the narrow edge of the cobble rather than on the face (Figure 20 and Plate 13). In the Chiriquí River specimens, the grinding facet may completely ring the cobble, or be restricted to a very small portion of one edge. Most commonly, two grinding facets occur on opposite sides of the cobble. Most edge-ground cobbles tend to be somewhat oval and flat, although a number do have triangular cross-sections. The sizes of the cobbles are quite variable (7 to 14 centimeters in length). The dimensions of the grinding surfaces themselves vary with the size and shape of the cobble and with the amount of use they have received (the more the use, the larger the grinding surface). The ground facets are slightly convex along their short axis and very convex to almost straight along their long axis. On the specimens from the Chiriquí River shelters these facets are quite smooth and regular, but because these tools have been so heavily weathered, it is not entirely certain that all facets were originally as smooth as they now appear. Nonetheless, it is reasonably clear that the facets were produced by some sort of grinding or mashing action. Certainly they do not in any way resemble the facets on the edge-battered cobbles except in their placement on the edge of the tool. I should point out here that several cobbles with edge-ground facets also have battered ends, showing that they have been used as·hammers as well as grinders. In addition, some show evidence of having been used as anvils. Multifunctional cobble tools are quite common in the Chiriquí River assemblages.

Edge-ground cobbles seem to be shaped simply through use. The continuum of tools from barely modified cobbles to ones whose entire periphery has been ground smooth indicates that this is so. The question of what the tools were used for remains to be answered. Because the edge-ground cobbles from the Chiriquí River shelters have eroded surfaces, I can provide no data on wear patterns beyond presenting the general appearance of the facet itself. However, similar tools occur in other New World sites including Cerro Mangote (McGimsey 1956), a preceramic shell midden, and Monagrillo (Willey and McGimsey 1954), an early ceramic shell midden. Numerous suggestions as to their uses have been offered, including shellfish processing, fiber softening, seed grinding, hide preparation and root-crop processing (see Sims [1971] for a current summary on "edged" cobbles). I am inclined to view the Chiriquí River edge-ground cobbles as tools for grinding or mashing root crops. They would have been used in combination with the grinding stone bases which were also recovered in both preceramic phases in the Chiriquí River sequence. These *grinding-stone bases* are simply flat boulders which have smooth central surfaces, sometimes slightly concave, which resulted from use. Experimental mashing of manioc tubers with an initially unmodified cobble and flat boulder did result in an "edge-ground" facet on the cobble and some slight smoothing of the boulder grinding base. Thus, these kinds of tools could have been formed in this fashion prehistorically, although, of course, they need not have been — Sims (1971) replicated edge-ground cobbles by working hides.

Rectangular Grinding Stones

Two brick-shaped grinding stones (*manos*) were recovered together in Boquete phase deposits in the Casita de Piedra (see Plate 15). All four sides of these cobbles have been ground, and the ends have been pounded. These multipurpose tools could have been used with the grinding-stone bases for preparing food and for hammering or pounding as well.

Cobbles with Offset-Grinding Facets

A very few grinding tools from the Boquete phase layers had grinding facets which, while on the faces of the cobbles, were slightly "off center" (see Plate 15). Such facets are relatively smooth, broad, and slightly convex, resembling those on the rectangular grinding stones more than the edge-ground facets. Still, in two instances, offset-grinding facets and edge-ground facets occur together on the same cobble.

Pestles

A few subcylindrical cobbles from Boquete phase deposits have had one or both ends used for pounding or mashing (see Plate 15). Each of the used ends has a ridge running slightly off center where two pounding surfaces meet at an angle of about 120°. This gabled end was apparently formed by having the pestle held at an angle of about 60° to the surface being struck, and reversing the tool in the hand a complete 180° while in use. At least, I was able to replicate the tool in this manner readily. Each section of the gabled facet is nearly flat, so that these tools (perhaps they should not be called pestles) could not have been used in the small stone mortars recovered from the Casita de Piedra. Perhaps they were pecking hammers.

Mortars

Two, possibly three, small stone mortars (outside dimensions of largest specimen; 8.7 by 7.7 by 5.4 centimeters) were found at the Casita de Piedra. The largest and best-made mortar came from Boquete phase deposits, while a fragmentary mortar plus a possible mortar came from Talamanca phase deposits (see Figure 21 and Plate 14). The smaller complete specimen is so heavily weathered that it cannot be determined with any degree of certainty whether or not it was intentionally manufactured.

Nutting Stones

Occurring in both preceramic phases are cobbles with one or more small (2 to 3 centimeters in diameter) depressions pecked into their surfaces (see Plate 14). Similar stones are used today in Panama for cracking nut

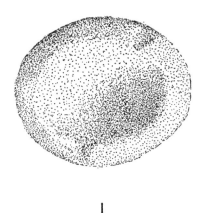

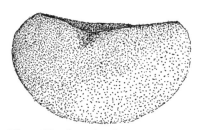

Figure 21.   Stone bowl or mortar, maximum outside diameter 8.7 cm

shells, particularly from the corozo palm. It may well be that the archaeological specimens served the same purpose because charred palm nut
fragments (many of them tentatively identified as corozo) were found
throughout the preceramic deposits.

Stone Bowls

Two fragments from stone bowls, a large body sherd (see Plate 14) and
a small incised rim sherd (see Plate 12) came from the Chiriquí River
excavations. The large (9.5 by 5.7 centimeters) fragment, from Talamanca
phase contexts, varies in thickness from 2.0 centimeters near the presumed base to a maximum thickness of 2.2 centimeters before tapering
to 1.2 centimeters toward the rim of the bowl. Both inside and outside
surfaces are smooth and regular. The incised-stone rim sherd dates from
the Boquete phase and does not at all resemble the larger bowl fragment.
It is, in fact, just a chip from the rim of a bowl (that is, no inside bowl
surface is present on the fragment), which had nearly vertical sides and a
fine incised line running parallel to the lip 0.8 centimeter below it.

SUMMARY AND CONCLUSIONS

Three major activities are documented in the preceramic occupation of the Chiriquí River canyon: stoneworking, woodworking, and plant processing. Of the three, stoneworking is the best documented and the easiest activity to analyze. Of overwhelming importance as a manufacturing technique was percussion flaking, using hammer stones either alone or in conjunction with anvils. By the use of these two classes of tools, every purposely manufactured stone implement from the Chiriquí River preceramic assemblages, with the exception of gravers and ground-stone tools, could have been produced. Pressure flaking was of minor importance, used only to isolate engraving spurs. Two additional stoneworking techniques known, but little used, were pecking and grinding. The ground-stone ax recovered was undoubtedly grooved by pecking, and perhaps it and other ground-stone tools were initially shaped by this technique as well. The ground stone tools were, of course, finished by grinding them with an abrasive-like sandstone. In summary, then, relatively few techniques and relatively few tools were used in a rather simple stoneworking industry.

In contrast, the number of different woodworking tools found in the Chiriquí River assemblages gives some indication of the complexity of the activity. These include wedges, scraper-planes, scrapers, knives, burins, gravers, choppers, axes, adzes, and chisels. Even allowing for a bias in this analysis (most of the functional experiments carried out were in woodworking), it is difficult to escape the conclusions that stone tools were made primarily for working wood. The possibility exists that the Chiriquí River shelters might have been, in part, specialized woodworking stations. Crabtree and Davis (1968) have observed that stone tools are quickly worn out when used for working wood and therefore one might expect to find workshops for manufacturing wooden objects near a source of stone suitable for making wedges, axes, adzes, chisels, etc. As I have pointed out, such sources are present throughout the Chiriquí River canyon. Whether the sites represent specialized stations or not, it is clear that woodworking is an important aspect of the cultural pattern which existed in western Panama from 5000 to 500 B.C.

The plant-processing tools found in the Chiriquí River shelters and the uses to which they were put present a special problem. Here I am referring to edge-ground cobbles, *manos*, cobbles with offset grinding facets, grinding-stone bases, nutting stones, and perhaps pestles and mortars. The heavily eroded surfaces of these tools make microscopic analysis impossible and thus the results of functional experiments equivocal because there are no wear patterns left on the archaeological specimens to which experimentally produced patterns can be compared. What is obviously needed are similar samples of cobble tools from sites where tool surfaces have remained intact for study.

In concluding, I should like to acknowledge that the approach to lithic analysis taken here is not particularly innovative, nor is it particularly well executed. Certainly, my experiments in replicating tools suffer in comparison to those carried out by a master craftsman and lithic technology expert like Crabtree (e.g. 1966, 1968, 1970). Likewise, my use of the microscope in the analysis of wear patterns lacks the sophistication brought to the subject by Semenov (1964). Nonetheless, the combination of making AND using stone tools, plus microscopic analysis of technological and functional attributes on both archaeological and replicated specimens, has much to recommend it. Crabtree and Davis (e.g. 1968) have brought new insights to old problems by combining technological and functional experiments. Semenov is at his best where he compares, by microscopic analysis, wear patterns on archaeological specimens with wear patterns produced experimentally (e.g. 1964:129–130). The combination of replicative experiments (both technological and functional) and microscopic analysis has proved to be of value in analyzing the Chiriquí River collections and should be of value in the analysis of other lithic assemblages as well.

REFERENCES

BEARD, J. S.
   1944   Climax vegetation in tropical America. *Ecology* 25:125–158.
   1955   The classification of tropical American vegetation types. *Ecology* 36 89–100.
CATAPAN
   1970   *Final Report on the Catastro Rural de Tierras y Aguas de Panama,* three volumes. Comisión de Reforma Agraria de Panamá.
CRABTREE, DON E.
   1966   A stoneworker's approach to analyzing and replicating the Lindenmeier Folsom. *Tebiwa* 9(1):3–39.
   1968   Mesoamerican polyhedral cores and prismatic blades. *American Antiquity* 33:446–478.
   1970   Flaking stone tools with wooden implements. *Science* 169(394):146–153.
CRABTREE, DON E., E. L. DAVIS
   1968   Experimental manufacture of wooden implements with tools of flaked stone. *Science* 159(3813):426–428.

GOULD, RICHARD A., DOROTHY A. KOSTER, ANN H. L. SONTZ

    1971   The lithic assemblage of the Western Desert Aborigines of Australia. *American Antiquity* 36(2):149–169.

HURT, W. R., T. VAN DER HAMMEN, G. CORREAL

    1972   Preceramic sequences in the El Abra Rock-Shelters, Colombia. *Science* 175:1106–1108.

MC GIMSEY, III C. R.

    1956   Cerro Mangote: a preceramic site in Panama. *American Antiquity* 22(2): 151–161.

RANERE, ANTHONY J.

    1972   "Early human adaptations to New World tropical forests: the view from Panama." Unpublished doctoral dissertation, University of California, Davis.

    i.p.   The preceramic of Panama: the view from the interior. *First Puerto Rican Symposium on Archaeology of the Caribbean Area.*

REICHEL-DOLMATOFF, GERARDO

    1965   *Colombia.* Ancient peoples and places series 44. Edited by Glyn Daniel. London: Thames and Hudson.

SEMENOV, S. A.

    1964   *Prehistoric technology: an experimental study of the oldest tools and artifacts from traces of manufacture and wear.* Translated by N.W. Thompson. New York: Barnes and Noble.

SIMS, CORT

    1971   Edged cobbles in the Pacific Northwest. *Tebiwa* 14(2):21–38.

STEWARD, JULIAN H., *editor*

    1948   *Handbook of South American Indians*, volumes two, three, and four. Bureau of American Ethnology Bulletin 143.

WILLEY, G. R., C. R. MC GIMSEY, III

    1954   *The Monagrillo culture of Panama.* Peabody Museum Papers 49:2. Cambridge, Mass.

A Study of Cuts, Grooves, and Other Marks on Recent and Fossil Bone: II Weathering Cracks, Fractures, Splinters, and Other Similar Natural Phenomena

GEORGE J. MILLER

INTRODUCTION AND REVIEW

In recent years, bones of animals other than human have assumed increasing importance on archaeological sites. Studies of primitive butchering (Brain 1969a; White 1952, 1953a, 1953b, 1954, 1955, 1956), domestication of animals (Drew, et al. 1970; Weide 1971, personal communication), bone pseudo-artifacts (Brain 1967a; Brooks 1967; Miller 1969a, 1969b; Sutcliffe 1970), together with the increasing interest of paleontologists, geologists, and archaeologists in paleoecology (Brain 1967b; Downs and Miller 1972; Miller 1970, 1971, 1972; Moriarty 1969), taphonomy, and bone accumulations (Brain 1967c, 1969a, 1969b; Dart 1957a, 1957b; Voorhies 1969) have helped to stimulate this interest. It was for these reasons, as well as the ever-present danger of misinterpreting bone that had been altered by natural causes as artifacts, that this study was initiated. The first paper in this series (Miller 1969b) briefly considered marks made on bone by carnivores and rodents.

The first part of this study appeared in the *Journal of the Idaho State Museum* (Miller 1969b).

I thank Dr. Earl H. Swanson, Jr. for his long and continued encouragement of this study and Professor John A. White for his guidance and advice. I am especially grateful to Professor Stuart Warter and to Mr. George T. Jefferson for permission to discuss briefly specimens prior to their own publications. My thanks for the critical reading of all or parts of the original manuscript go to Robert S. Begole, F. Gaynor Evans, George T. Jefferson, William C. Seidel, Ruth De Ette Simpson, Stuart A. Warter, and one of the pioneers in studies of this kind, Theodore E. White. This study could never have been completed without the generous help in terms of time and energy, as well as the permission to study specimens on their property, of Mr. and Mrs. Robert A. Crawford. Photographs are by the author.

For Plates, see pp. xxxi–xl, between pp. 102–103

Experiments with putting fresh bone in the cages with captive animals, together with field observations, attempted to show how some of the marks found on fossil bones could be misinterpreted.

It was found, for example, that marks on the shaft of long bones that had in the past been attributed to rodent gnawing could also be produced by canids, such as the coyote (*Canis latrans*) and the wolf (*Canis lupus*). Members of the dog family will normally gnaw on the shaft of long bones using the incisors, which leave very shallow grooves in the bones transverse to the longitudinal axis. The shape of mammalian long bones, generally round or oval and elongated, prohibits most mammals from gnawing in other directions. The morphology of the mammalian mouth and dentition, with the gnawing incisors placed anteriad, makes it difficult for such an animal to use the incisors, or the canines for that matter, on an object that is oriented so as to be larger or longer than the distance that the mouth can be opened. The machairodonts, with their ability to drop the lower jaw over ninety degrees, may be the exception to this rule (Miller 1969c). It would also appear that the rodents and lagomorphs, with their protruding incisors, might be capable of gnawing a bone parallel to the longitudinal axis. However, I have been unable to find any evidence that they do so. The grooves that were produced on the long bones by the canids were so much like the marks produced by gnawing rodents that it is extremely difficult to determine which animal was responsible. A useful clue, visible only under magnification, is the minute striations, sometimes found in the grooves parallel to the direction of the bite, that are made by rodent teeth. However, the only time that one can say with any degree of certainty that the bones were gnawed by rodents is when only two parallel grooves with the minute striations are found on the shaft in a position transverse to the longitudinal axis, and even this effect has been produced by canids, apparently when they have only gnawed once on the bone. The occurrence of only two parallel grooves in close juxtaposition, that is close enough together to have been made by the two rodent incisors, is so infrequent that in the great majority of cases one is only safe in saying that the bone had been gnawed by unidentified animals. This interpretation becomes quite important when the investigator makes inferences about past events based on the "fact" that rodents were present on the site shortly after the time of death of the man or other animal whose bones are being studied.

The habit of many predators and scavengers, including the canids and felids, of chewing the ends off bones can sometimes be used to infer their presence on the site. The fact that the cancellous bone is much softer than the compact bone and that it is located in a position where it is relatively easy for the animals to work on seems to account for this preference. Witness the location of the olecranon process of the ulna and the calcaneum for example. The position of these is such that a carnivore can easily maneuver them into position so that they may be attacked with the carnassials. Field observations have shown the following order of preference is used by the coyote when scavenging a large herbivore, such as the domestic horse (*Equus caballus*) or cow (*Bos taurus*): First, the external ear is chewed off and devoured. Second, the mandible is torn off — presumably to get at the tongue. Mandibles have been found that were dragged or carried by coyotes as far as thirty feet away from the rest of the carcass in cases in which the only other part of the carcass that had been consumed was the external ear.

Considerable variation in eating habits seems to follow although the internal organs are among the prime targets. After the soft parts have all been devoured, the first parts of the skeleton to be worked on are usually the olecranon process, the calcaneum, the ribs, and the spinous process of the vertebrae — all relatively soft, cancellous tissue. Although the coyotes observed in this study have been remarkably consistent in their order of preference, many other animals do not follow any set procedure and in many cases the same animal does not show the same preferences in consecutive performances. Tigers (*Panthera tigris*) observed by Schaller (1967) usually start on the hind quarters and next proceed to the forequarters. Bones are gnawed or ingested at any time — when first exposed or when all the soft parts have been consumed. Bones of young animals were completely consumed, whereas in adult animals only the thin or soft parts, such as the edge of the scapula, ends of the ribs, tip of the sternum and the nasal bones, were consumed (Schaller 1967).

Individual bobcats (*Lynx rufus*) show considerable variation in the order of ingestion of parts of the carcass; the preferred parts are, however, the tongue and brains, the intestines and other internal organs, with the rest of the body, including the bones, being consumed last (Miller and Carron 1969). In cases in which the carcass is that of a mammal such as the cotton tail (*Sylvilagus sp.*), jackrabbit (*Lepus sp.*), or chinchilla (*Chinchilla laniger*), which are smaller than the bobcat, the bones were usually ingested along with the soft parts; the only parts not consumed were the metapodials and the phalanges.

Many different scavengers become involved in the postmortem, pre-burial history of a dead animal, and many of them leave their marks to add to the confusion. After the bone has become dry and powdery, I have known beavers (*Castor canadensis*) and even the desert tortoise (*Gopherus agassizi*) to gnaw on them and leave their marks. Brain (1969a), in an experiment with the Kuiseb River Hottentots, first purchased a domestic goat (species not stated) from them and then gave it back to them to eat with the stipulation that they must give all the remains to him instead of to their dogs as they would normally do. This was to eliminate the possibility of the dogs chewing and leaving marks on, or consuming, the bones. The Hottentots consumed the caudal vertebrae and also chewed and swallowed the ends of the femora and the metapodials. Brain postulated that Early Man who, in most cases, had much healthier teeth than the Hottentots, would have consumed even more of the bone. Thus it seems obvious, that one must use extreme caution in making any extrapolations based on animal tooth marks on bone.

It was also found in the previous study that when fresh bones of the domestic horse and cow were put in their cages, the large carnivores would use the canine teeth when consuming the bone. The distance of the canines from the fulcrum of the jaws would lead one to think that the necessary force to penetrate a bone by biting would not be available. However, it was found that captive lions (*Panthera leo*) and tigers (*Panthera tigris*) as well as wolves (*Canis lupus*) frequently used the canines for this function and were able to produce round holes in the bone. By the time such bones are found on an archaeological site, so much weathering, abrasion, and other alteration have taken place that it is difficult to determine whether these holes were drilled by man or inflicted by the carnivore canine. It was found that in most cases the two kinds of holes could be distinguished. The man-made hole was almost invariably smooth around the periphery and marks from the "drill" could sometimes be found inside the hole, oriented parallel to the surface in which the hole was started. In contrast, the holes made by the carnivore canine would have a rough outline with small fractures in the bone around the periphery of the opening. Marks inside the hole, while extremely rare, were oriented perpendicular to the surface. These differences were caused by the variation in the direction and intensity of the forces applied. In the case of drilling, the force is applied downward with a rotary motion producing a cutting or grinding effect, whereas in biting all of the force is applied downward with no cutting or grinding to relieve the fracture-producing stress exerted on the surface of the bone. It is obvious that the rotary motion of a rough stone tool would tend to produce scratches whereas the downward motion of a smooth canine would not.

Some of this information was used in a study of suspected bone artifacts from the Rancho La Brea of Los Angeles, California (Miller 1969a). Several bones of extinct animals were found that had cuts, grooves, and other marks that appeared unique. A tibia of the sabretooth (*Smilodon*

californicus) that was dated at 15,200± 800 years Before Present (Berger
and Libby 1968) had two parallel grooves as well as two holes in the shaft.
Although the evidence for the artifactuality of the specimen is still not
conclusive, it was possible to show with some degree of certainty that
some of the marks were not made by the teeth of any known animal.
Other marks on some of the bones were tentatively identified as being
made by large carnivores. One in particular, a large spall broken off the
shaft of the sabretooth tibia, was almost identical to a spall broken off the
shaft of the recent horse (*Equus caballus*) tibia by a caged tiger (*Panthera
tigris*) using the upper canine tooth.

This paper will attempt to show ways in which the degree and form of
weathering evidence on bones may be correlated with the marks made by
predators and scavengers.

LONGITUDINAL AND TRANSVERSE CRACKS AND FRACTURES

The modification of bones by weathering before preservation or fossilization takes place (see Plate 1) can bring about some effects that can easily
be mistaken for human workmanship. Postmortem fractures in the form
of cracks parallel and transverse to the longitudinal axis of long bones
brought about by exposure to the atmosphere can produce splinters and
other fragments that might be mistaken for artifacts. This is especially true
if the fragments are subjected to a natural abrasive force such as that of
wind-blown sand, water transport, movements within the earth, or a combination of one or more of these actions. The splinters produced by
weathering (see Plate 2) often resemble those produced by the groove
and splinter technique. The technique of cutting parallel, v-shaped grooves
in antlers and metapodials (Clark and Thompson 1953) was used in Upper Paleolithic and Mesolithic Europe while the same or a similar technique was used on mammoth ivory in the Upper Paleolithic of South
Russia (Gvozdover 1953) and Siberia (Gerasimov 1941) as well as on
caribou antler and on ivory by the Eskimos (Clark and Thompson 1953).
Brain (1967a, 1969a) reports a case that occurred on the Namib Plain of
South Africa, which is an area of extreme aridity with less than one inch
of rain per year. When bone fragments are left lying in fully exposed positions on the gravel surface, they become bleached and degreased within
three months. Weathering of the bone surface produced by exposure to the
sun results in the development of a soft, chalky, superficial layer. The bone
fragments are often gnawed by gerbils (*Desmodillus sp.*). The fragments

lying on and in the sand by a waterhole are disturbed by the feet of the many animals that come there to drink. Many of the fragments become pointed and a "remarkable polish may develop on their surfaces" causing them to resemble a much used man-made tool.

Field Studies

The study area is located in the Tierra Blanca Mountains of the Colorado Desert in San Diego County, California. Elevation ranges from 600 to 1800 feet above sea level. Temperature ranges from a minimum of −12 degrees centigrade to a maximum of 54 degrees centigrade with the average range being from 0 to 49 degrees centigrade. Rainfall per year is less than three inches. Rainfall for 1971 was 0.67 inches and for 1972 through September was 0.12 inches. The area has been undergoing an extreme drying trend since 1945 with an overall drying trend for several thousand years. All rocks in the area are entirely granite in varying stages of decomposition; the mountains are made up of granite boulders and the valleys of fine granitic sand. All specimens studied were on the floors of the valleys and thus in the granitic sand. Range cattle had foraged in the area from 1933 until the present. When cattle and horses died, they were allowed to remain where they had fallen and had remained undisturbed by man until examined by the author in August and September of 1972. With the rancher's records of when the animals died, this made a unique situation to study the effects of weathering on bone under natural conditions in a desert environment.

The most common predators and scavengers known to be in the area were coyotes (*Canis latrans*), foxes (*Vulpes velox* and *Urocyon cinereoargenteus*), mountain lions (*Felis concolor*), bobcats (*Lynx rufus*), raccoons (*Procyon lotor*), badgers (*Taxidea taxus*), skunks (*Spilogale putorius*), ring-tailed cats (*Bassariscus astutus*), the usual desert rodents including the pack rat (*Neotoma desertorum*), the kangaroo rats (*Dipodomys deserti* and *D. merriami*), the ground squirrels (*Citellus terreticaudus* and *Ammospermophilus leucurus*), and the common desert birds such as the raven (*Corvus corax*) and the red-tailed hawk (*Buteo jamaicensis*). It should be noted here that most desert animals seem to be more omnivorous than their close relatives from less harsh environments, and animals that normally do not eat meat will be found to do so under these conditions.

After the death of an animal, the first thing to take place is the removal of the soft parts by predators, scavengers, invertebrates such as worms and bacteria, wind scouring, and dessication. Next the deterioration and modification of the bone begins to occur. This is brought about by the gnawing of animals, by wind scouring, and by weathering. Later if the bone becomes buried, replacement of the organic constituents by minerals in solution in the permineralization or fossilization process takes place. In this study we will be interested mainly in the weathering process. The terms "weathering" and "weathered," as used in this report, refer to the effects on bone of saturation, dessication, and temperature changes and do not include wind abrasion.

Weathering cracks in long bones begin to appear shortly after the bones become exposed. Small cracks, parallel to the longitudinal axis of the bones, begin to occur even before the periosteum has been completely removed. Animals that have been dead for less than one year (see Plate 3) show less than 5 percent of the periosteum removed from the still articulated bones with not more than one small longitudinal crack per long bone. Bones that have been removed and scattered by scavengers usually have almost all of the periosteum removed, are thoroughly bleached, and have many longitudinal cracks. It appears likely, although the only evidence is the lack of periosteum on the scattered bones, that the periosteum may be chewed or gnawed off by the scavengers. The inefficiency of the scavengers in the study area probably accounts for the long time lapse before weathering sets in because the periosteum tends to protect the bones from dessication. Carcasses of animals that had been dead for as much as six months were found to have coyotes still working on them. In one case, coyotes and possibly other scavengers, dug "trenches" up to forty-five centimeters wide by sixty centimeters deep by 1.52 meters long to get at parts of the carcass from underneath. This occurred approximately four months after the animal had died. It would appear that in an area where there were larger scavengers and predators present, the soft parts of the carcass would be disposed of in a much shorter period of time; thus the bones would be exposed to the atmosphere much sooner.

After an animal has been dead for one year, about 25 percent of the periosteum is gone; exposed portions of the bone are thoroughly bleached to a brilliant white; from two to three longitudinal cracks have appeared on the bones. These cracks go through the compact bone and into the marrow cavity. It is not until after the second year that transverse cracks begin to appear. After four years, the periosteum is all off, except in places where the bone has been covered by sand. In these cases, the parts of the bone that were in contact with the substrate still had some well-dried periosteum adhering to them and were not completely degreased. Some of the long bones were still articulated and held together by small pieces of ligament. All of the exposed bone was thoroughly bleached and there were many longitudinal and transverse cracks going through the compact bone and into the marrow cavity. Exfoliation was just beginning to take place, and the surface of the bones was beginning to become very slightly powdery (see Plate 4).

After eighteen years, most of the organic material was gone, although parts of the bone that had been covered with sand still retained a brownish color. From this stage on, the bones rapidly lost the brilliant white color of the freshly bleached specimens and started to change to a dull, grayish color. Exfoliation increased rapidly and many cracks and splinters were produced (see Plate 5). Animals examined, dead for thirty-one and thirty-four years respectively, showed severe deterioration, a dull gray color, many cracks and splinters, and the bone so badly weathered that it is doubtful if fossilization could take place. Bones that have been exposed to the atmosphere for over one hundred years in the Colorado Desert often retain their identity enough to be recognizable. I have found bones of horses along the old overland stage routes of the 1840's and at long abandoned stage stations in recognizable condition. However, they were in such a poor state of preservation that it would have been difficult to collect them, even using the most refined techniques. It would appear that bones that had been exposed to the atmosphere for over twenty years, at least in the study area, had become so deteriorated that they would no longer be a contributing factor in the production of pseudo-artifacts. Bone splinters, for example, are so badly weathered that even if they were to become fossilized, which is quite unlikely, they would not be mistaken for artifacts (see Plate 2).

Laboratory Studies

Experiments with freezing-thawing and wetting-drying have produced breaks parallel and transverse to the longitudinal axis of long bones. These fractures appear to be identical to those produced under natural conditions as discussed above. Plate 6 shows a photomicrograph of fractures produced in long bones of domestic cows under both conditions for comparison. Note that the surfaces of both have the same rough texture with no observable cleavage plane.

All experiments were conducted with long bones of freshly butchered cattle (*Bos taurus*). Experimental bones were tibiae and metapodials. The bones, when obtained, had already been disarticulated and thoroughly cleaned of all soft parts. All specimens were taken immediately from the slaughter house to either the deep freeze or to the soaking vats. The exact time that had elapsed between butchering and the start of the experiments could not be determined. It is believed to be less than twenty-four hours in all cases. The experiments were conducted for a period of three years at irregular intervals.

Sixty tibiae and eighteen metapodials were used in the experiments. Differences between right and left tibiae and right and left anterior and posterior metapodials were not taken into consideration because no differences in the kind of fractures produced on the different bones were observed. Some differences in the location of the fractures, i.e. anterior-posterior, proximal-distal were observed, but these were not constant among specimens and thus were not deemed pertinent to this study.

Thirty tibiae and nine metapodials were put in a commercial deep freeze where the temperature was maintained at –20 degrees centigrade for three weeks. Fifteen tibiae and five metapodials were then removed from the freezer and placed outside in direct sunlight where they were allowed to thaw and dry at temperatures ranging from 10 to 24 degrees centigrade. The other fifteen tibiae and four metapodials were air-dried indoors at 24 degrees centigrade. In both cases, cracks or fractures parallel to the longitudinal axis of the bone began to appear within twelve hours. Drying was continued for seventy-two hours.

Observations made at irregular intervals during the thawing and drying time showed that many of the cracks would go through the compact bone to the marrow cavity while others were only surface cracks not over one millimeter deep (see Plate 7). Although the experimenter was not present when all of the fractures occurred, those observed seemed to take place with an "explosive" effect. A loud "pop" was heard and then a new fracture was found. This suggests that considerable force was involved.

In the other series of experiments thirty tibiae and nine metapodials were soaked in distilled water at temperatures ranging from 18 to 24 degrees centigrade for three weeks. The specimens were then subjected to the same drying procedure as above. Fractures did not appear in these bones until after twenty hours had elapsed. The "explosive" effect also occurred in this series, suggesting that the force involved was related to drying rather than to thawing.

An additional sampling of six tibiae and two metapodials was stored indoors in sealed containers at 20 degrees centigrade for three weeks and then subjected to the same drying conditions as the two experimental series. This sample produced the same kind of fractures and cracks but in a much smaller quantity and with a much less intensive "explosive" effect. Fractures did not begin to take place until after twenty-four hours.

OBLIQUE OR SPIRAL FRACTURES

Oblique or spiral fractures commonly occur in the metapodials of large cursorial mammals during life. This kind of fracture is usually caused by a three twisting or torsional force. Twisting or torsion is a combination of the three primary forces: tension, compression, and shearing (Evans 1964). In most cases, the fracture tends to spiral around the shaft of the bone at an angle of approximately 45 degrees to the longitudinal axis. Although this kind of fracture occurs most frequently in the perissodactyls it also occurs occasionally in the artiodactyls (see Plate 8). The shape of the bone seems to be a contributing factor to the difference in frequency between the two groups. For example, the "oval" cross section of the equid metapodial, wherein the lateral diameter is much greater than the antero-posterior diameter, as contrasted with the more "square" cross section of the artiodactyl metapodial appears to be a type of structure that is more susceptible to oblique fractures. The ratio of lateral diameter to antero-posterior diameter at a point equidistant from the proximal to the distal ends of the metapodial in *Equus caballus* is generally about 6:5 as opposed to that of *Bos taurus*, which is normally approximately 1:1. Other variations in the gross anatomy as well as in the microscopic structure of the bone may very well be contributing factors because "the behavior of any body under load is a function of the size and shape of the body, especially its cross section, as well as the mechanical properties of the materials composing it" (F. Gaynor Evans 1968, personal communication).

Field Studies

Numerous domestic horses and cows that have died under natural conditions (and have been allowed to remain on top of the ground) in the study area discussed above, as well as on many other sites in California and Idaho, have also been examined; in no instances were there found spiral fractures that had occurred postmortem.

Although no large mammals have been exhumed, three carnivores, two coyotes (*Canis latrans*) and one bobcat (*Lynx rufus*), that had been buried for five years, were excavated, cleaned, and examined. No oblique or transverse fractures or cracks and very few longitudinal fractures were found. These animals had been covered with approximately seventy centimeters of granitic sand, the native sediment. This seems to suggest that burial tends to retard drying and minimizes other changes, such as temperature, to the extent that very few cracks or fractures occur.

Laboratory Studies

The previously discussed experiments with freezing-thawing and wetting-drying did not produce oblique, spiral fractures. Breaks and cracks parallel and transverse to the longitudinal axis of the bone were induced, as discussed above. After the experimental bones had been allowed to dry for seventy-two hours, there were so many fractures parallel to the longitudinal axis that it would have been difficult, if not impossible, for oblique fractures to take place.

These experiments were designed to be as comprehensive and intense as practical compared to any preburial conditions that bones might be subjected to in nature. Because no oblique or spiral fractures were produced, it seems to be safe to assume that, under natural conditions, these fractures occur very rarely, if at all, postmortem and prior to burial.

C. K. Brain (1967b, 1969a) in his studies of bone accumulations in Hottentot villages along the Kuiseb River in the Namib Desert of South West Africa reports that the shafts of limb bones of domestic goats that had been butchered by the natives were broken through by hammerstone impact and spiral fractures were common. A similar situation was reported by R. A. Dart (1957a) in antelope long bones found on an Australopithecine site at Makapansgat. I have tried to duplicate this condition by smashing green long bones of cows with large cobbles and have been unable to produce spiral fractures. However, it seems that this effect could be duplicated with green bones of goat, antelope, or other small artiodactyls (which I have so far been unable to obtain). Size of the animal does not seem to be relevant in these postmortem fractures that have been caused by weathering. Plate 9 shows bones of a coyote that had been killed while scavenging on a horse that had just died. The bones had been exposed for thirty-one years. The same kind of longitudinal and transverse fractures and cracks were found in the long bones of both animals.

PRACTICAL APPLICATIONS

An example of an oblique or spiral fracture is shown in Plate 8, a fossil camel (*Camelops sp.*) metapodial. The specimen was recovered from basal sediments of Pleistocene Lake Manix by Mr. Schmidt (Jefferson 1968). Stratigraphic correlations suggest the specimen is from 60 to 70,000 years old (Basset 1971; George T. Jefferson 1972, personal communication). Evidence, which could be interpreted as aboriginal modification and or use prior to fossilization, is visible at the break. Scratches, which appear to be from abrasive use, possibly from use as a scraper, are transected by preburial longitudinal weathering cracks. This seems to suggest that the bone was used as a tool while fresh and then discarded. It could then have remained on the surface of the ground long enough for weathering cracks to occur before it was buried. The transverse cracks could have occurred at the same time as the longitudinal cracks, as has been discussed above. It should be noted that the evidence is not unequivocal. It has been suggested that the break, which was probably a compound fracture, would have protruded through the skin. In this case, if the leg, or parts of it, were dragged along the ground by a large scavenger, the exposed bone would become scratched, thus producing the same effect as if the scratches had been produced by usage. However, my experiments in cutting of green bones indicate that a much greater force than that brought about by dragging a bone over the ground is needed to produce such scratches on it. Green compact bone, unless soaked in water for a considerable length of time, is extremely difficult to work and does not scratch easily. The possibility of the scratches being self-inflicted by the camel attempting to walk is obviously ruled out by the fact that the scratches are on the proximal end of the bone while the distal end is intact.

A case of bone pseudo-artifacts occurred recently on the Rancho La Brea Project in Los Angeles, California. Several objects that appeared to be bone needles or awls were found in association with the extinct fauna of Rancho La Brea. Of the many highly qualified archaeological consultants called in to examine the specimens, several (no names are mentioned for obvious reasons) were of the opinion that the objects were artifacts and some could even detect signs of usage. Minute lines or scratches on the ends parallel to the longitudinal axis of the objects, such as those that are found on bone needles and awls and are caused by the in-and-out motion used when pushing a thong through a hole, were observed. The specimens, most of which were broken, measured up to nine centimeters in length, two millimeters in width, and less than one millimeter in thickness and were splint-shaped and highly polished (see Plate 10). From my studies of bone splinters I felt that there was some doubt that the objects were what they appeared to be. Because microscopic examination revealed small orifices on several of the specimens that suggested stomata on what superficially resembled pine needles, I sent them to the project paleobotanist, Dr. Janet Warter, for examination. However, it was ornithologist Stuart Warter who solved the problem. Dr. Warter identified the objects as being ossified bird tendons, such as are found in turkeys and certain large raptors. This is the first instance that I know of in which ossified bird tendons have been identified on either a paleontological or on an archaeological site. The close resemblance to polished bone splinters would probably cause most paleontologists to overlook or discard such specimens. Conversely, were they to be found on an archaeological site, they would probably be collected as "suspected artifacts." Comparison with ossified tendons from Recent domestic turkeys showed no signs that would indicate that the specimens had been used as needles or awls. They were morphologically identical to the Recent specimens. In regard to the polished appearance, even Recent specimens appear polished as do most other bird bones. A polishing effect probably also occurs from the movement within the tar deposits due to fine grains of sand that are suspended in the asphalt. I have deliberately given only a cursory description of these specimens and no locality data because Dr. Warter will be dsicussing them more fully in a forthcoming publication.

DISCUSSION

Natural bone splinters and even ossified bird tendons may very well be mistaken for artifacts. Although ossified bird tendons, to the best of my knowledge, have been found only at Rancho La Brea, it is quite possible that they may occur on other sites as well. This would appear to be particularly true of archaeological sites because ossified tendons are known to be present in such a human food item as a turkey. The unusual quality of the Rancho La Brea fossil preservation (Miller 1970) probably accounts for the presence of ossified tendons on that site; however, now that we know that they have been preserved on one site, a meticulous examination of bone splinters at other sites might be expected to add to their presence in the fossil record. Another source of pseudo-bone needles and/or awls has been shown by Sutcliffe (1970). Bone fragments ingested and later regurgitated by hyenas produced not only needlelike splinters but bones with holes in them from the action of stomach acids which "could be mistaken for human artefacts" although "they are generally distinctive..." Because the hyena niche in the Western hemisphere seems to have been at least partially filled in Pleistocene times by the dire wolf (*Canis dirus*), the possibility of similar habits producing similar effects on bone must be considered. In view of these findings, it would seem advisable to reevaluate some collections of bone needles and awls and to exercise extreme caution when making collections and identifications in the future. Other pseudo-tools, such as those that could be produced by the oblique, spiral fracture that gives bone a sharp, gouge-shaped end, should in most cases be detectable when a thorough analysis is made.

It is readily admitted that this continuing study has barely scratched the surface, and it is hoped that others will become interested in pursuing the subject. In view of the difficulty of obtaining large samplings with adequate field information, the need for more students and more studies in different localities and different environments seems obvious.

REFERENCES

BASSET, ALLEN
  1971   Radiocarbon dates of Manix Lake, Central Mojave Desert, California. *Geological Society of America Special Paper, Abstract to Meetings.* (Abstract of paper submitted for the meeting in Riverside, California.)
BERGER, RAINER, W. F. LIBBY
  1968   UCLA radiocarbon dates VIII. *Radiocarbon* 10:402–416.
BRAIN, C. K.
  1967a Bone weathering and the problem of bone pseudo-tools. *South African Journal of Science* 32:1–11.
  1967b "Procedures and some results in the study of Quaternary cave fillings," in *Background to evolution in Africa.* Edited by Walter W. Bishop and J. Desmond Clark, 285–301. Chicago: University of Chicago Press.
  1967c Hottentot food remains and their bearings on the interpretation of bone assemblages. *Scientific Papers of the Namib Desert Research Station* 32:1–11.
  1969a The contribution of Namib Desert Hottentots to an understanding of Australopithecine bone accumulations. *Scientific Papers of the Namib Desert Research Station* 39:13–22.
  1969b Faunal remains from the Bushman Rock Shelter, Eastern Transvaal. *South African Archaeological Bulletin* 24:52–55.
BROOKS, RICHARD H.
  1967   A comparative analysis of bone from Locality 2 (C1–245) Tule Springs, Nevada. *Nevada State Museum Anthropological Papers* 13:402–411.
CLARK, J. G. D., M. W. THOMPSON
  1953   The groove and splinter technique of working antler in Upper Palaeolithic and Mesolithic Europe. *The Prehistoric Society* 6:148–160.
DART, R. A.
  1957a "The Makapansgat Australopithecine Osteodontokeratic culture," in *Proceedings of the Third Pan-Africa Congress of Prehistory*, 161–171.
  1957b The Osteodontokeratic Culture of *Australopithecus prometheus*. *Transvaal Museum Memoir* 10:1–105.
DOWNS, THEODORE, GEORGE J. MILLER
  1972   "Asphalt cemetery of the Ice Age," in *Encyclopedia Brittanica yearbook of science and the future*, 50–63. Chicago: Encyclopedia Brittanica.
DREW, ISABELLA M., DEXTER PERKINS, JR., PATRICIA DALY
  1970   Prehistoric domestication of animals: effects on bone structure. *Science* 171:280–282.

EVANS, F. GAYNOR
1964   "Significant differences in the tensile strength of adult human compact bone," in *Proceedings of the First European bone and tooth symposium, Oxford, April 1963*, 319–331. Oxford: Pergamon Press.

GERASIMOV, M. M.
1941   Obrabotka kosti paleoliticheskoi. stoyanke Malta. *Materialy i isledovannia po arkeologii SSSR* 2:65–85.

GVOZDOVER, M. A.
1953   Obrabotka kosti i kostyania izdeliqa avdeevskoy stoyanki. *Materialy i isledovannia po arkeologii SSSR* 39:192–226.

JEFFERSON, GEORGE T.
1968   "The Camp Cady local fauna from Pleistocene Lake Manix, Mojave Desert." Unpublished master's thesis, University of California at Riverside.

MILLER, GEORGE J.
1969a Man and Smilodon: a preliminary report on their possible coexistence at Rancho La Brea. *Contributions in Science* 163:1–8.
1969b A study of cuts, grooves, and other marks on recent and fossil bone. I. Animal tooth marks. *Tebiwa, Journal of the Idaho State University Museum* 12:20–26.
1969c A new hypothesis to explain the method of food ingestion used by *Smilodon californicus* Bovard. *Tebiwa, Journal of the Idaho State University Museum* 12:9–19.
1970   The Rancho La Brea Project: 1969–1970. *Los Angeles County Museum Quarterly* 9:26–30.
1971   Science and education at the tarpits, part one. *Ward's Bulletin* 11:1–6.
1972   Science and education at the tarpits, part two. *Ward's Bulletin* 11:1–4.

MILLER, GEORGE J., RICK CARRON
1969   "On food ingestion in the bobcat (*Lynx rufus*)." Unpublished manuscript.

MORIARTY, JAMES R., III
1969   The San Dieguito Complex: suggested environmental and cultural relationships. *Anthropological Journal of Canada* 7:1–18.

SCHALLER, GEORGE B.
1967   *The deer and the tiger*. Chicago: University of Chicago Press.

SUTCLIFFE, ANTONY J.
1970   Spotted Hyaena: crusher, gnawer, digester and collector of bones. *Nature* 227:1110–1113.

VOORHIES, MICHAEL R.
1969   Taphonomy and population dynamics of an Early Pliocene vertebrate fauna, Knox County, Nebraska. *Contributions to Geology* 1:1–69.

WHITE, THEODORE E.
1952   Observations on the butchering technique of some aboriginal peoples, 1. *American Antiquity* 17:337–338.
1953a A method of calculating the dietary percentage of various food animals utilized by aboriginal peoples. *American Antiquity* 18:396–398.
1953b Observations on the butchering technique of some aboriginal peoples, 2. *American Antiquity* 19:160–164.

1954   Observations on the butchering technique of some aboriginal peoples, 3, 4, 5, and 6. *American Antiquity* 19:254–264.

1955   Observations on the butchering technique of some aboriginal peoples, 7, 8, and 9. *American Antiquity* 21:170–178.

1956   The study of osteological materials in the plains. *American Antiquity* 21:401–404.

PART FOUR

Discussion

Discussion

COMMENT *by Joffre Coe*

One of the most interesting aspects of the current archaeological effort is the emphasis on understanding the manufacture and use of stone tools. It has been apparent to most prehistorians, at least since the time of Bouche de Perthes, that of all the efforts of man it is the objects he made of stone that are most likely to survive. The papers of this symposium* begin with this premise, some stating that "99.5 percent of the history of mankind is represented by the Stone Age," and that stone tools, in a real sense, do "represent fossilized human behavior patterns" (Crabtree). The archaeologist is now charged to extract "the maximum possible understanding of human behavior from this limited data" (Collins). I am sure that the value of comprehensive studies in lithic technology is fully accepted today. Yet it has only been within the last decade that Don Crabtree and François Bordes have received proper recognition for their persistent effort. In reading these papers it would seem that lithic technology has just been discovered by the "new archaeologist." Virtually all the citations in the bibliographies are for the year 1963 or later. Only Crabtree mentioned an earlier experimenter like Halvar Skavlem; only Collins and Newcomer cited an early source like W. H. Holmes. I wonder, therefore, how many of the people who have recently become interested in the techniques of stone work know about the experiments conducted at the Mantes Cement factory in 1902 by Marcellin Boule; or that Abbé Breuil became

---

* Don Dragoo's paper was accepted for publication after this symposium was prepared and therefore could not be discussed.

quite expert in fabricating paleolithic hand axes (this is a replica he made over fifty years ago); or that there was a lithic laboratory established in Columbus, Ohio in the 1930's? Science has been developing along all of its perimeter; therefore, techniques are available to the archaeologist today that could hardly have been foreseen in earlier years. My point is only that we should make use of all the resources that are available to us — the experiences of the earlier investigators as well as the techniques of modern science.

Neither time nor competence will permit more than a few brief remarks concerning the subject of some of these excellent papers. What I do say, however, will reflect my own interest rather than any priority assigned to the papers.

Crabtree has presented the basic problems of lithic technology in his usual clear and forthright style. Considerable space was devoted to an explanation of the role that materials play in the achievement of a final product. He also reminded the observer that "the worker must either modify or develop techniques which conform and respond to the material being used," a fact that seems to be frequently overlooked. He concluded his statement with a list of twenty-five questions that might be answered by a careful study of lithic debris, one of these questions being: "what is indicated by a series of use flakes of certain character — termination, change of angle, incurred resistance, improper use, beginners, apprentices, or mishandling?" When the archaeologist can answer questions of this sort with assurance, then he most certainly will have arrived at a new plateau in his understanding of past human behavior.

Collins' paper, while covering many of the same concepts as Crabtree, reads as though it has been written by a sociologist. Terms such as "product groups," "activity sets," and "artifact populations" will be a little hard for some of the older archaeologists to read, and statements like "there is the potential operation of a 'feedback' relationship between steps in the manufacturing process as changes in output requirements in one step may necessitate changes in earlier steps" will be even harder for them to understand. Nevertheless, Collins presents a carefully reasoned outline or model that should help in the orderly presentation of data. The problem with any system based primarily on inference or analogy is that by its very nature it is selective and biased. Use, meaning, and value are not inherent in the form of any given object. They are inferred by the archaeologist who, unfortunately, can never hope to see them through the eyes of the original maker. He can only judge them in the light of his own experience and hope it is meaningful. The function and value of any man-made product changes through time and many items can serve more than one purpose at any given time. There is, as yet, no magic formula that can revitalize the fragments of the past, that is archaeological data, and reveal them to us as a total, viable cultural system.

Crabtree and Collins have been concerned, I believe, with a holistic approach. Gunn, on the other hand, has suggested a method for "finger printing" artifacts or the identification of the individual craftsman's style. The ability to identify the work of one person could open many new avenues of knowledge in prehistory. Gunn has demonstrated that individual styles can be isolated in his control group. It will be interesting to see this method applied to specific archaeological problems where the number of variables and unknowns will be greatly increased.

The heating of stone to improve its flaking quality is known to have occurred in many archaeological situations, Crabtree, Purdy, and others have been experimenting with various stones and methods of heating with interesting results. In his present paper Crabtree is concerned primarily with detecting the use of heat. Purdy, however, describes the results of a series of controlled experiments with Florida cherts and has concluded that heat treatment was more than a casual affair. To be successful it appears that man needed to be precise in his utilization of fire and that the method and critical temperature would vary, depending upon the material used. Further observations were made on the type of fractures that resulted from heat stress. This information should help the archaeologist identify spalls and splinters that were not part of the actual knapping process.

Newcomer, Green, and Kobayashi have applied the principles of experimentation and lithic technology to specific problems. Newcomer states that his intent was "to introduce a modification of the terminology used to describe the experimental manufacture of palaeolithic flaked stone artifacts." He defines three levels of "abstraction" — method, mode, and technique. This may be useful, but I was more impressed with his statement that "experimenters often find that several different techniques will produce identical artifacts and waste flakes, and we can be properly sceptical when it is claimed that only one technique will produce the described results."

Green's effort is more typological. He states that the "points identified as McKean are not McKean, but are of the Little Lake Series found in the northern Great Basin," and then proceeds to document his case with careful analysis and description. This may be the case of a rose by any other name, but it also illustrates the fact that type descriptions of stone tools have been woefully inadequate in the past.

Kobayashi's experimental effort in producing and defining bipolar flakes and cores, while directed toward the early palaeolithic in Japan and China should also be of value to the Americanist since bipolar techniques have been reported from various parts of the New World. I would like to be able to compare the specimens I am familiar with in the Southeast with Mr. Kobayashi's experimental results.

Bradley is rightly concerned with the loose or inadequate terminology used in the current literature. He has supplied us with a set of definitions and an example of their use. I am afraid, however, that any attempt to standarize terminology will meet with little success. Over the past forty years there have been many such efforts. Committees have been appointed and much has been written on the subject. Variety however, seems to be the nature of language. The attempt to change the term "temper" to "aplastic" in pottery description was no more successful than was the French Academy's effort to reform the French language many years earlier. We must, however, be able to understand our terms in order to communicate intelligently.

Miller's paper on bones does not deal directly with lithic technology but is certainly one that should be read by all archaeologists. The ability to distinguish between the marks made by the gnawing of an animal and those made by the tools of man would seem to be elementary. Yet in a relatively recent publication of the Smithsonian Institution a photograph showing rodent gnawing on a skull was labeled "cut marks on surfaces, suggesting removal of scalp and brain before burial."

Finally, I enjoyed reading Johnson's long and detailed paper on the lithic tools from northern Chile. It was not the results of her computer analysis, since even she admits that "the results from the core analysis may seem somewhat meager," but her clear understanding of basic problems and procedures that impressed me. At one point she states that "an archaeologist who is a flint knapper may be overcautious in his analysis, but he is not likely to make completely implausible or impossible interpretations of his data." In another place she states that: "all the computer does is to find the order present in the data as it has been presented by the archaeologist. It is the job of the archaeologist to find out the causes and significance of the order." It is all too easy to construct straw problems to suit hypothetical situations. It is another matter to exact meaningful interpretations from the cold stones of reality.

COMMENT *by Jeremiah F. Epstein*

The papers offered for this symposium are, in one way or another, a trib-
ute to Don Crabtree and his contribution to what he has called in his own
paper the "Science of lithic technology." Whether or not this field is perhaps more properly called a science, rather than a discipline or subdisci-
pline within anthropology, is not important. What is important is that we
have reached the level where the detailed analysis of lithic debris, attempts
to replicate aboriginal chipped stone artifacts, and all the theoretical
problems involved in this research have been accepted by the profession
as a legitimate form of inquiry. This inquiry has been placed on a firm
foundation by Crabtree, and it is demonstrated by the fact that almost
every paper given here either quotes him, refers to his work, or in one way
or another emphasizes the experimental approach which he has so effectively advocated.

   As with most discussions or studies, the symposium papers can be
classed as either primarily theoretical of empirical in their outlook. Among
the former, I see two major groupings; those that are addressed to the
problems of synthesis and definition (Newcomer, Bradley, and Collins)
and those that deal with the perennial problem of typology, either without
the computer (Green) or with it (Johnson and Gunn). On the empirical
level, four papers are concerned specifically with experiments on lithic
materials (Crabtree, Kobayashi, Purdy, and Lenoir), while one more
(Miller) consider bone which either served as a tool, or was affected by
human action.

   Newcomer approaches the problem of understanding lithic reduction
by three processual categories which he calls method, mode, and technique. For Newcomer, the first is viewed as the steps used in making the
artifact (i.e. production of Levallois flakes, fluted points, etc.). Mode is
the kind of flaking employed (hard hammer versus soft hammer). Both
method and mode can be determined, he believes, by the experimental
approach. Technique, however, involves so many variables, (for example,
in holding the piece, or the hammer), that Newcomer doubts whether it
can be perceived experimentally. I certainly agree with him in regard to
this last statement. At this point in time I even wonder how precise we can
be in the determination of mode. Where large flake samples are available,
modes can be statistically demonstrated, but in small collections or in
samples composed of a single flake, we often cannot be so positive.

   Bradley, who is also concerned with process and communication, has
offered a series of definitions for our lithic technological vocabulary.
Among the terms are familiar words such as blank, implement, and stage,

which he correctly points out imply that we know the intent of the flint knapper. Apparently he feels that his intent is usually discernible. This may well be. For my part, I would like to use terms of this nature at the end of my analysis rather than in the initial classification of the flint sample. Blanks and preforms are interpretations of our data, and the distinction between one's data and its initial interpretation can be lost very easily by classifications using terminology such as suggested here.

In Collins' approach artifacts and debitage must be related. He establishes seven categories of lithic activity and uses them to explain the changes in lithic assemblages from two localities: one in Texas, the other in France. Like Bradley, Collins' lithic reduction categories involve judgement of intent. The impression his synopsis gives is that the results are easily reached. I do not doubt that Collins' categories represent valid stages in the lithic sequence, but they also indicate very sophisticated judgements on the part of the analyst. While most of us would agree that all seven categories probably exist in most archaeological sites, I wonder if we would also agree as to which specific artifacts belong to each group.

Presumably, any projectile point typology based on form alone can be improved by a technological approach. This is what Green attempts in his paper (originally given at the 25th Northwest Anthropological Conference, Portland, Oregon, 1972). The lanceolate and stemmed indented base points of southern Idaho that have been called McKean are reclassified and placed in the Little Lake Series of the northern Great Basin. We are told that the primary distinction between McKean and the Humbolt-Pinto groupings is in the technology employed, but while he describes the latter in terms of preforms and blanks, he does not employ this terminology in his discussion of McKean. The argument would be more convincing if the characteristics of the various point types were presented in parallel columns so that each feature could be easily compared. Green's paper connects to the perennial problem of defining a types. Frankly, I lament the fact that with the abundant literature on this subject and his own commitment to one particular approach, Green failed to devote even one paragraph to this fundamental issue.

Those concerned with the applications of computers to archaeology should find pleasure in both Johnson's and Gunn's papers. Johnson's study is not, as its title suggests, a discussion of a lithic complex, but only of the core technology employed in some sites in Chile. The two computer programs used in the analysis are carefully discussed, along with the types of data used for input. The final conclusions seem quite obvious. We are told, for example, that the most common use of the cores was for flakes, and that the production of blades was attended to with more care than that of flakes.

Joel Gunn's paper (originally prepared for the 1972 Plains Conference) discusses the problem of finding the individual knapper by identifying the patterning of flake scar orientation on the pieces he has flaked. The scar patterns are analyzed by creative use of laser diffraction, and the data is fed into the computer. The approach, while not conclusive, suggests that the individual may indeed emerge if we look for him.

While both papers show considerable sophistication and creativity in converting the sample to a final printout, I have reached the point where I wonder whether all of this was necessary. Johnson's conclusions seem so obvious, so simple, that I suspect they were perceived before the data was punched. Similarly, I am not at all convinced that the individual identifications made by Gunn's laser/computer could not be accomplished as well by a meticulous observer. Have we reached the point where our students no longer trust their own judgement, but rely on the non-partisan electronic monster? I suspect the next decade will see ourselves so converted to the machine that a photograph of the punched-out fortran card will be considered more reliable than a photograph of the artifact.

Don Crabtree's paper is the delightful distillation of the knowledge that in one way or another all of us are trying to achieve. While for many what he says is already understood, it is still the kind of paper one can come back to again and again. In our headlong search for higher and higher levels of abstraction, it is all too easy to forget, or lay aside, the fundamentals. Crabtree brings us back to earth with a discussion of what we know, and some questions we all should ask. He ends by encouraging all of us to learn by experimenting. There is here something for everyone.

Kobayashi's experimental study is filled with the kind of data so urgently needed for an understanding of bi-polar flaking. I regret that the report is so brief for his data raises a series of tantalizing problems. For example, he distinguishes three lettered flake types and notes that the ratio of A to C flakes changes in his two flaking experiments. Whether this reflects a conscious difference in techniques used or a general improvement in manual skill is not noted. I regret that Kobayashi was not at this meeting to elaborate on his contribution. Purdy's fascinating paper describes the effects of heating Florida cherts, with observations made of the types of fractures that occur in various combinations of slow to rapid heating and cooling situations. She backs up Crabtree's original heat treating experiments with concrete experimental data and concludes that man had to be very precise in his utilization of fire to alter lithic materials. Unfortunately, there is no description of the techniques used to heat the flint and to measure its properties afterwards. Also, speculation on how Florida Indians may have accomplished all this would have been appropriate.

Lenoir's paper deals with his own experiments in duplicating what Bordes has called *fracture en languette* [tongue fracture]. He suggests that the cause is not simple and that various elements may be involved including the use of too hard a percussor, too strong a blow, or the heterogenous nature of the material. What Lenoir fails to submit is statistical data, and so it is almost impossible to evaluate his conclusions.

Miller's paper on bone is in two parts. The first section dealing with cuts and grooves, was actually published in 1969; the section dealing with weathering is new. Miller is concerned with the problem of distinguishing between human and non-human induced fractures, or marks on bone, and his data is basic to anyone concerned with interpreting osseous material in or out of an archaeological context. Among his observations is the statement that oblique or spiral fractures are not the result of weathering, but can occur when an animal twists its limb. Goat bones, broken by Hottentots using hammerstones, are reported to show spiral fractures, and so are antelope bones from the Makapansgat locality. He ends with a discussion of a spirally fractured camel metapodial from Manix lake. There is the possibility that the bone may have been used as a scraper. Since the specimen came from the basal sediments of Lake Manix, which has been considered as much as 60,000–70,000 years old, the possibility of its use as a tool by man is especially intriguing. Unfortunately, Miller's discussion leaves us hanging. The impression given is that he believes the bone was once a tool, but he notes the data is not unequivocal.

I regret that Ranere's study on the materials from his excavations in western Panama arrived too late to be discussed in this symposium. Ranere duplicates most of his chipped stone tools, experiments with them on wood, and finds similar patterns of wear on both the duplicated and original specimens. This is a delightful study and in many ways a model for future archaeological reports.

I find in reviewing my own remarks that I have taken an approach bordering on the hypercritical. In many instances I have criticized not what was done, but what was not done. This is somewhat unfair, but necessary. I hope my comments can be used constructively. Lithic technology has grown up in the last decade, but there is still room to mature.

REPLY *by James P. Green*

I would like to briefly reply to Epstein's comments on my paper. I shall reply in the order of his comments.

I agree that a balanced descriptive schema would have been preferable;

however, one works with the material he has at his disposal. While I was concerned with projectile points and the flaking patterns manifest on their surfaces, I could not overlook other technological clues provided by the collections at hand. The McKean collection, as I noted, consisted of seventeen projectile points from the type station. The technological system developed for members of the Little Lake Series came from the handling of more than twenty Great Basin collections. The manufacturing stage indicators, "blank "and "preform" were not utilized in the description or reconstruction of the McKean material because of the small sample. However, I noted that not many sites provide the entire manufacturing sequence. This was the reason for examining a large number of Great Basin collections containing Little Lake and so-called McKean material.

Any type of visual aid which organizes the data under discussion greatly adds to the presentation of a paper. A diagram noting the distinguishing characteristics of the point types in question may have added to my argument. Instead of a diagram or other schematic representation, I chose to present very respectable line drawings and photographs. I still feel that a good photograph is worth a thousand words. Unfortunately, these were not included in the copy Epstein reviewed.

Epstein's final comment regarding my not discussing the subject of typology is also worthy of a reply. I feel that I have a particular approach to typology and that this approach is made up from several theoretical positions, although Epstein notes that I use "one particular approach." As of the writing and rewriting of the paper, it was deemed important to avoid falling into an unnecessary scuffle of being placed into one of the several theoretical camps. This aside would have only overshadowed the objective of the paper, that of establishing a data base, a "technological corpus" if you will, from which to initiate an assault on some of the problems of typology. The data base will be complete with the analysis of the lithics from the Stahl Site and Pinto Basin. When this facet of the study is finished, statements on the theoretical aspects of typology can and will be made.

REPLY *by Joel Gunn*

The only comment I would like to make is with regard to Jeremiah Epstein's questioning whether the trouble Lucy Lewis and I went to was worth it for the conclusions we reached.

I would like to point out that for any topic to be studied "scientifically," it should be done so in a systematic and highly reproducible manner.

First, the trouble that was gone to in the two papers largely had to do with studying artifacts according to a methodology which could be replicated in any laboratory and explicating that methodology so that anyone else interested in the same topic could do so. If the conclusions we arrived at seem obvious to the impressionistic archaeologist, they are probably equally obvious to us. We, however, have gone to the trouble to circumvent impressionistic methodology to better the scientific qualities of the art of lithic analysis.

Second, Epstein's criticism accuses the results as being simplistic. Another way of saying it is that the problems are plasmodic in nature. By rights they should be, as the application of numerical analysis to archaeological problems is in its nascent stages. It is not yet appropriate for us to go beyond what is intuitively graspable. That is not to say that the methods used are not capable of going fully beyond simplistic conclusions. The methods are there, but we are not. Soon we will pass beyond the realm of easy intuitive analysis and a lot of people will wish for the good old simple days. I expect, however, that leaping into the nonintuitive beyond will be fully worth the trouble in terms of a better understanding of how human cultures of the past operated.

REPLY *by L. Lewis Johnson*

In general, I found the commentaries by Coe and Epstein to be a valuable addition to the session. The major comment I would like to make concerns Epstein's discussion of the papers by Joel Gunn and me. I think Epstein is expecting too much of the first fumbling excursions into a new mode of analysis. Both Gunn and I stress that these are preliminary analyses aimed at exploring a new method to see if it is applicable to the study of ancient technology. If I may quote the last paragraph of my paper:

Finally, I wish to stress that the analysis of the collection is not complete. Although the results from the core analysis may seem somewhat meager for an elaborate analysis, the cores are only one segment of the collections and the analysis of the others, particularly of the retouched artifacts, will provide more information about the technology and should lead to the formation of higher order hypotheses.

My hopes for the analysis of the remainder of the collection proved valid, particularly in the formation of further hypotheses; the results may be studied in Lewis (1973) and Johnson (i.p.).

REPLY *by Hiroaki Kobayashi*

Dr. Jeremiah F. Epstein points out the ratio of A to C flakes changes in my two flaking experiments. This is to the point. This change reflects a general improvement in manual skill and does not reflect a conscious difference in technique used. I regret that I could not fully represent my consideration in writing my paper in English.

REPLY *by M. H. Newcomer*

Since the points I tried to make in my paper "'Punch technique' and Upper Palaeolithic blades" are only lightly touched upon in the comments provided by Drs. Coe and Epstein, this reply will be brief. I still think the time is ripe for reviewing the ways in which we apply the results of experimentation (or ethnographic observation) to archaeological material and wish this aspect of lithic technology could have been discussed at length at the symposium. Dr. Epstein's précis of this part of my paper is fair, but I would hasten to add that it was never my intention to apply my system to small numbers of artifacts or "samples composed of a single flake."

My only regret about the meetings was that there was too little time to develop some of the themes which I see as important for experimental archaeology: the roles played by experimentation and ethnographic parallel in reconstructing technologies; the difficulties in using experiments to infer the functions of stone tools; and the relationship between the study of form (typology) and technology.

I would like to conclude this reply with a note of sincere thanks to Dr. Earl H. Swanson for his invitation to the symposium and his helpful advice and encouragement.

REPLY *by Barbara A. Purdy*

Drs. Coe and Epstein seem to have the impression that these reports represented the group's entire knowledge pertaining to this subject. On page 229, Dr. Coe says: "In reading these papers it would seem that lithic technology has just been discovered by the 'new archaeologist.' Virtually all the citations in the bibliographies are for the year 1963 or later." This was not true of my paper but, because of its specific nature, I did not cite historic accounts or experimenters. I did, however, cite my dissertation and a *Science* article, both of which contain many early references. A similar remark can be addressed to Dr. Epstein. On page 235, he says: "Unfortunately, there is no description of the techniques used to heat the flint, and measure its properties afterwards." This information is contained in my dissertation. The Congress paper did not deal with thermal alteration specifically, but with fractures resulting from destructive application of heat. On page 236-237, Dr. Epstein says: "I have criticized not what was done, but what was not done." Some of it has been done, Dr. Epstein.

In general, the comments of Drs. Coe and Epstein were interesting and provide a worthwhile summary of the Lithic Technology Symposium.

REFERENCES

JOHNSON, L. LEWIS
   i.p.   "The Aguas Verdes industry of northern Chile," in *Advances in Andean archeology*. Edited by David L. Browman. World Anthropology. The Hague: Mouton.
LEWIS, L. G.
   1973   "A computer-aided attribute analysis of a lithic industry from northern Chile." Unpublished dissertation, Columbia University.

Biographical Notes

BRUCE BRADLEY (1948, U.S.A.). Educated at the University of Arizona and the Cambridge University, in anthropology and archeology. Author of several papers on lithic technology and experimental archeology.

JOFFRE COE. No biographical data available.

MICHAEL B. COLLINS (1941, U.S.A.). Educated at the Universities of Texas and Arizona; currently assistant professor of anthropology at the University of Kentucky. He is author or co-author of several papers on physical anthropology and on prehistory in North America and Europe.

DON E. CRABTREE (1912, U.S.A.). Don Crabtree began experimental flintworking as a youngster in east central Idaho. Before World War II, he was associated with the Ohio State Museum Lithic Laboratory and with vertebrate paleontological expeditions of the University of California at Berkeley. He is a Research Associate of the Idaho State University Museum, where his research has been supported by a series of National Science Foundation grants. He has been featured in six documentary films, five prepared at Idaho State University and one made in collaboration with François Bordes at the University of California. He is the author of numerous papers, including "An introduction to flintworking," "Experiments in flintworking," "Experiments in replicating Hohokam Points," and "A stonework's approach to analyzing and replicating the Lindenmeier Folsom." He is the Director of an experimental Flintworking School for graduate students in anthropology.

DON W. DRAGOO (1925, U.S.A.). Educated at Indiana University and the University of New Mexico and is now Curator of Anthropology at the Carnegie Museum of Natural History, Pittsburgh, Pennsylvania. He has worked extensively in the prehistory of North America and Old World prehistoric contacts. He is the author of the book *Mounds for the dead* and numerous monographs and articles. He has done fieldwork and research in the United States, Canada, Arabia, Australia, Japan, and many other areas.

JEREMIAH F. EPSTEIN (1924, U.S.A.). Educated at the University of Illinois, Urbana, and the University of Pennsylvania, is currently Professor of Anthropology at the University of Texas at Austin. He has published various monographs and papers on the archeology of Texas and Northeastern Mexico.

JAMES P. GREEN (1953, U.S.A.). Received his undergraduate anthropology training at California State University at Hayward. Studied under Don Crabtree as an M. A. student at Idaho State University, and now completing doctoral work at Washington State University, where his research areas are Great Basin prehistory and lithic technology.

JOEL GUNN (1943, U.S.A.). Received training in anthropology at the University of Pittsburgh and is now Assistant Research Professor and Co-director of the Meadowcroft Project at the same institution. The author is primarily interested in high resolution data analysis techniques which will facilitate sophisticated modeling of prehistoric lifeways. Publications include "An envirotechnological system for Hogup Cave," and "Dynamic typology: a model for functional classification of prehistoric stone tools with an application to French paleolithic burins."

L. LEWIS JOHNSON (1943, U.S.A.). Educated at Carleton College and Columbia University (B.S. 1966; Ph.D. 1973), she has taught at the Polytechnic Institute of Brooklyn and is now an Assistant Professor at Vassar College. Her major research focus is on understanding the process of manufacture of lithic implements.

HIROAKI KOBAYASHI (1947, Japan). Educated at Tohoku University, he is now studying for his doctorate at the Laboratory of Archaeology at Tohoku University. His particular field of study is the Early Paleolithic in Japan, and he is the co-author of some papers in this field.

MICHEL LENOIR (1947, France). Now studying for his Ph.D. at the Laboratoire de Géologie de Quaternaire et de Préhistoire, Université de Bordeaux 1, he has published several papers in the areas of prehistory, quaternary geology, and lithic technology and is presently doing research on paleolithic industries at sites in Gironde.

GEORGE J. MILLER (1921, U.S.A.). Educated at California State University at Long Beach and Idaho State University. Presently Curator of Paleontology at Imperial Valley College Museum, El Centro, California. Has published numerous papers on sabretooth cats and on bone artifacts.

MARK NEWCOMER (1942, U.S.A.). Educated at Columbia University and the University of London, and is now Lecturer in Prehistoric Archaeology at the Institute of Archaeology, London. He is interested in Paleolithic technology and is currently excavating in the Near East.

BARBARA A. PURDY (1927, U.S.A.). Educated at San Diego State University, Washington State University, and the University of Florida, she is currently Assistant Professor of Anthropology and Social Sciences and is Assistant Curator at the Florida State Museum, University of Florida. Research interests in primitive technology and archeometric applications to the solution of archeological problems.

ANTHONY J. RANERE (1942, U.S.A.) Educated at Harvard University, Idaho State University, and the University of California at Davis; now Assistant Professor of Anthropology at Temple University. Author of several articles on the archeology of western North America and lower Central America.

EARL H. SWANSON, JR. (1927, U.S.A.) Educated at Carleton, Arizona, Washington, and London. Professor of Anthropology and Museum Director, Idaho State University since 1957. Fulbright awards 1954, 1955, 1972. Directed five documentary flintworking films, and founded the journal *Tebiwa*. Author and editor of numerous papers and books, including *Birch Creek: human ecology in the cool desert of the northern Rocky Mountains 9,000 B.C. - A. D. 1850, Languages and cultures of western North America*, and *Utaztekan prehistory*.

Index of Names

Adovasio, J., 35
Aikens, Melvin C., 168
Alba, Richard D., 81, 84
Andersen, Adrian, 148

Baden-Powell, D. F. W., 99
Basset, Allen, 221
Beard, J. S. ,176
Begole, Robert S., 211
Berger, Rainer, 215
Berry, L. G., 16
Binford, Lewis R., 35
Binford, Sally R., 35, 100
Bleed, Peter, 35
Bordaz, J., 100
Borden, Charles E., 149, 151
Bordes, François, 1–2, 5, 30, 57, 64, 97, 98, 99, 100, 101, 109, 113, 114, 129, 151, 229, 235
Boule, Marcellin, 229
Bradley, Bruce A., 5–13, 232, 233, 234
Brain, C. K., 211, 213–214, 215, 221
Breuil, Henri, Abbé, 229
Brezillon, Michel, 64
Brooks, H. K., 133, 139
Brooks, Richard H., 211
Broyle, Bettye J., 147
Bryan, Alan Lyle, 161
Butler, B. Robert, 40, 162
Butts, Steven, 78

Cann, J. R., 20
Cherdyntsev, V. V., 151

Chia Lan-po, 115
Clark, G., 19
Clark, J. G. D., 98, 215
Clarke, David L., 66
Clements, Thomas, 149
Clewlow, C. W., Jr., 162, 165, 168
Coe, Joffre L., 147, 229–232, 238, 239, 240
Collins, Michael B., 15–33, 229, 230–231, 233, 234
Combier, J., 100
Correal, G., 178
Coutier, L., 99
Crabtree, Don E., 1–2, 12, 35, 38, 40, 57, 63, 64, 65, 97, 99, 100, 101, 105–114, 134, 135, 207, 208, 229, 230–231, 232–233, 235
Crawford, Robert A., 211
Crook, W. W., Jr., 149

Dart, R. A., 211, 221
Davis, E. L., 207, 208
Davis, John, 35, 41–42, 49
Davis, M., 19
Deetz, J., 37
De Jarnette, David L., 150–151
De Lumley, Henry, 64
Derevianko, A. P., 151
Dibble, D. S., 26, 27
Downs, Theodore, 211
Dragoo, Don W., 145–158
Drew, Isabella, 211

Epstein, Jeremiah F., 232–236, 237–238, 239, 240
Evans, F. Gaynor, 211, 220

Fitting, James E., 152
Flannery, K. V., 19
Folk, R. L., 138
Friedman, Herman P., 78–81

Gerasimov, M. A., 215
Goodman, M. E., 16
Gordus, A. A., 19
Gould, Richard A., 64, 111, 195
Green, D., 41
Green, James P. 159–171, 231, 233, 234, 236–237
Griffin, J. B., 19
Gruhn, Ruth, 161–162; "Test Excavations at Sites 10–OE–128 and 129, Southwest Idaho," 161
Gunn, Joel, 35–61, 231, 233, 224–235, 237–238
Gvozdover, M. A., 215

Harary, Frank, 81, 83, 85
Harrington, Mark R., 149, 167
Harris, R. K., 149
Haynes, C. Vance, 147
Heizer, Robert F., 159
Hempel, C., 37
Hester, Thomas R., 113, 168
Hodson, F. Roy, 78
Hole, F., 19
Holmes, W. H., 19, 229
Humphrey, R. L., 147
Hurt, W. R., 178

Ikawa, Fumiko, 154
Irving, W. N., 148
Irwin-Williams, Cynthia, 148

Jefferson, George T., 211
Jelinek, A. J., 23
Jennings, Jesse D., 159, 168
Johnson, L. Lewis, 63–95, 232, 233, 234–235, 237, 238
Josselyn, Daniel, 149–150

Kehoe, Thomas F., 160
Knudson, Ruthann, 114
Kobayashi, Hiroaki, 115–127, 231–232, 233, 235, 239
Kragh, Anders, 113–114

Krieger, Alex D., 148, 149

Layton, Thomas N., 168
Leakey, L. S. B., 105, 149
Lenoir, Michel, 129–132, 233, 235
Leroi-Gourhan, André, 64
Lewis, L. G. See L. Lewis Johnson
Lewis, Lucy. See L. Lewis Johnson
Libby, W. F., 215
Linares, Olga F., 173
Lively, Matthew, 149–150

McBurney, C. B. M., 100
McCarty, Richard, 173
McCary, Ben C., 152
MacDonald, George F., 151, 152
McGimsey, C. R., III, 178, 204
McNealy, Robert, 173
MacNeish, Richard S., 148, 153, 154
McPherron, Alan, 35
McPherron, Margaret, 35
Malde, Harold E., 148
Martin, Paul S., 146–147
Mason, B., 16
Mewhinney, H. 64
Miller, George J., 211–226, 232, 233, 236
Miller, Susanne J., 168
Moriarty, James R., III, 211
Müller-Beck, H., 148
Mulloy, William, 159, 163, 164; "McKean Site, The," 162
Mulvaney, D. J., 154
Muto, Guy, 35, 37, 40

Neill, W. T., 64
Newcomer, M. H., 32, 97–102, 229, 231, 233, 239
Newton, Isaac, 110–111

Oakley, Kenneth P., 63
Okladnikov, A. P., 151
Orr, Phil C., 148

Piggott, S., 19
Pressler, E. E., 138, 139
Preston, F., 41
Preston, F. W., 134–135, 137
Prinz, Beth, 35
Purdy, Barbara A., 133–141, 231, 233, 235, 239–240

Ranere, Anthony J., 173–209, 236
Ranere, Joan, 173
Reichel-Dolmatoff, Gerardo, 178

Renfrew, C., 20
Richardson, James, 153
Rohlf, F., 58
Ronen, A., 19
Rouse, I., 37
Roust, Norman L., 168
Rubin, Jerrold, 78–81

Schaller, George B., 213
Schiffer, M., 23, 24–25
Seidel, William C., 211
Semenov, S. A., 64, 208
Serizawa, Chosuke, 115, 154
Shafer, H. J., 23
Shaerer, W. L., 138, 139
Shephard, R. N., 78
Shutler, Richard, 149
Simpson, Ruth De Ette, 149, 211
Sims, Cort, 204
Skavlem, Halvar, 113–114, 229
Smith, P. E., 30, 32
Speth, J. D., 16
Spier, R. F. G., 23
Sprague, Roderick, 159
Steward, Julian H., 178
Sutcliffe, Antony J., 211, 223
Swanson, Earl H., Jr., 1–2, 35, 114, 115,
    159, 160, 211, 239

Thomas, David H., 168
Thompson, M. W., 215
Titmus, Gene, 35, 113–114
Tixier, Jacques, 97, 98, 99, 100, 114

Van der Hammen, T., 178
Veldman, D., 58
Vinci, Leonardo da, 64
Voorhies, Michael R., 211

Wahlstedt, W., 49
Warter, Janet, 222
Warter, Stuart, 211, 222–223
Weaver, C. E., 138
Wheeler, Richard P., 160; "Note on the
    McKean Lanceolate Point, A.," 162
White, Anta M., 70
White, John A., 211
White, Theodore E., 211
Willey, Gordon R., 148, 149, 204
Wilmsen, E. N., 20
Witthoft, John, 152
Wormington, Marie, 114, 145–146, 147–
    148, 149, 151
Wright, G. A., 19

Young, C. C., 115

Index of Subjects

Afontova Gora site, Siberia, 151
Africa, 8, 151, 221
Aguas Verdes complex, Chile, 67, 69, 90–93
Alabama, 147, 149–150, 151, 152–153
Alabama Archaeological Society, 149
Alaska, 11, 147
Amazon River, 178
American Anthropological Association, 145
Anathermal period, 161, 168
Archaic culture, 26, 140, 147, 150
Arctic Anthropology, 145
Arenosa Shelter, Texas, 26–30
Arkansas, 134
Asia, 145–158
Assemblage, defined, 5
Atacama Desert, Chile, 67
Aurignacian period, 100
Australia, 153–156, 195
Australian aborigines, 111
Ayacucho complex, Peru, 153

Baikal, Siberia, 151
Bering Straits, 146
Bipolar technique, 115–127; defined, 115
Black Rock Desert Survey, 164
Blackwater Draw site, New Mexico, 146
Blank, defined, 5
Boise, Idaho, 161
Boquete phase, 177, 184, 190, 195, 199, 200, 201, 204–205, 206
Bordeaux, 2
Borneo, 154

Brandon blades, 100
British Columbia, 151
Brown's Bench, 164

Calama, Chile, 67
Calico Mountains site, California, 149, 168
California, 159, 220
Capsian culture, 114
Casita de Piedra, Panama, 176–178, 181, 186, 201–202, 204, 205
Cassia County, Idaho, 160
CATAPAN, 176
Caulapau site, Mexico, 148
Celebes, 154
Cerro Mangote, 204
Chiao-Ch'eng site, China, 154
Chile, 63–95, 234
China, 115, 154, 155, 231
Chiriquí River, Panama, 173–209
Chiu Chiu, Chile, 67
Chou-Kou-Tien Loc, China, 115
Clactonian period, 99
Clovis culture, 2, 35, 146, 147–148, 151, 152
Clus program, 78–81, 87, 93
Colorado Desert, California, 216, 218
Columbia University, Bureau of Applied Social Research, 78
Columbus, Ohio, 229
Complet program, 78–93
Cooperton site, Oklahoma, 148
Corbiac site, France, 99
Coyote Flats, Idaho, 162, 164

Crump site, Alabama, 150

Danger Cave, 164–165, 168
Debert site, Nova Scotia, 151, 152
Decrepitate, defined, 136
Desert Culture period, 26
Divostin Project, University of Pittsburgh, 35
Dordogne, France, 99

"Early Man in North America, New Developments: 1969–1970" (symposium, American Anthropological Association, San Diego, 1970), 145
Eskimo, 215
Ethiopian blade technique, 114

Fenho Valley, China, 154, 155
Flea Cave, Peru, 153–154
Flintridge, Ohio, 110
Florida, 133–141, 231, 235
Folsom point, 64
Ford Foundation, 173
Fractures: and archaeologists, 133–141; *languette*, 129–132

Georgia, 150
Glass Buttes, Oregon, 39
Glenns Ferry, Idaho, 160
Gottweig period, 155
Great Basin, North America, 35, 159–171
Gumu-sana assemblage, 8–12

Hirose River, Japan, 116
Hogup Cave, 164–165, 168
Holcombe site, 152
Hopewell cores and blades, 110
Horacio Gonzales site, Panama, 177
Hoshino complex, Japan, 154
Humboldt Cave Base projectile points, 159, 162, 165, 234
Humboldt Sink, Nevada, 165

Idaho, 159–171, 220
Idaho State University, 35, 113; Flint-knapping School, 35, 40; Museum, 2, 40, 113, 115
Idial style, 37–38
Implement, defined, 5
Iwajuku complex, Japan, 154

Japan, 115–127, 153–156, 231
Java, 154
Journal of the Idaho State Museum, 211

Kansas Geological Survey, 35; Geologic Research Section, 42
Kersey, Colorado, 114
Kuiseb River Hottentots, 213–214, 221
Kukiksait assemblage, 11–12

Laugerie Haute Ouest site, France, 30–32
Les Eyzies, France, 30, 114
Lewisville site. Texas, 149
Lindenmeier site, Colorado, 146
Lithic period, 147, 150–151
Lithic Dalton points, 150
Little Lake (Pinto) projectile points, 159, 162–165, 169, 231, 234, 236
Llano Estacado, Texas and New Mexico, 20
Lao River, Chile, 67, 68
Lovelock Cave, 164
Lovelock Lake Bed site, Nevada, 164, 165

McKean-Humboldt Concave Base A-Pinto projectile points, 162–169
McKean projectile points, 159–171, 231, 234, 236
"McKean Site, The" (Mulloy), 162
Makapansgat site, 221, 236
Malad Hill, 164
Mal'ta site, Siberia, 151
Manix, Lake, 221, 236
Mantes Cement factory, 229
Marion County, Florida, 133–141
Method, defined, 97
Mexico, 146
Mississippi, 150
Miyagi Prefecture, Japan, 116
Mode, defined, 97–98
Modification, defined, 5
Monagrillo, 204
Morphology, defined, 6
Mousterian period, 151
Museum of Natural History, Paris, 114

Namib Plain, South Africa, 215–216, 221
Nevada, 159
New Guinea, 154
North America, 145–158
Northwest Anthropological Conference (1972), 159, 234
"Note on the McKean Lanceolate Point, A" (Wheeler), 162

Ohio Valley, 153

Old Crow Flats, Yukon, 148
Olduvai, 105
Oregon, 161
Owens Valley, California, 167
Owyhee County, Idaho, 160

Paccaicasa complex, Peru, 153
Panama, 173–209, 236
Panamá, Dirección de Património Histórico, 173
Pecos River, Texas, 26, 29
Perigordian period, 99
Peru, 153–154
Philippines, 153–156
Pinto Basin, 137
Pinto projectile points. *See* Little Lake projectile points
Pioneer Basin, 164
Plano cultures, 163
Preform, defined, 6
Preliminary modification, defined, 6
Primary core, defined, 6
Primary flake-blank, defined, 6

Rancho La Brea, California, 214, 222-223
Raw material, defined, 6
Rock Creek projectile points, 159
Rock Creek site, Idaho, 159, 164, 168

Salar Brinkerhoff, Chile, 68
Santa Rosa Island, California, 148
Schoolyard site, Panama, 177
Secondary core, defined, 6
Secondary flake-blank, defined, 6
Sendai, Japan, 116
Shoop site, 152
Siberia, 147, 151, 215
Sigma Xi, 173
Silent Snake phase, 168
Simons Site Cache, Idaho, 39–61
Smithsonian Institution, 232
Smithsonian Tropical Research Institute, Balboa, Canal Zone, 173
Snake River Plain, Idaho, 162
Solutrean culture, 30–32, 109, 112
South America, 145–158
South Fork Shelter, 164
Southwestern Idaho Survey (1959), 164

Sozudai site, Japan, 115–127
Stage, defined, 6
Stahl site, California, 167, 237
Step, defined, 6
Stutz Bluff shelter site, Alabama, 150–151
Surprise Valley, 164

Taiwan, 154
Talamanca phase, 176–177, 184, 186–187, 190, 192, 195, 199, 201, 205, 206
Tanimoto coefficient, 79
Technique, defined, 98–99
Tennessee, 147, 150, 152–153
"Test Excavations at Sites 10-OE-128 and 129, Southwest Idaho" (Gruhn), 161
Tierra Blanca Mountains, California, 216–218
Timor, 154
Ting Ts'un site, China, 154
Tohoku University, 115
Trapiche Shelter, Panama, 176–178, 181, 186
Tule Springs site, Nevada, 149
Turkish blades, 100
Twin Falls County, Idaho, 160

United States, National Science Foundation, 173
University of Kansas, Lawrence, Center for Research, 42
University of Pittsburgh, 153; Divostin Project, 35

Valsequillo area, Mexico, 148
Vezere River, France, 30

Wells Creek site, Tennessee, 151, 152, 153–154
Weston Canyon Rockshelter, Nevada, 164, 169
Williamson site, 152
Wilson Butte Cave, Idaho, 161–162, 164
Würm (Wisconsin) period, 155

Zarsiadero Shelter, Panama, 177
Zeya River, Siberia, 151